Child Maltreatment

Contemporary Issues in Research and Policy

Volume 12

Series Editors

Jill E. Korbin
Schubert Center for Child Studies
Cleveland, OH, USA

Richard D. Krugman
University of Colorado School of Medicine
Aurora, CO, USA

This series provides a high-quality, cutting edge, and comprehensive source offering the current best knowledge on child maltreatment from multidisciplinary and multicultural perspectives. It consists of a core handbook that is followed by two or three edited volumes of original contributions per year. The core handbook will present a comprehensive view of the field. Each chapter will summarize current knowledge and suggest future directions in a specific area. It will also highlight controversial and contested issues in that area, thus moving the field forward. The handbook will be updated every five years. The edited volumes will focus on critical issues in the field from basic biology and neuroscience to practice and policy. Both the handbook and edited volumes will involve creative thinking about moving the field forward and will not be a recitation of past research. Both will also take multidisciplinary, multicultural and mixed methods approaches.

More information about this series at http://www.springer.com/series/8863

Ilze Earner • Alexandra Telitsyna
Editors

The Development of Child Protection Systems in the Post-Soviet States

A Twenty Five Years Perspective

Springer

Editors
Ilze Earner
Silberman School of Social Work
Hunter College
New York, NY, USA

Alexandra Telitsyna
National Research University Higher School
of Economics
Moscow, Russia

ISSN 2211-9701 ISSN 2211-971X (electronic)
Child Maltreatment
ISBN 978-3-030-59587-6 ISBN 978-3-030-59588-3 (eBook)
https://doi.org/10.1007/978-3-030-59588-3

This Springer imprint is published by the registered company Springer Nature Switzerland AG.
The registered company address is: Gewerbestrasse 11, 6330 Cham, Switzerland

Acknowledgments

The editors wish to thank a few individuals and organizations who made this project possible. We thank the Higher School of Economics Basic Research Program, Center for Studies of Civil Society and the Nonprofit Sector at the National Research University Higher School of Economics and its Director Dr. Irina Mersianova, the Hunter College Presidential Travel Program, and Elena and Gennady Timchenko Foundation and its Director Maria Morozova. Lastly, we thank Rebecca Gee for her excellent editorial assistance in the preparation of the manuscript and the staff at Springer International for their advice and guidance.

Introduction

Introduction

Samarkand, Yerevan, Tashkent, Almaty, Baku—ancient cities that for most Westerners are familiar in connection with the Silk Road, the fabled trade routes of exotic goods, and ideas, which flowed from the East to the West. Today, these are modern cities in the emerging states of Central Asia, which, along with Baltic and Eastern European states, are the focus of our look at a different kind of journey, the development of systems of child protection in the post-Soviet world. Fifteen countries emerged in 1991 from the former Union of Soviet Socialist Republics (USSR), each with individual histories and cultures as well as political and economic affiliations. As social scientists, the development of different national policies, practices, and programs to serve children and families from a previous single model of child protection provides us with a unique and unusual opportunity to examine the trajectory and the influences that shape current social service praxis in these 15 countries. What has this meant for children? For families? What service models are being emulated? How are unique cultural perspectives shaping ideas about the definition of a child and the role of families? What are the challenges and what have been the successes in ensuring the well-being and safety of children?

The protection, well-being, and safety of children is a vital concern of all human societies. The questions, of course, have always been who is a child, whose children are protected, what defines well-being, and under what circumstances can an authority outside of the family intervene to assure the safety of children? Modern societies have expended a great deal of effort in defining who is a "child," what is a "family" and identifying the social expectations of families, the rights and responsibilities of parents and children, and guaranteeing the social security of families and children. In the modern state, there are also circumstances, defined in child protection policies, in which the state can become involved in the life of a child despite or even against the parents' wishes. These questions, and the answers, are deeply embedded in historical, cultural, social, economic, and political factors. To further complicate matters, the answers are neither uniform nor equitably applied. It is no wonder then that the question of how children are protected is such a robust field of inquiry in social science.

Numerous scholars have engaged in cross-national research on social policies that focus on the family and children. The seminal works of Alva Myrdal (1942), Sheila Kamerman and Alfred Kahn (1978), and Neil Gilbert (1997) laid the groundwork, created models of analysis, and underscored the importance of cross-national comparative studies; it is in comparison that we can best understand how and why social services and social policies develop to address the needs of target populations. Myrdal focused almost exclusively on national policies as they affected families and children. Her work specifically identified ways in which a comprehensive "welfare state" that met the social needs of all families, not just the poor, could facilitate family formation, stability, and child development (1942). Kamerman and Kahn took this format a step further in their comparative analysis of European social welfare systems and provided the first descriptive analysis of national policy approaches to supporting families across 14 countries. Their major contribution to understanding family policy was to differentiate between "universal" and "categorical" benefits that support child and family well-being. In their analysis, social insurance (or universal) policies represented a progressive approach to ensuring that all families and children were protected from unforeseen or dire circumstances. Neil Gilbert's international comparative work (1997) formulated a matrix of social, economic, and political forces that promoted the protection of children from abuse and neglect with the primary responsibility resting with the state rather than private entities.

In more recent years, cross-national studies of child protection have more narrowly focused on specific topics in the development of policy, for example the growing role of the private sector in child protection (Gilbert et al. 2011; Spratt et al. 2015; Merkul-Holguin et al. 2019); the professionalization of practice and service providers (Klevens et al. 2018); or specific populations at risk such as migrating children (Skivenes et al. 2015). With a few exceptions, cross-national and comparative studies in child protection have focused almost exclusively on Western Europe, North America, and Australia with the result being an unfortunate lack of diverse or global perspectives in the existing literature (Brown et al. 2017). We believe the models of policy analysis and understanding the development of systems of child protection prevalent in the Western world could be greatly enhanced by examining what happened in the post-Soviet states—how did a sudden shift to market capitalism affect the well-being of children and families? And how were older models of child protection, such as a preference for institutionalization, changed in the context of emerging economic and political systems as well as re-emerging traditional and cultural definitions of family roles and responsibilities? One of our goals here is to bring new voices into the global discussion of child protection.

A Step Back in Time: What was Child Protection in the Soviet Union?

To understand how child protection evolved in the post-Soviet states and the policies and programs as well as practices, it is necessary to understand what the "Soviet model" was, what it looked like as a service delivery system, for whom, and how it was already changing prior to 1991. In the chapter on Russia (Semya, Telitsyna, and Garifulana), the authors trace the medieval history of laws and policies that governed family and social relationships, the "Russkaya Pravda" through the period of Catherine the Great and the establishment of orphanages for the illegitimate children of the nobility largely for the purpose of protecting property and inheritance rights (Vladimirskii-Budanov 2005; Yablochkov 1876). Inspired by the progressive ideas of her confidant and supporter, the school reformer Ivan Ivanovich Betski, foster homes and orphanages were opened throughout Moscow and St. Petersburg for a larger demographic of children built on the dream of creating a utopian estate.

Picking up with the upheavals of World War I and a prolonged period of social unrest, by 1917 the phenomenon of "abandoned children" was first recognized and government intervention turned to the most expedient option—government-sponsored orphan homes. In 1918, the Russian Democratic Federative Republic adopted strategic policy initiatives on the protection of children and signaled a change in the focus of the purpose of state guardianship of orphans—it was no longer a matter of protecting property but rather the "care of the person" (Tottenborn 1919).

In post-revolutionary Russia, the concept of parental rights as being inviolable was soon discarded. For example in a popular magazine, *Proletarian Revolution*, an article on children surrendered to institutional care advises that information about the child's family is better left absent, "you should not be afraid of outraging the rights of absent parents" (Tottenborn 1919). Concurrent policy debates focused on whether parental rights could also be terminated if it was deemed that parents raised their children contrary to the new ideology of communism. In the 1919 People's Commissariat of Social Security, a clause was included that parental rights could be terminated if parents continued to educate their children "in the way which is apparently contradictory to the main principles of communism and indoctrinate in their children enmity to communism and develop counter-revolutionary sentiments in them" (Tottenborn 1919). A period of radical institutionalization emerged in the 1920s; orphan protection ranged from labor colonies and commune schools such as the Bolshevskaya commune portrayed in the film, *Road to Life* (Ekk 1931). As more extreme measures of repression occurred throughout the 1930s, a new wave of "orphaned" children appeared—those whose parents were deemed "betrayers of the nation." Institutions set up for educating and providing care for children outside of large urban centers were overwhelmed, and ironically, nascent forms of kinship foster care began to evolve. Permission was granted to place the children of repressed parents with relatives in 1937 (Besschetnova 2011). This continued until 1968 when kinship foster care was abolished and institutional care was reestablished as a primary form of child protection.

By the last decades of the twentieth century, the number of children raised in residential care homes in the Soviet Union began to decline. In 1988, a resolution by the Council of Ministers was issued "On the organization of family-based care homes." This policy called for the establishment of "children's towns" for families who fostered at least ten children. By 1990, there were 3500 children in 347 established family-based care homes. It was assumed that this form of foster care would enhance assistance to children by providing a more comprehensive combination of social, collective, and family forms of childrearing (Bessachetnova 2011).

In a reprise of the turn of the previous century, after 1990 the number of abandoned children started to grow steadily (2001). By 1991, their numbers grew to 59,154; by 1995, over 113,000 children needed out of home care. In 2000, 123,204 children were in various forms of residential care homes. Most of the children placed in residential care homes were "social orphans"—their natural parents were alive but were either deprived of parental rights or abandoned their child to the care of the state.

Studies suggested that the reasons for the growth of the number of children in institutions were social and economic instability, which led to the impoverishment of a large part of the population in the 1990s. Once again, family-based forms of placement that had begun to be established late in the Union of Socialist Soviet Republics did not continue to develop in the first few years of the post-Soviet period. As in the 1920s, the response to overwhelming numbers of abandoned and homeless children was institutional care (Tyndik and Buryakova 2014). A pattern that remained in place in many of the former republics as well.

How This Project Evolved: Moscow, November 2019

Between 2013 and 2015, the editors of this book met through a project sponsored by the Eurasia Foundation in Washington, D.C. that brought together academics, policy-makers, and researchers in child protection from the USA and the Russian Federation. In a series of international meetings, excursions, and fact-finding trips, this project produced the first comprehensive comparison of child protection systems in the USA and Russia. Both Dr. Alexandra Telitsyna and Dr. Ilze Earner as well as other authors who contributed to this book presented at several international conferences on our joint work (Earner et al. 2019, 2018, 2017, 2016). In 2018, we decided to expand our focus beyond a US and Russian comparative lens to look at what has happened to child protection in the post-Soviet states since 1991. We thought this would be an unusual—and useful—comparative study because all of the emerging states started out with the same policy and practice model of child protection in place.

With support from the Higher School of Economics in Moscow, the Moscow State University of Psychology and Education, and the Silberman School of Social

Work at Hunter College in New York and a generous grant from the Timchenko Foundation, we organized the first ever roundtable on child protection with representatives from all of the post-Soviet states on November 19, 2019, in Moscow (XV International and Practical Conference, Moscow, November 20–22, 2019, p. 5). Most of the contributors to the chapters in this volume attended that conference. The importance of this roundtable is significant—not only was it the first-time researchers, academics, and policy-makers from all of the former Soviet states were brought together to discuss child protection, but for the participants it was a genuine and intimate forum to discuss mutual concerns and resources and share experiences, as well as frustrations, in their work. The need is clearly there for the continuation of these types of forums to facilitate the building of a knowledge base, theoretical perspectives, and body of research that is distinctly post-Soviet and addresses the unique and varied needs of this part of the world. While Western-based foundations, as well as the European Union and UNICEF, have expended a great deal in terms of resource development, expertise, and technical assistance in helping to formulate policies, programs, and practice in child protection in many of these states, it is also important to recognize that there are regional, national, and historical concerns that are unique to each region. Now is the time to develop a platform of what is increasingly termed an "indigenous" approach to child protection (West Coast Leaf 2019). This approach recognizes and incorporates the voices, knowledge, practices, and perspectives of ethnic and regional populations.

So what has happened in child protection since 1991 in the post-Soviet states? The picture that emerges is one of differential interpretations and implementations of the United Nations Convention on the Rights of the Child, to which all of the countries are signatories. Some states have a dedicated ministry charged with oversight of child protection; in others, the responsibilities are scattered across several governmental agencies both at the national and local levels. Cultural traditions and historical practices have figured prominently in addressing child protection policies that have in turn led to ongoing negotiations on how to balance tradition with modern ideas about the roles of parents and children and how best to protect children. In some states, concern about the decline in population due to emigration has embedded child protection into social insurance programs in an attempt to support and stabilize families through economic and social supports. The challenges to de-institutionalization as a primary form of child protection are numerous. As one example, in an overwhelming majority of states, disabled children remain more likely to be institutionalized. Nevertheless, there are also emerging successes with new stakeholders in the arena of child protection: NGOs are playing an increasing role in devising and implementing innovative family and children's services programs, foster families are increasingly being relied upon to provide services to children who cannot remain in their own families, and a new cadre of social workers with specific skills in the field of child welfare are being educated and trained.

This book is by no means a definitive work on child protection in the post-Soviet states. If anything, it is a primitive baseline, descriptive study that serves to identify the specific challenges and concerns in each of the countries included in this volume. Our methodology and analysis was based on the presumption that academicians, researchers, practitioners, and policy-makers in child protection from each state were the experts. All of the participating authors were provided with an outline to describe their current policies, programs, and practices. We also asked authors to identify challenges and successes and to identify a model program that demonstrates promising practices for the future. Our greatest hope is that a cross-national and comparative study like this might inspire an ongoing process, as well as a vehicle, for future collaboration and cooperation between these new countries on the issue of child protection as they continue to evolve their national and regional policies and practices. It would add greatly to the understanding of child protection if there were a resource center, a research consortium, and an educational exchange between the states of the former Soviet Union as they develop approaches to family and children's services and child protection. A regional peer-reviewed journal would enhance the international profile of national experts in this field. The global field of child welfare would benefit too, from hearing and learning about the challenges and concerns of practitioners, researchers, and academics from this part of the world. Let the journey begin.

Ilze Earner
Alexandra Telitsyna
Anastasia Milakova

References

Besschetnova, O. V. (2011). Orphanhood in Russia: From charity to deinstitutionalization. *Sociological Research, 11*, 106.

Brown, L., Lei, J., & Strydom, M. (2017). Comparing international approaches to safeguarding children: Global lesson learning. *Child Abuse Review, 26*, 247–251. https://doi.org/10.1002/car.2486.

Earner, I. (2019). *De-Institutionalization in the Russian Federation and services to at-risk youth: A long way home.* Strengthening Families: Moving to a Global Perspective CWLA, Washington, DC, April 13, 2019.

Earner, I., & Telitsyna, A. (2018). *The Anti-Café: Anti-dote to social isolation for vulnerable and at-risk youth.* International Society for the Prevention of Child Abuse and Neglect 16th European Regional Conference Prague, Czech Republic, August 31–September 5, 2018.

Earner, I., Morse, J., Telitsyna, A., Semya, G., Shulga, T., & Lvoff, O. (2017). *The use of digital story-telling and other media in training and skill-building of child welfare workers, social work students, mentors and foster parents: The child's voice revisited.* International Society for the Prevention of Child Abuse and Neglect 15th European Regional Conference, The Hague, Netherlands, October 1–4, 2017.

Earner, I., Lalayants, M., Baranova, Z., & Baranov, A. (2016). *Towards competency-based workforce development: Collaboration between United States and Russian Federation Child Welfare Faculty.* International Society for the Prevention of Child Abuse and Neglect 21st International Congress, Calgary, Canada, August 28–31, 2016.

Ekk, N. (1931). *Film. Road to life.* Release September 30, 1931. USSR.

Gilbert, N. (Ed.). (1997). *Combating child abuse: International perspectives and trends.* New York: Oxford University Press.

Gilbert, N., Parton, N., & Skivenes, M. (2011). *Child protection systems: International trends and orientation.* New York: Oxford University Press.

Kamerman, S. B., & Kahn, A. J. (Eds.). (1978). *Family policy: Government and families in fourteen countries*. New York: Columbia University Press.

Klevens, J., Ports, K. A., Austin, C., Ludlow, I. J., & Hurd, J. (2018). A cross-national exploration of societal-level factors associated with child physical abuse and neglect. *Global Public Health, 13*(10), 1495–1506. 10.1080/17441692.2017.1404622

Merkul-Holguin, L., Fluke, J. D., & Krugman, R. D. (Eds.). (2019). *National systems of child protection: Understanding the international variability and context for developing policy and practice*. Cham: Springer International Publishing.

Myrdal, A. (1942). Nation and family. *Population Index, 8*(1), 10–12. Retrieved July 4, 2020, from www.jstor.org/stable/3030599

Pathways in a Forest. (2019, September). *Indigenous guidance on prevention-based child welfare*. http://www.westcoastleaf.org/wp-content/uploads/2019/09/Pathways-in-a-Forest.pdf

Skivenes, M., Barn, R., Kriz, K., & Poso, T. (2015). *Child welfare systems and migrant children: A cross country study of policies and practices*. New York: Oxford University Press.

Spratt, T., Nett, J., Bromfield, L., Hietamäki, J., Kindler, H., & Ponnert, L. (2015). Child protection in Europe: Development of an international cross-comparison model to inform national policies and practices. *The British Journal of Social Work, 45*(5), 1508–1525. https://doi.org/10.1093/bjsw/bcu109

State report on the children situation in the Russian Federation. (1998). *Moscow: Synergy*, 1999 (p. 40).

The Resolution of the Council of Ministers of the USSR dated 17 Aug.1988 N 1022 "On the organization of family-based care homes" dated 17 August 1988.

The Russian Federation in 1992 (Statistical Yearbook). (1993). Moscow. Republican information and publishing center (p. 251).

The Russian statistical yearbook: Stat.SB. (2001). State Statistical Committee of Russia (p. 212). Moscow.

Tyndik, A. S., & Biryukova, S. (2014). On overcoming the risks of social exclusion of orphaned children and parentless children in modern Russia. In V. Schmidt, E. Yarskaya-Smirnova, & Zh. Chernova (Eds.), *Family and childhood policy in post-socialism: Collective* (p. 211). Monograph. Moscow.

The XV International Scientific and Practical Conference: Psychology of Education: Best Practices of Working with Childhood (November 20-22, 2019). Moscow: Russian Federation.

Contents

Chapter 1
Armenia

Lilit Asoyan

1.1 Introduction

Armenia is a land-locked country that is located in the geographic Transcaucasus region between Europe and Asia. A rich and ancient history has also included numerous episodes of invasion and conquest. In 1915 the Ottomon Empire was responsible for a campaign of deportation and massacres that continued into 1918. The Soviet Republic of Armenia was established in 1920; on September 23, 1991 Armenia declared independence from the former Soviet Union. As with many of the former republics, established social institutions, including those for the protection of children, began to undergo a gradual transformation.

In 1993, Armenia ratified the UN Convention on the rights of the child, an international legal document that defines the rights of children to education, recreation and leisure, to enjoy cultural achievements and to provide other services to children by UN member States. All States that have ratified the instrument must regularly submit reports on the implementation of the relevant rights to the coordinating and monitoring Committee on the rights of the child. States must submit an initial report 2 years after accession to the Convention, followed by periodic reports every 5 years. The Committee reviews each report and presents its views and recommendations to the state party in the form of "concluding observations".

In 2003 the number of children in social institutions and guardianship institutions increased because of economic and social conditions in Armenia. This was a cause for great concern. With technical support from international organizations such as the United Nations, the family code in Armenia has been revised to ensure the

L. Asoyan (✉)
International Scientific Educational Center, National Academy of Sciences RA, Shirak State University After M. Nalbandyan, Gyumri, Armenia
e-mail: lilitasoyan@rambler.ru; lilicat08@mail.ru

I. Earner, A. Telitsyna (eds.), *The Development of Child Protection Systems in the Post-Soviet States*, Child Maltreatment 12,
https://doi.org/10.1007/978-3-030-59588-3_1

protection of children through non-institutional care as well as to start work on the introduction of foster families. Since 2008, Armenia has committed itself to funding and expanding the use of foster families as a primary institution for the care of children who cannot remain in their own families. A strategic program was developed to reform institutions dealing with child protection described by the phrase "unloading orphanages". The government has taken many concrete steps in this direction in 2016, but many mechanisms have not been clarified. Current barriers include the ongoing reliance on institutional care, especially for disabled children and lack of funding for community-based support services.

1.2 The Definition of a Child

The definition of the term "child" is given in article 41 of the Republic of Armenia Family Code[1]: "A child is considered to be a person who has not reached the age of eighteen." Often the term "minor" is used instead of the term "child", but in both cases it refers to a person who has not reached physical and social maturity, as a result of which he/she cannot fully realize and his/her rights. In this case, the guarantor of the rights of the child, as well as all citizens, is the state that takes care of the social protection of children. On December 29, 2003, the government adopted the National Program for the Protection of Children's Rights 2004–2015 as a mechanism to establish a framework for the development of child protection in Armenia.[2] To develop this document, an interdepartmental Commission was created, the working group of which included representatives of the ministries of Foreign Affairs, Social Security, Justice, Health, Education and Science, Youth and Culture, as well as the representatives of the police, the National Assembly and Non-governmental organizations (NGOs) ("Im Iravunk" ("My right"); "Orran" ("Cradle"); "Huisi Kamurj" ("Bridge of hope"); "Association for children's health", "Children First". This program was developed in accordance with the provisions of the UN Convention on the Rights of Children, the recommendations of the UN Committee for the protection of children's rights, as well as within the framework of Armenia's obligations under the Vienna Declaration and programme of action.

A three-stage child protection system was introduced in Armenia in 2005, including the National Commission for the Protection of Children's Rights at the national level, the Division for the Protection of the Rights of Families, Women and Children at the regional level, and the Commission for Guardianship and Guardianship and Protection at the Community Level. The mission of the regional divisions is

---

[1]Family code of the Republic of Armenia, adopted on November 9, 2004//available URRL// https://www.arlis.am/DocumentView.aspx?docid=62819 (accessed 04.09.2019).

[2]See "Decision of the RA Government N 1745-Ն of December 18, 2003 on approval of the national program on protection of children's rights in the Republic of Armenia for 2004–2015" (in Armenian), available URRL// https://www.arlis.am/DocumentView.aspx?docid=11712 (accessed 04.09.2019).

to guarantee the rights of children left without care, to implement policies aimed at protecting the rights of women and children, and to implement targeted social protection programs for the latter. However, current criticism of this framework is that the number of staff and funding at each level do not adequately contribute to the rapid identification of vulnerable groups and provide necessary services.

The local Commissions for Guardianship and Protection at the Community Level operate mostly on concepts left over from the Soviet period. These commissions are under the leadership of the city mayor or village mayor and they are in charge of appointing guardians for children left without parents. They have the right, if necessary, to ensure the removal of the child from the family and to apply to the court for restriction or deprivation of parental rights if it is detected that a child needs protection from abuse or neglect. The decision of these commissions is legally bound. Territorial social security institutions, which employ more than 500 civil servants across Armenia, monitor compliance with the law on social support. These institutions "identify low-income families, put them on record in the system of assessing poverty, implement the assignment of benefits and support, and independently or jointly with public organizations develop projects for social and psychological rehabilitation, participate in the development and implementation of projects for the social development of the service area, provide information and advice to citizens, and if necessary, send citizens to the appropriate institutions for more detailed specialized assistance."

1.3 Institutional Care

Prior to 2005 children's homes—institutional care facilities called 'orphanages' provided for children that were either abandoned, neglected or those who were truly orphaned. Until recently, there were six public and four private orphanages, two of which were operated by SOS Children's Village. Another private facility was named after Mother Teresa—"Tiramayr Ayastan Center". However, as part of the reforms in child protection begun in 2005, the state has gradually closed these institutional children's homes and introduced out of home care through the use of foster families and social workers.[3] From 2005 to 2009. The Center for Child Support of the Armenian Aid Foundation, in cooperation with the Ministry of Labor and Social Affairs of the United Nations Children's Fund (UNICEF) in Armenia implemented a pilot program for the establishment of the institution of guardianship. Through this pilot program 32 children found shelter in 30 foster families. The purpose of this pilot program was to place children in a foster home if it

[3]See Read more "Orphanages are closed, where will our children be?" (in Armenian)// https://armarlur.com/70612-2/

was impossible to return to the biological family to the detriment of the child's interests.[4] Since 2018, the state has continued the program of closing institutional care facilities with the main focus now being on returning children to biological families or making replacement guardianship arrangements through foster families. If for some reason the previous two options are not possible, the child will be able to live in small family group homes, which are not only less expensive to operate but, also provide children with a more home-like environment.

The question of what to do about institutional care for children is an ongoing issue. The National Assembly in May 2019 took up the issue of transferring children, as well as some functions for the custody of children to public organizations were discussed,[5] since a rather serious amount is spent on the maintenance of children in specialized children's institutions. So, one child on average provided from 8 to 10 thousand AMD (15–20 US dollars at the exchange rate in 2019), whereas for the child in foster (foster) family is allocated 250 thousand drams per year (approx $500) are allocated for the child in foster (foster) family, which also includes the salary of the parent for the care and maintenance of the child.[6] As of 2017, there were 24 children in 21 foster families. By 2018, 65 children had found shelter in foster families, some of whom left the family when they reached adulthood.[7]

1.4 "Residential Care Homes" or Boarding Schools and the Issue of Disability

In addition to children's homes, there are also boarding schools in Armenia, which are officially called "Boarding Institutions for the care and protection of children", of which 8 are state-owned, and one is a charitable private organization. These institutions were re-organized in 2007. When enrolling a child in a boarding school, the family must be registered in the social program of "Family Poverty Allowance". These boarding school institutions which were common throughout Central and Eastern Europe now exist only in Armenia. Currently, children from 6 to 18 years of age undergo social rehabilitation in boarding schools. In contrast to institutional care homes or orphanages, where the guardian of the child is the state, in a boarding school the guardian is a parent or other official representative. Children spend the whole week at boarding schools, but weekends and holidays can be spent with the

[4]Melikyan G., Gevorgyan A., From the orphanage to the family: how much does child care cost?// https://ampop.am/orphanages-and-foster-families-in-armenia/ (available 19.09.2019).

[5]See more "public organizations will deal with issues of orphanages in Armenia – Minister"// https://news.am/arm/news/515394.html, 29.05.2019.

[6]Melikyan G., Gevorgyan A., From the orphanage to the family: how much does child care cost?// https://ampop.am/orphanages-and-foster-families-in-armenia/ (available 19.09.2019).

[7]Melikyan G., Gevorgyan A., From the orphanage to the family: how much does child care cost?// https://ampop.am/orphanages-and-foster-families-in-armenia/ (available 19.09.2019).

family. Specialized boarding schools for children with disabilities are also functioning in Armenia under the Ministry of Education and Science. As they are funded by the number of pupils, allegations have been made that the flow of children to such institutions is poorly controlled and may not only include children with disabilities, but also socially disadvantaged children from poor families. According to the results of research in 2019, out of 260 children in four boarding schools, only 20 needed the services of specialized institutions, because their level of disability made it is impossible for them to live in a family. Based on this, the government of the Republic of Armenia decided to close such boarding schools, which, of course, was perceived ambiguously by the society, not only for ethical reasons: There is a question of employment of workers of boarding schools, and also the future of pupils. As noted by the Deputy Minister of Labor and Social Affairs Zhanna Andreasyan: "The process of disbanding boarding schools is not a separate decision, but part of a policy aimed at creating conditions for children to live in families. This process will not stop, eventually it will also include children's homes and specialized institutions for child care and custody.[8]" At the moment the issue of closing four boarding schools is being considered. The government has set a course to strengthen the institution of the family, introduce the institution of guardians, foster families, and send children to the so-called "children's villages".

The provision of support to families with disabled children through models based on "children's villages" are not without controversy. On August 8, 2019, the government of Armenia decided to grant the territory of the Ararat region to the charity organization "Armenian Caritas" for the construction of a city for 600 children from socially disadvantaged families and children with disabilities, where they will be provided with care, treatment, and education. Educational programs will also be implemented in the city. The City of Children project is based on a model of a city for adults with its own infrastructure-a kindergarten, a middle and high school, a hospital, a sports complex and other institutions designed for people with mobility problems. Residents of the city should be able to acquire a profession, learn crafts, computer skills that they can develop in the established processing, craft industries, guest houses, restaurants and other places.[9] However, the Human Rights Defender of Armenia expresses concern about social inclusion of disabled children regarding this program, as it contradicts the best interests of the child. The implementation of the program in this version will contribute to the strengthening of stereotypes and prejudices against children with disabilities and socially disadvantaged children. In particular, the Ombudsman of Armenia raised concerns stating that removing disabled children from their communities and placing them in a specially built

[8]See Paytyan M., after the disbanding of boarding schools, the turn will reach children's homes, 05.09.2019// https://armeniasputnik.am/society/20190905/20281902/gisherotikneri-lutsarumic-heto-herty-nayev-mankatnerin-e-hasnelu.html

[9]"City of children" for eight thousand people will be built in Armenia, 12.08.2019// available URRL// https://ru.armeniasputnik.am/society/20190812/20035656/Gorod-detey-postroyat-v-Armenii.html (accessed 04.09.2019).

"villages" opposes the equal rights of persons with disabilities as to liberty of movement and freedom of choice of residence.

According to the Human Rights Defender, the Republic of Armenia should be guided by the high mission of protecting the rights of the disabled. The state must promote, protect and ensure the full and equal enjoyment by all persons with disabilities of all human rights and fundamental freedoms, as well as respect for their dignity. The position of the Armenian Ombudsman was presented to the government with a proposal to finalize the program in the best interest of the child.[10]

1.5 Community-Based Care: Day Care and Inclusive Schools

In Armenia, there are public day-care centers for children, as well as centers organized by the NGO "Huisi Kamurj" ("Bridge of hope"). There are also public/private partnership centers through "Caritas", "Orran", "Children of Armenia Foundation", "World Vision" providing services to children from socially disadvantaged vulnerable families and the disabled.

With the support of the UN Children's Fund, international organizations, local public organizations, and the Ministry of Education and Science, pilot programs on inclusive education have been implemented in Armenia. Children with disabilities have the opportunity to study in regular schools. Currently 2500 disabled children are being educated in 100 schools throughout Armenia. There is now public support to move to full inclusive education.

Health and rehabilitation centers perform important work to improve the health of children with disabilities, reducing the risk of falling into special institutions, as well as decreasing the risk of complications. There are eight such centers in Armenia, which receive some subsidy from the state.

Local public organizations, such as "Aravot" ("Morning") take an active part in the program for closing orphanages and boarding schools, providing support to foster families, as well as providing a package of material support to the biological families of children from boarding schools.

[10]"The City" for children program contradicts the best interests of the child—the position of the Armenian Ombudsman, aysor.am, 30.08.2019// https://www.aysor.am/ru/news/2019/08/30/%D0%BE%D0%BC%D0%B1%D1%83%D0%B4%D1%81%D0%BC%D0%B5%D0%BD/1601631 (accessed 04.09.2019).

1.6 Promising Practices for the Future

In December 2015, reforms in the sphere of children's rights protection in Armenia were discussed at a meeting of the National Commission for the Protection of Children's Rights. "The goal of all these procedures is to make the system of protection of children's rights more effective and efficient, and to organize the care and protection of children in families," said Minister Artem Asatryan. He also stressed the importance of the assistance and support that the Armenian government receives from the United States and other foreign countries. Tanya Radokay, UNICEF representative in Armenia, in her turn noted that many things are changing for the better in Armenia in the field of child rights protection: there is a transition from the large institutions that remained after the Soviet Union to alternative services and care for children in families. It is extremely important that the whole process is properly planned and implemented to ensure the best quality of care for children, otherwise these children may again be in the above-mentioned institutions, and this is desirable to avoid. In his turn, Advisor to the Minister of Labor and Social Affairs of Armenia, David Hakobyan noted that within the framework of reforms in the sphere of protection of children's rights, 5 draft decisions of the government and 1 draft decision of the Prime Minister were developed. The Commission will discuss these projects today, along with the need for their approval and the expected results, and the projects will be submitted to the government in the near future.[11]

In September 2017, Armenia launched a five-year public campaign "Replace Violence with Love" aimed at eliminating violence against children. Ten Armenian non-governmental organizations engaged in the protection of children's rights joined the initiative.[12]

Armenia submitted its first report on the implementation of children's rights in 1997. The Committee submitted its comments on the report in 2000, proposing a number of changes in the protection of children's rights. In 2003, the government of Armenia submitted a second, and in 2011 a third and a fourth report on the implementation of the Convention, which were examined by the Committee and in 2013 new recommendations were made in the form of "concluding observations". On June 12, Human Rights Defender Arman Tatoyan presented an extraordinary report on Armenia's compliance with its obligations to the UN Committee on the rights of the child. According to the Ombudsman's report, the recommendations of the Committee were not implemented by Armenia or were partially implemented. "Our research shows that Armenia did not pay due attention to the proposals sent to it by the UN Committee on the rights of the child under the Convention and related protocols. Many of these proposals were either not implemented or were partially

[11]Armenia is discussing reforms in the sphere of protection of children's rights, golosarmenii.am, 18.12.2015// https://golosarmenii.am/article/36036/v-armenii-obsuzhdayut-reformy-v-sfere-zashhity-prav-detej (accessed 04.09.2019).

[12]"Public campaign to eliminate violence against children", moj.am, 06.09.2017// http://moj.am/ru/article/1839 (accessed 04.09.2019).

implemented. Moreover, the Armenian public is not sufficiently aware of the Convention," Tatoyan said. The Ombudsman listed several areas in which the monitoring did not follow the recommendations of the UN Committee on the rights of the child.

Gender discrimination "Overcoming the problem of selective abortions in Armenia has not been implemented by informing the public that premature termination of pregnancy is a manifestation of discrimination. Artificial termination of pregnancy based on sex selection is prohibited, but it is very difficult to control illegal selective abortions in the era of rapidly developing technologies," Tatoyan said. According to him, the problem cannot be solved only by long-term bans. In addition, the sex ratio in Armenia continues to be high (according to the latest data, there are 115 men per 100 women in Armenia-ed.), which in itself indicates that selective abortions are secretly performed under the ban. "The legislation on the prohibition of discrimination is almost forgotten, and its mention in some institutions is unacceptable. It is not by chance that the RA law enforcement practice rarely finds court decisions that apply the RA law "on equal rights for women and men". This law, as a rule, does not apply to decisions on guardianship and protection," the Ombudsman said.

"**Despite the measures taken, children in difficult situations continue to be discriminated against**," Tatoyan said. According to him, discrimination against children in difficult situations is largely due to barriers, lack of awareness, stereotypes in society, as well as the lack of comprehensive judicial practice and, in general, legal norms to prevent it. "It should be mentioned that the concept document of the state for the protection of children's rights does not mention any restrictions. However, the services provided to ensure equal rights and opportunities for children in difficult life situations are mainly provided not with regard to the rights of the child or his/her interests, but to meet his/her needs," he said. According to the Ombudsman, despite the steps taken, access to certain medical services between urban and rural communities is not systematically resolved. In addition, most of the buildings of educational institutions are not adapted for children with disabilities.

Custody issues "in Armenia, cases when children are sent to orphanages on the initiative of their biological parents have become more frequent. For example, parents temporarily refuse to take care of their child if they have a disability or are socially vulnerable. As a result, the child ends up in a social institution. Very often, parents do not give up their rights, leaving their children in orphanages, which does not allow them to be adopted by other families in the future.",—said Tatoyan. According to the Ombudsman, it was necessary to create a legislative framework for the care of children temporarily out of the family, taking into account the already established practice and its necessity. The consent of the parents to adopt a child must be expressed in a statement by a notary or the head of the organization in which the care of at least 69 children left without parental care is performed.

As for the reduction of funding for children's education and health "not only has there not been significant progress in providing funds for health and education since 2013, moreover, the number of deductions has decreased, and this is despite the fact that back in 2007 the UN Committee on the rights of the child recommended increasing funding for these industries," says the Ombudsman. Health spending in 2017 was about 1.5% of GDP, while education spending fell to 2.34% of GDP. According to the medium-term program of public spending for 2018–2020, by 2020 it is proposed to reduce the share of GDP allocated to health to 1.06%, and education-by 1.85%.

Strategy for the protection of children's rights "significant part of the activities envisaged in the Strategic plan for the protection of children's rights in the Republic of Armenia and its implementation schedule are steps that require funding from other sources not prohibited by law. However, the strategy for the protection of children's rights does not have a clear budget assessment, which makes it impossible to assess what resources are needed for its implementation," Tatoyan said. According to the Ombudsman, the activities of the National Commission for the protection of children's rights have become ineffective in recent years. "In fact, no regular sessions are convened. The last post on the Commission's website was published on January 31, 2013," he said.

The position of the Armenian office of UNICEF "The most basic proposals of the UN Committee on human rights, in particular, the creation of a coordinating body, the formation of a common policy and the proper financing of health and education, have Not been implemented. This is reflected in the overall situation. Investments and assistance from abroad and the Diaspora are not as important as increasing the share of education and health from the budget and national GDP. In this matter, proper monitoring of the situation is necessary, which, unfortunately, is not available," said Tanya Radochay, a representative of the Armenian office of NISEF. According to her, Armenia has enough time to implement the Committee's recommendations before the next report, which is due in 2019. The Convention on the rights of the child is the first and main international legal instrument that addresses the rights of the child at the level of international law. The document consists of 54 articles detailing the individual rights of young citizens aged from birth to 18 years to fully develop their capabilities in conditions free from hunger and need, cruelty, exploitation and other forms of abuse. The Convention on the rights of the child has been ratified by all UN member States except the United States and Somalia. The Committee on the rights of the child is a body of 18 independent experts who monitor the implementation of the Convention by State parties. The Committee also monitors the implementation of the two Optional protocols to the Convention on the involvement of children in armed conflict and on the sale of children, child prostitution and child pornography.[13]

Nevertheless, in the ranking "Index of motherhood" the best countries for mothers and children according to the International NGO "Save the Children" among 178 countries, Armenia ranked 95th place, ahead of in the region of Georgia

[13] Armenia has not fulfilled part of its obligations to the UN Committee on the rights of the child-Ombudsman, AMI "news-Armenia", 12.06.2018// https://newsarmenia.am/news/analytics/armeniya-ne-vypolnila-chast-obyazatelstv-pered-komitetom-oon-po-pravam-rebenka-ombudsmen/ (accessed 04.09.2019).

(98) and Azerbaijan (99th place).[14] Armenia's well-being index is calculated according to the system proposed by the UN, which includes the following criteria:

1. economic/financial well-being of the family;
2. the state of the child's relationship with family and peers;
3. health condition of the child;
4. behavior of the child, including leading to a decrease in the level of safety of his/her life (use of drugs, alcohol, etc.);
5. educational achievements of the child;
6. inclusion of the child in the life of the group, community (participation in educational, economic and political institutions);
7. emotional well-being of the child.[15]

August 28, 2019 Minister of Justice of the Republic of Armenia Rustam Badasyan received a delegation headed by the representative of the UN Children's Fund in Armenia (UNICEF) Tanya Radochay. The representative of UNICEF called a brilliant example the fact that Armenia is one of the countries with the lowest number of minors convicted in prison, and a good example is the creation of the Juvenile Justice Council, which, according to Tanya Radochay, works quite effectively. The next positive example of the representative of UNICEF, concerning Armenia, concerned the commitments made by the country to eliminate violence against children. During the discussion of issues related to the protection of children's rights, Minister Badasyan assured that one of the priorities of the government is the protection of human rights and solutions to the issues raised will find a place in the new national strategy for the protection of human rights and the resulting action program for 2020–2022.[16]

According to the new program of the government of Armenia, approved in February 2019, Schools should become development centers that contribute to the revival of social and cultural life of society, become open, free and creative centers. In the General education sector, the government's goal is to increase access to education by 2023, bringing to 70% the involvement of children over the age of three in all communities.[17]

On December 29, 2003, the government adopted the national programme for the protection of children's rights 2004–2015 as a mechanism.[18] To develop this

---

[14]Armenia is the leader among the countries of the region in the rating "index of motherhood"// https://www.panorama.am/ru/news/2014/05/08/armenia-rating-maternity/292334

[15]See Index of children's well-being// http://www.demoscope.ru/weekly/2014/0609/analit01.php

[16]Badasyan discussed issues of children's rights protection with UNICEF representative, armenpress.am, 28.08.2019// https://armenpress.am/rus/news/986181.html (available 04.09.2019).

[17]"The new government's program. 20 main points", radiovan, 2019.02.08// https://radiovan.fm/station/article/7586 (accessed 04.096.2019).

[18]See "Decision of the RA Government N 1745-Ն of December 18, 2003 on approval of the national program on protection of children's rights in the Republic of Armenia for 2004–2015" (in Armenian), available URRL// https://www.arlis.am/DocumentView.aspx?docid=11712 (accessed 04.09.2019).

document, an interdepartmental Commission was created, the working group of which included representatives of the Ministries of Foreign Affairs, Social Security, Justice, Health, Education and Science, Youth and Culture, as well as representatives of the police, the National Assembly and Public organizations ("Im Iravunk" ("My right"); "Orran" ("Cradle"); "Huisi Kamurj" ("Bridge of hope"); "Association for children's health", "First for children"—translated from Armenian L. A.). This program was developed in accordance with the provisions of the UN Convention on the rights of children, the recommendations of the UN Committee for the protection of children's rights, as well as within the framework of Armenia's obligations under the Vienna Declaration and programme of action.

Chapter 2
Azerbaijan

Rashad Huseynov and Farida Abbasova

2.1 Introduction: The Context of Child Protection in Azerbaijan

Azerbaijan is the former Soviet country sandwiched between Russia and Iran along the coast of the Caspian Sea. Azerbaijan is considered upper middle-income country by World Bank standards with significant revenue from the oil industry. The oil revenue also helped to increase the state budget. From 2003 within 10 years, state budget expenditure increased more than 20 times from AZN 887 million (£557 million) to AZN 22.9 billion (£14.37 billion) in 2013.[1] However, increased spending has not been directed towards human and social development. The main spending directions were infrastructure projects, general government services, and defence. Even in relative term the social security, education and health expenses fall from 18.2%, 23.7% and 11.6% in 2003 to 9.7%, 11.6% and 4.3% in 2009 respectively. In absolute term with the raising state budget, it means growth for these sectors, but in relative term, it proves that these sectors were not prioritised by the government. Although, government started to address this gap from 2009 and increase funding of these sectors, overall the social spending is still non-adequate compared to other European and some CIS countries.[2] Azerbaijan social spending as of GDP (health education and social security) for 2011 was 6.4%. To compare the same indicator for

[1]The World Bank, (2015). World Bank Group Azerbaijan Partnership Program Snapshot. World Bank Group.

[2]Aliyev, G., Valiyev, A., & Rustamova, S. (2011). Social Protection and Social Inclusion in Azerbaijan. European Commission. pp. 8–9.

R. Huseynov (✉) · F. Abbasova
SOS Children's Village Azerbaijan Association, Baku, Azerbaijan
e-mail: Rashad.Huseynov@sos-az.org

I. Earner, A. Telitsyna (eds.), *The Development of Child Protection Systems in the Post-Soviet States*, Child Maltreatment 12,
https://doi.org/10.1007/978-3-030-59588-3_2

the same year in Russia and Kazakhstan was 20% and 10.1 respectively[3] EU average of social spending (pension and social security) of GDP for 2017 was 18.8%.[4] It is also worth mentioning that the salary of personnel in the health and social services sectors and of the education sector is below the national average. However, in the last 2 years there is a notable increase in social spending by the government. For 2018, the social expenditure comprised 33.5% of total budget expenditures, which is more than previous years. Even more, for 2020 the share of social expenditures in the budget expenditures will be 40.7%, which is 9.9% or 2 billion 664.2 million AZN more than in 2019. It reflected itself in increases in the 2019 budget allocations for education (up by 13%) and health care (by 44.5%), which are important steps in terms of improving human capital.[5]

2.2 Child Protection System

Like in all post-Soviet countries, children deprived of parental care, disabled children, and abandoned children were traditionally provided by the state. The child welfare system was characterized by large residential care institutions.[6] Child protection system in Azerbaijan is still heavily based on Soviet concepts and ideology when "The State is above you and protects you" philosophy is widely believed and spread. The concept of welfare state is usually applied for parliamentary democracies and market economies but not for communist countries. However, in communist societies, the collective responsibility for the welfare of citizens also existed, and the relevant institutions were set up. The state was not the only agent taking responsibility for the well-being of citizens, but it had an exceptional significance in the welfare mix. Despite the past 20 years of regime change, welfare, and particularly Child welfare system and reforms are the ones that undergone the transition and changes the least.

In a nutshell, Azerbaijan still has a long way to go to achieve welfare state. Consequently, all these also associated with child welfare system. This is mainly due to gaps on social service provision in the country, which continues to reflect the heritage of Soviet approach. This makes demand and supply matter quite conflicting and overcoming stagnation and inaction with is still complicated.

[3]McCullaugh, M. E. (2013). From Well to Welfare: Social Spending in Mineral-Rich Post-Soviet States. Doctoral dissertation, University of California, Berkeley.

[4]https://ec.europa.eu/eurostat/statistics-explained/index.php/Government_expenditure_on_social_protection

[5]https://fed.az/az/dovlet/2020-ci-il-budce-layihesi-acilandi-meblegler-reqemler-63315

[6]Gross, Rebecca (2009) Return to Investment in Child Welfare Reform: the CEE/CIS Region, KSC Research Series (USAID: Washington, DC), April 10.

2.2.1 Existing Legislative Framework

The population of Azerbaijan in 2019 became 10,000,000. Of this number, nearly 3,000,000 or 30% are children. According to the State Statistical Committee of Azerbaijan, there are 13,117 children in various institutions under Ministry of Health, Ministry of Labor And Social Protection and Ministry of Education. This figure was 23,869 in 1991 and mainly after implementation of State Programme of Fosterage of Children from State Child Institutions (De-Institutionalisation) and Alternative Care (2006–2015) dropped two times and fluctuated between 10 and 13 thousand in the last decade.[7] However, the state program on De-Institutionalization was not fully successful as there still 45 boarding schools and residential care facilities in the country. The 95% of children spending their most of the time in public institutions have a family or at least one living family member. The number of disabled children are around 73,000 comprising the 2.4% of children population.[8] Out of these children, only 13% receive education at home, and 7% attend special schools. Access most of children's with severe disability to any form of education is denied.[9]

As globally accepted, every child has a right to adequate care and supervision and to be free from abuse, neglect, and exploitation and responsibility of parents/care givers and welfare system is to provide and protect the fundamental right of every child in safe upbringing. Article 24 of the Constitution of the Republic of Azerbaijan provides that everyone, from the moment they are born, possesses inalienable rights and liberties. The Family Code provides that parents are responsible for the child's "health and psychological, physical and moral development" and have an obligation to protect the child's rights and interests.

Children without parental care are under the special protection of the state. The law of the Republic of Azerbaijan on "Social protection of orphan children and children deprived from parental care" defines the measures of protection of children of this category during their secondary and higher education.[10]

The Republic of Azerbaijan ratified Convention on the Rights of the Child on 21 July 1992. The CRC is incorporated into national law. In 1993, the Republic of Azerbaijan signed Universal Declaration on "Survival, protection and development of children". The President of the Republic of Azerbaijan signed two Optional Protocols of the Convention—"Involvement of children in armed conflicts" and "Sale of children, child prostitution and child pornography" of the CRC in 2000. In 2004 Parliament of the Republic of Azerbaijan ratified the Convention №182 on "Elimination of the worst forms of child labour" and Recommendation №190 of the International Labour Organization and the Hague Convention on International adoption of children.

---

[7] State Statistical Committee of the Republic of Azerbaijan, 'Demographic Indicators', 2019.

[8] State Statistical Committee of the Republic of Azerbaijan, 'Demographic Indicators', 2019.

[9] https://qaziler.az/news.php?id=57639#.XZjPFEYzZPY

[10] http://www.mfa.gov.az/en/content/

The issues concerning social and legal protection of children are regulated by the Constitution of the Republic of Azerbaijan and number of laws. The main document in this sphere is the Law of the Republic of Azerbaijan on Child Rights adopted on 19 May 1998. The law was prepared in accordance with international documents such as Universal Declaration on "Human Rights" (1989), Declaration on Child Rights, UN Convention on the Rights of the Child (1989), Universal Declaration on "Survival, protection and development of children" (1990) and reflects rights of children approved at the international level and obligations of the state to realize these rights.[11]

Local relevant legislation

- Law of the Republic of Azerbaijan on Social Services, 2011
- The guaranteed level (scale) of free public social service to Persons (families) in hardship, 2014
- The guidelines for the provision of the home-based (mobile) social services, 2013
- The Guidelines for the referral of vulnerable persons to the state social service facilities 2013,
- The Law of the Republic of Azerbaijan on the Regulation of Commissions on Minors' Affairs and Protection of Minors' Rights, 2002
- Law on Social Protection of Children Deprived of Parental Care, 1999
- The Law of the Republic of Azerbaijan on the Rights of the Child, 1998
- The Family Code of the Republic of Azerbaijan, 1999
- The Law on Prevention of domestic violence, 2010
- The law on social adaptation of persons released from prisoners
- Law on Disability Prevention and Disabled Persons (Rehabilitation and Social Protection), 1992
- The Law of the Republic of Azerbaijan on Targeted Social Assistance, 2006
- The Law of the Republic of Azerbaijan on Compulsory Medical Surveillance of Children, 2013

2.2.2 Existing Child Protection Practice

There is no fixed definition of what child protection services should cover but Article 19 of the UNCRC gives a definition. It requires states to provide protection to children from "*all forms of physical or mental violence, injury or abuse, neglect or negligent treatment, maltreatment or exploitation, including sexual abuse*". It also postulates t—"*all appropriate legislative, administrative, social and educational measures . . . to provide necessary support for the child . . . as well as for other*

[11]Republic Of Azerbaijan Ministry Of Foreign Affairs, 2013.

forms of prevention and for identification, reporting, referral, investigation, treatment and follow-up of instances of child maltreatment".[12]

Similarly, to other ex-CIS states, the child protection system in Azerbaijan based heavily on the use of institutionalisation. Nevertheless, institutionalisation is still the main child protection extent.

There is a developed National Plan for Protection of Children's Rights in Azerbaijan, but it does not stress and instrumentally address poverty reduction and family support services and strategies. There are addition documents addressing Child Welfare System: National Action Plans on Trafficking in Human Beings[13] and on Street and Neglected Children,[14] State Programs on De-institutionalisation and Alternative Care (2006–2015)[15] and on the Improvement of Refugees' Living Conditions and Work Opportunities.[16]

However, neither the law nor the Action Plans or Programmers demands the executive body to take pro-active measures to identify and work with families in need of social assistance and support. In addition, since the reforms have been taking place, there has been no consistent development of community-based services, prevention mechanisms to support and assist at risk group of children, families and communities. Moreover, there is still lack of supportive mechanisms to help children and risk of abuse, neglect and separation.

To analyse the lack of state-funded community services, it is clear that there is no specific direction or appointed actor from the government to take charges and responsibilities for all essential care mechanisms. Instead, the services and very fragmented and lack of centralized or localized coordination and harmonisation makes them even more sporadic, chaotic, and at times completely irrelevant meeting child's needs.

The same in a way applies to the NGO sector[17] that has tried to address this gap in provision and development of services particularly community based. However, as majority of them had due to the limited funding sources, limited number of trained and qualified staff, limited support from other state actors, this gap has become hard to address.

Another issue, the country has been facing is lack of accurate and adequate facilities for provision of well-grounded care services. Facilities are not equipped properly, not child and child with special needs friendly, in many cases not accessible form distant and remote places, do not have or have limited trained professionals.

[12]Convention on the Rights of the Child, *adopted* 20 Nov. 1989, G.A. Res. 44/25, U.N. GAOR, 44th Sess., Supp. No. 49, U.N. Doc. A/44/49 (1989) (*entered into force* 2 Sept. 1990), *reprinted in* 28 I.L.M. 1448 (1989), art. 19(2).

[13]Adopted 26 June 2005.

[14]Adopted in 2003.

[15]Adopted 29 March 2006.

[16]Adopted in October 2007.

[17]In particular, Caspian, Mushfig, Rainbow, Origami and UAFA.

2.2.3 Who Is a Child at Risk?

Most states provide a definition, generally in the terms used in Article 19 of the UNCRC, of children who are considered to be 'at risk' and thus in need of referral to the child protection authorities. This includes children who are subject to physical or mental violence, injury or abuse, neglect or negligent treatment, maltreatment or exploitation, including sexual abuse.

Article 51(5) of the Family Code provides that a child has the right to make an application to the executive body for protection of his or her rights and, upon reaching the age of 14, to make an application to the court. Under the law on the Commissions of Minors' Affairs and Protection of Minors' Rights, the Commission[18] can "*receive minors, their parents and other legal representatives, to hear their complaints or applications to understand their personal case*".[19]

2.2.4 Main Actors and Mechanisms of Provision Child Welfare Services

The Ministry of Health of Azerbaijan Republic is entirely responsible for the care of babies from 0 to 3 years (including in particular abandoned children) and for health assistance to children with disabilities and chronic diseases. Institutions and service centres under the Ministry of Health are:

The **emergency unit for babies abandoned** at birth, known with the Russian acronym of OMD. Located in Baku, it provides the first health assistance to children neglected in maternity hospitals.

4 baby homes (2 in Baku, 1 in Ganja, 1 in Nakhchivan), including 1 home for babies with "psycho-neurological problems." Set up according to a heavily 'medicalized' model, baby homes employ medical staff (physicians and nurses, working in lab coats) to take care of children up to 3 years.

Sanatoriums for children with chronic/infectious diseases and psycho-neurological problems. Although the hospitalisation period should be limited only to the time needed for the health treatment, sanatoriums have to be seen as residential institutions.

The Ministry of Education has the widest responsibility over children's residential institutions, with the exclusion of the few facilities that are not expected to exercise an educative function.

3 institutes for children deprived of parental care (orphanages), out of which two including a boarding school (and thus becoming 'total institutions', since children are deprived of any contact with external services).

---

[18]Which is presumed to be one of the executive power organs.

[19]The Law on Commissions of Minor's Affairs and Protection of Minors' Rights, 2002, art. 5(8).

10 Special Boarding Schools for Children with Disabilities**.** The education system in Azerbaijan was inherited from the Soviet times and despite recent efforts to initiate inclusive practices, does not allow for the mainstreaming of children with special needs.

24 boarding schools of the general type, where children are supposed to stay only during the school year. In reality, in a vast number of cases children are left in the institutions during almost the whole year; frequently the delicate bonds with the family, often very poor and living far away from the schools, are completely cut.

Among these institutions it is worth mentioning the two 're-education' schools with a special regime for boys with 'disruptive behaviours.'

3 centres for home education (located in Baku, Ganja and Sumgayit) register children entitled to receive the service and send teachers to their homes.

Institutions under the Ministry of Labor and Social Security The Ministry of Labor and Social Security assists needy families and children more in terms of financial support than in social services.

The **Department of Social Support**, from where resources are transferred to the districts for the distribution of allowances to all the entitled categories of citizens (among which is the already-mentioned generic allowance for children, allowances for IDPs and refugees, the ones for children with disabilities, and several other—however minimal—contributions);

3 residential institutes for children with severe learning disabilities. The main function of such institutions is to provide children with shelter and basic material life conditions; they are not supervised by the Ministry of Education since they are not supposed to provide any form of education since the children are considered "unable to learn."

9 Institutions under the Executive Committees. The welfare services in Azerbaijan are administered, at district level, within the Executive Committees. Within the committees, several commissions and offices are relevant for the protection of children, not always directly corresponding to the previously listed national commissions/departments.

The **Commissions on Juvenile Issues and Protection of Minors' Rights** (Commission on Minors). Established in 2002 with the intent to provide children with a higher level of protection, the commissions are composed of 2 full time employees (generally 1 lawyer and 1 administrative staff), and involve other professional figures on a case basis. Supervised at district level by the Heads of the Executive Committee, the Commissions on Minors report directly to the Deputy Prime Minister of Humanitarian Issues in the Cabinet of Ministers. The Commissions on Minors are involved with the police in juvenile justice issues, and pronounce their determining opinion in the identification of proper care solutions for children deprived of parental care. The main objective of the commissions as mentioned in regulation is to protect the rights and legal interest of children and to prevent juvenile delinquency and to coordinate related activities of relevant the local and state structure, body and institutions. Article 51.7 of the Family code if Azerbaijan also stresses that relevant local executive authorities control the protection of the rights of children.

The **Commissions on Guardianship and Adoption** composed of one child protection Inspector and one administrative staff in each district; here all the children abandoned or deprived of parental care are registered. The identification of tutors/guardians or adoptive families can be done at local level after a pronunciation by the court. If a solution is not found within a month, children are logged in a national register, and the case is managed by the relevant ministry (Health or Education). More than 90% of these children are taken care of by guardians (generally relatives, since the practice of fostering is not officially recognized in Azerbaijan) or adoptive families.

State Committee for Family, Woman and Child Issues is the main executive body of the Republic of Azerbaijan implementing state child policy. The Committee was established by the Decree of the Republic of Azerbaijan on 6 February 2006. The Committee is responsible for protection of children, improvement their welfare, provision of their rights and freedoms and also coordination of state policy in this sphere.

There are 11 Children and Family Support Centers (including regions) functioning under The State Committee on Family, Woman and Children Affairs of Azerbaijan Republic. Children and Family Support Centers is the alternative care model supporting children, women and families at risk, referring them to other services in the community and ensuring the provision of community based services in initial level as well as relevant support in case of Force Majeure. The centres are working the vulnerable group of population.

2.2.4.1 NGOs

From 2012 every year, the state contracts about **30** NGOs to provide various social services namely Day Care Services, Community based social services for disabled children, and various awareness raising campaigns in different regions of the country. However, the process is not sustainable, starts with delays and does not cover the whole country. Social workers are mainly recruited in these NGOs, where they work with family and children. Yet most of them are not social workers with diploma but trained paraprofessionals.

2.3 Alternative Care Models

Mentioned earlier, the **Commission of Minors and Guardianship Authority** are the main bodies responsible for safeguarding provision for children without parental care. However, the division of authority and responsibility is not always clear.

These actors are responsible to looking after the children child deprived of parental care. This can be via family based or residential care services. Where a child is placed in a residential institution, consent to placement will generally have to be obtained from the ministry responsible for the institution.

2.3.1 Guardianship

Under the Civil Code of Azerbaijan, the Guardianship Authority shall act as guardian to a child when he or she has no parents; where the parents have been deprived of their parental rights by a court,[20] and in cases where parents neglect their parental responsibilities or fail to protect the rights and interests of the child.[21] Under the Family Code of Azerbaijan, this also includes refusal to take a child back from a residential institution.[22] The Guardianship Authority is generally the initial guardian for the child, but within 3 months, a guardian (if the child is under the age of 14) or trustee (if the child is aged 14–18) should be appointed for the child.[23] Where a child is placed in an institution for children, the director of the institution may be appointed guardian.[24]

However, the Civil Code does not contain any details of the procedure to be followed by the Guardianship Authority in appointing a guardian and the authors were unable to find any regulations covering procedure.

Based on the Civil Code, any adult may become a guardian, provided: he/she is able to work, has no medical and or physical limitations, has not been deprived of parental rights before and is not an alcohol or drug addict.[25] The code also stresses 'morals' and ability to fulfil the obligations of a guardian, as well as the wishes of the child and the guardian's relationship with the child.[26]

In practice, the majority of children deprived of parental care appear to be in guardianship, many of them under the guardianship of the director of the residential home in which they are placed.[27] Where a child is placed in the care of an individual

[20] Civil Code of the Azerbaijan Republic, approved by the Law of the Azerbaijan Republic № 779-IG of December 28, 1999, entered into force 26 May 2000 according to the Law of the Azerbaijan Republic № 886-IG of 1 September 2000, Art. 33.

[21] Civil Code of the Azerbaijan Republic, approved by the Law of the Azerbaijan Republic № 779-IG of December 28, 1999, entered into force 26 May 2000 according to the Law of the Azerbaijan Republic № 886-IG of 1 September 2000, Art. 33 and Art. 35(1).

[22] Family Code of Azerbaijan, 2000, Art. 114(1).

[23] Family Code of Azerbaijan, 2000, Art. 137(2); Civil Code of the Azerbaijan Republic, approved by the Law of the Azerbaijan Republic № 779-IG of December 28, 1999, entered into force 26 May 2000 according to the Law of the Azerbaijan Republic № 886-IG of 1 September 2000, Art. 33.

[24] Civil Code of the Azerbaijan Republic, approved by the Law of the Azerbaijan Republic № 779-IG of December 28, 1999, entered into force 26 May 2000 according to the Law of the Azerbaijan Republic № 886-IG of 1 September 2000, Art. 35.4.

[25] Civil Code of the Azerbaijan Republic, approved by the Law of the Azerbaijan Republic № 779-IG of December 28, 1999, entered into force 26 May 2000 according to the Law of the Azerbaijan Republic № 886-IG of 1 September 2000, Art. 35.2; Family Code of Azerbaijan, 2000, Arts. 137(3) and 144.

[26] Family Code of Azerbaijan, 2000, Art. 137(2).

[27] See State Statistical Committee of the Republic of Azerbaijan, 'Demographic Indicators'. Government statistics do not break out the number of children in guardianship separately, including children in fostering and in guardianship into the same figure. However, it is generally thought that the vast majority of these children are in guardianship.

guardian, this is generally an extended family member. Where a child is placed under guardianship or trusteeship, the child shall live with that person. When a child reaches the age of 16, he or she may live separately from the trustee with the consent of the Guardianship Authority, provided that this will not have any adverse effect on his upbringing and the protection of his rights and interests.

2.3.2 Fostering

Fostering is a relatively new concept in Azerbaijan, introduced into the Family Code in 2000.[28] Children who are without parental care as well as children in educational, treatment and social protection institutions may be placed with foster families. However, the process of placement is briefly set out in Article 145.2:

The foster family should reach agreement to take a child or children with the executive power organ (not clear who is that organ and what are the procedures of foster care implementation): Siblings must be placed together except where this is not in the best interests of the child. If the child is over the age of 10, the child must consent to the placement.

The placement shall be for the time period agreed but this may be shortened if circumstances change or the placement breaks down. Foster parents should be paid a monthly grant for each child, determined by legislation.[29]

The executive body has a duty to monitor the placement, though the nature and extent of that monitoring is not clear. There is little detail in the Family Code on how a foster parent shall be selected, though Article 144 of the Family Code sets out the categories of persons who may not be considered or used as foster parents.

The State on De-Institutionalization (2006–2015) highlights the development and support of fostering, especially for children who are being de-institutionalised.[30] However, the regulation of foster care developed within state program was not approved by the Cabinet of Ministries. This is the main reason, which prevent the development of fostering services at local level and inhibits the expansion of foster care in the country.

2.3.3 Small Group Homes

The Small Group Home (SGH) as alternative care model were firstly introduced in Azerbaijan in 2013 within the "State Programme on alternative care and

[28]See Art. 142.

[29]See Family Code of Azerbaijan, 2000, Art. 145.6. It was not possible to find the legislation containing details of how much is to be paid.

[30]State Programme on alternative care and Deinstitutionalization (2006–2015).

Deinstitutionalization" and unlike the foster care the Cabinet of Ministries approved its regulation. The SGH aims to ensure the right of the children deprived of parental care to adequate housing. In comparison with state orphanages, in group homes children have their own bedrooms, personal belongings and writing tables. Social workers (care assistants) care for children in several shifts here. Up to 12 children can live in until they turn 18. Those who decide to continue their education are allowed to continue to live in the group home. The children living small group homes go to nearby general education facilities (schools). Government took the turkish model, by separating group homes for girls and boys in Azerbaijan. However, there are only two small group homes built so far, one for girls in Baku city and one for boys in Lankaran city.[31]

2.4 Best Practice Models

Diversion Centre and Legal Clinic that was established in Narimanov District, Baku, by UNICEF Azerbaijan, the Ministry of Internal Affairs, the Ombudsman, the NGO Alliance and the British Embassy, in consultation with the Children's Legal Centre in 2007. The Diversion Project aims to provide a pre-trial diversion option to ensure that, in accordance with international human rights law, children are dealt with outside the formal criminal justice system, wherever possible. Children being at risk of offending are referred to the project by Commission on Minors and Police. In different years with the availability of funding the project expanded to different regions. Currently it operates only in Baku. It recruits social worker, psychologist, pedagogue and sport teacher. There is evaluation of this centre done in 2010 available in English, which finds that "On the whole, referring institutions were very positive with their feedback on the effectiveness of the Diversion Centre. In most cases, they felt that the Centre helped children to get their 'normal lives' back" (Unicef 2010).

SOS children Villages Azerbaijan as an umbrella organization of SOS KDI is one of the unique models and organizations that works in three different layers of child protection, namely Care, Prevention and Advocacy. It has hands on experience in working with children and families mainly in its Family Based Care and Family Strengthening (FS) Program. From 2001, it provides Family like care to 150–200 children annually. With its Family Strengthening program from 2006 it supports about 400 beneficiaries in three cities. The main objective of the project was to strengthen the families by supporting them and prevent the abandonment of children. SOS AZE is one of the rare organizations in the country, which applies case management system (multi team approach, assessment tools, Individual Plans, Data base system etc.) in working with its beneficiaries. FS projects are also being successfully implemented in other CEE/CIS countries.

[31]The Ministry of Education, 2016.

Agency for Sustainable and Operational Social Security *(Azerbaijani: Dayanıqlı və Operativ Sosial Təminat Agentliyi (DOST))* is a public legal entity which was created by order of President in order to improve governance in employment, social protection, labor. "DOST" centers provide employment services, labor, social protection and guarantees, as well as other services in accordance with the activities of the Ministry of Labor and Social Protection of Population of Azerbaijan. It collects all the services of Ministry of Labor and Social Protection of Population of Azerbaijan at one place using Single Window System.[32] Over 30 DOST Centers to be created in Azerbaijan until 2025. Despite the fact that it is not directly related with child protection system but with overall welfare system, surely with its expanding range of services it will have positive impact to protection of vulnerable children.

2.5 Transforming Child Adoption in Azerbaijan

In 2019, government of Azerbaijan decided to tackle the existing problems in child adoption process such as negative image of adoption process due to clarity and complexity, low number of adoptions (~40 p.a.) and increasing number of children in care institutions.

It is proposed to centralize the adoption process and digitalize it. The proposed adoption implementation process has detailed stages:

Child Placement—Adoptive parent application (assessment/training and exam)—Matching and visiting child at residential care—Trial period—Court-Monitoring.

Starting November 1, 2019, the MLSPP will the only responsible body for the policy and implementation of internal and inter-country adoption on country level. New process requires several jobs to be performed in each stage, which will be done by professional MTD (Social workers, psychologists, doctor, lawyer etc.). The responsible body for the process at the MLSPP level will be The Central Division of Adoption, and the field level the department of Adoption and Children Deprived of parental care of the DOST Agency.

Due to the new implementation plan, most of the articles on Family Code that regulates adoption process have changed and amended. According to the new law, the responsibility for the central registration of the children deprived of parental care is under the MLSPP and will be run through central electronic information system. All process that cover adoption will go through this electronic information system and there will be integrated information cross-government agencies.[33]

[32]The Ministry of Labor and Social Protection, 2019.

[33]The Ministry of Labor and Social Protection, 2019.

2.6 Future Objectives

2.6.1 Gaps in Legislation

Above mentioned actors are aimed to provide protection for children at risk of abuse, neglect or exploitation, in reality the existing model of Welfare it provides only a general framework, with no details on how children are to be identified, referrals investigated, child protection procedures initiated, decisions taken or measures to be applied. Neither does the legislation articulates clearly the roles and responsibilities of the respective bodies at local and national level. It does not specify clearly, which body has responsibility for the protection of children or for the provision of services that make up an integrated child protection system. In addition to the mentions there is still no monitoring body evaluating the services and the no minimum quality standards.

2.6.2 Lack of Child Centred Approach

The existing child welfare system in the country is shaped on a service-centred, rather than needs centred, model: the services according are still delivered to cover fixed referral procedures; the service providers react only when the problem reaches their premises. The provided services are limited, has no monitoring mechanisms, and often has pre-defined scenario without taking the need of child into professional account. The case management and outreaching methodologies do not characterize the welfare system in Azerbaijan.

2.6.3 That the Lack of Clear Responsibility at Central Government Level

There is lack of clear responsibility at central government level for the development of policy on child protection and it has been limited structural change in provision of child protection services at local level since independence. There needs to be a consensus at central government level as to which ministry or body has responsibility for development of national policy and ensuring the delivery of child protection services at local level. This body should also be responsible for setting national minimum quality standards in partnership with ministries and NGOs providing child protection services.

A child protection service should be established at local level and should have responsibility for promoting and safeguarding the welfare of children. Every local child protection service should provide a minimum guaranteed level of services to children at risk of abuse, neglect, exploitation and institutionalisation, and should be staffed appropriately to undertake this task. This body should absorb the current functions of the Commission on Minors and the Guardianship Commission. The minimum guaranteed level of services offered at local level should include identifying, investigating, assessing and providing care plans for children in need of protection, as well as the services necessary to meet those needs.

2.6.4 *The Lack of Data*

Due to the limited case management and gate keeping services, there is no duty to keep records of child protection referrals or their outcomes. Another serious barrier in reforming the system is lack of an effective data collection system and aggregated, disaggregated statistical data on child protection cases. There is no or limited national database for child protection cases. It should be a national, uniform policy on recordkeeping for all cases of child abuse, as well as staff training to understand its importance. In addition, consideration should be given to establishing a national database for child protection cases.

2.6.5 *Lack of Alternative Care Options*

Despite community-based alternatives, residential care remains the main placement for children without parental care. The criteria for admission to residential care are broad and there is a lack of written guidance to assist decision makers in determining whether institutionalisation is the appropriate placement for a child. In practice, many children are admitted to an institution at the request of their parents, for financial reasons, without any assessment of the child's needs or consideration of their best interests. Residential institutions for children are not covered by minimum quality standards, nor are they subject to a regular regime of inspection. The proper alternative care option should at least comprise foster care, small group home, respite care, family support and training centres, day care centres, rehab centres etc. Family strengthening and support services should in the heart of the child welfare services. Fostering should be a key component of the child protection system, and can be an effective gate-keeping mechanism when used to prevent the institutionalisation of children—particularly young children.

2.7 Conclusion

The purpose of the current study was to examine the existing child protection system in Azerbaijan and the path it has passed since independence. It also brings together different welfare services to tackle the problem of the child in need. The study finds found out that generally the child protection system of Azerbaijan is a subject to path dependency as the crucial role and responsibilities of child welfare system is not clearly structured and adequately developed yet. As globally accepted, the role of child protection is to provide and protect the fundamental right of every child in safe background and ensure that every child has adequate care and supervision and is free from abuse, neglect, and exploitation. Article 24 of the Constitution of the Republic of Azerbaijan[34] provides that everyone, from the moment they are born, possesses absolute rights and autonomies. The Family Code provides that parents are responsible for the child's "*health and psychological, physical and moral development*"[35] and have an obligation to protect the child's rights and interests.[36] However, the responsibilities and the borders in the decision making of all parts, which taking part in the process should be clearly set and defined. Despite the recent reforms like DOST services, transformation of adoption system, considerably increase in child related social benefits (by five time on average compared to 2005), the government has to show more commitment and implement reforms to achieve and establish proper child protection system in the country.

[34]The Constitution of the Republic of Azerbaijan, Art. 24.

[35]Family Code of Azerbaijan, 2000, Art. 58(1) and (2).

[36]Family Code of Azerbaijan, 2000, Art. 59.1.

Chapter 3
Estonia

Inna Klaos and Ekaterina Carrie

3.1 Introduction: Overview of Estonia

Estonia is the northern- most of the Baltic States. Culturally and linguistically it is most closely connect to Finland, although like its southern neighbors shares a history of invasions and conquests by the German Livonian Knights, Denmark and Russia. On February 24, 1991 Estonia declared itself independent from the former Soviet Union. In 2019 the population was 1,291,954 persons. Of these, 46.7% of the population is male and 53.3% is female.

In January and February 2020, 2075 children were born. Overall, the population growth in Estonia is −570. Of the total number of children in Estonia, approximately 13,000 are children identified with special health problems.

Population of Children in 2019

Age	Number of children
From 0 to a year	14,395
From 1 to 4	56,340
From 5 to 9	74,176
From 10 to 14	72,512
From 15 to 19	61,227
In total	278,650

I. Klaos (✉) · E. Carrie
Teadlik Lapsevanem MTÜ, Tallinn, Estonia
e-mail: inna@teadliklapsevanem.ee

I. Earner, A. Telitsyna (eds.), *The Development of Child Protection Systems in the Post-Soviet States*, Child Maltreatment 12,
https://doi.org/10.1007/978-3-030-59588-3_3

3.2 Socio-economic Profile of Estonia

Estonia is a member of the European Union since 2003. In the 15 years since Estonia joined the EU the country's net average wage has more than tripled from 363 € to 1098 €, and the minimum gross wage has increased more than 3.4 times from 158.50 € to 540 € (516.45 €, net). Estonia's GDP (PPP) doubled from 2004 to 2019 from $23.790 billion to $46.587 billion.

In Estonia, there are separate minimum wage rates for secondary school teachers, kindergarten teachers, and cultural workers with higher education. The average salary for employees of these professions will be equal to 120% of the average salary in the country.

3.3 Social Benefits and Allowances for the Population

Every family with a child receives a monthly child benefit which in 2019 is 60 € for the first child, 60 € for the second child, and 100 € for the third child and each subsequent child. The monthly allowance for a child as of 2019, whose parent is undergoing urgent or alternative service, is 300 € per month for each child until the end of the parent's term of service.

From 2020, the amount of the allowance for a child with a moderate degree of disability will be 138.08 €, and for a child with a severe degree of disability—161.09 €. An allowance of 241.64 € will be paid for a child with a severe medical condition.

About 13,000 children with disabilities live in Estonia. In comparison with 2009, their number has almost doubled. In 2017 child benefits at moderate level of disability was received by 5000 children; 7164 children with a severe level of disability, and 732 children with a profound degree of disability. Estonia has the longest 100% paid maternity leave in the world, with 62 paid weeks of maternity leave. Under Estonian law, not only the mother but also the father has the right to maternity leave. From July 1, 2020, paternity leave with 100% payment will be 30 days.

3.4 History of Social Protection of Children

Prior to the establishment of the Republic of Estonia in 1919, social protection laws and institutions in Estonia were based on the national laws of the Russian Empire. Hospitals also often functioned as social welfare institutions, where issues of custody and guardianship at the public level were closely intertwined. The social protection of children and their well-being were regulated by provincial and municipal laws adopted in 1775. These provincial laws also allowed for the creation of social security institutions for individuals, associations, cities and villages. In 1866, the

Social Security Act was passed which distributed social funds among three levels: primary welfare, which was handled by urban and rural communities, County-level welfare, which was handled by district and provincial welfare, and provincial-level social welfare. The parish community was responsible for the care of orphans, victims of violence, and infirm children who had no relatives to help. In 1925 The Riigikogu (Estonian parliament) passed a welfare legislation that provided financial assistance to individual people in need during periods of unemployment and provided support to poor families. Charitable and social welfare organizations came under the direction of the Ministry of Labor and Social Security. In 1934 the Riigikogu allowed private and religious charitable organizations and foundations to operate freely in providing assistance to individuals, families and children. After the Soviet occupation in 1940, private charities and charitable societies were liquidated.

3.5 Modern Child Protection System in Estonia

Since 1991, the system of protecting children in Estonia is governed by the Republic and is administered through the Council for the Protection of Children, the Ministry of Social Affairs, the Social Insurance Department, County elders and local self-government units under the Child Protection Act. The tasks of the government of the Republic include the development of draft legal acts and state strategies in the field of child protection, as well as budget planning.

The Council for the Protection of Children is a government Commission that focuses on collecting data and information in the field of child protection, on the basis of which family and child policy is formed. The tasks of the Ministry of Social Affairs include the organization of state protection of children and the formation of family and child policy.

The tasks of County offices include the implementation of state supervision in the counties when organizing the protection of children.

Through the Department of Social Insurance, families with children can apply for appropriate state benefits and services. The child protection division of the Department of Social Insurance offers support to specialists working with children and organizes national preventive work and cooperation between various spheres (social sphere, education, health, legal protection).

The local government organizes the protection of children at the local level and creates the necessary conditions in its city or municipality to ensure the rights and well-being of children.

Child protection services are provided at the local level through regional offices. These regional offices are tasked with ensuring that the state policies on child protection are being implemented, statistics are collected, a 24 h hotline is available and appropriate services such as counseling, mediation and preventive services are offered to families and children.

Fig. 3.1 The regional centers of the child protection division serve the following working regions: **North Regions** *Harju, Rapla and Järva counties*, **Eastern Region** *Ida-Viru and Lääne-Viru counties*, **Southern region** *Jõgeva, Põlva, Tartu, Valga, Viljandi and Võru counties*, **Western region** *Saare, Hiiu, Pärnu and Lääne counties*

The regional centers of the child protection Division are located in four Estonian cities-Tallinn, Jõhvi, Tartu and Pärnu (Fig. 3.1).

The legal basis for child protection services is based on principles of family law in Estonia that everyone has the right to inviolability of family and personal life and that government agencies, local self-government bodies and their officials must not interfere with the family or private life of anyone, except to protect the health, morals, public order or the rights and freedoms of others, to prevent crimes, or to detain a criminal in cases and in accordance with the law. Further, parents have the right and duty to raise and care for their children. This is balanced with the Convention of the Rights of the Child which codify the following:

Rights and responsibilities of the child

- Equal rights and obligations for all persons residing in the Republic of Estonia-Chapter II of the Constitution

- The child has the right to grow up in the family, and parents have the right and duty to raise the child and take care of it, ensuring full development, according to the age characteristics and development of the child.
- An orphan and a child left without parental care have the right to state support
- The child has the right to self-determination from, belonging to a nationality, and cultural and education in their native language
- A child has the same right to help and care, regardless of gender and nationality, regardless of his or her family, and regardless of whether he or she is healthy, ill, or has special health and development needs.
- Children have the right to freedom of thought, conscience, religion and expression
- The child has the right to a period of rest and leisure that he/she uses for age-appropriate enjoyable activities, depending on health, desires and opportunities
- The child has the right to privacy-privacy, communication and friendship. Slander on the honor and dignity of the child is not allowed
- The child must be protected from economic, physical and mental exploitation, as well as from work that is excessive or detrimental to his or her development or learning
- The child has the right to participate in the development of child protection programs

3.6 Children Who Are Under the Care of the State

At the end of 2018, the total number of children in substitute homes and families was 2468, of which 906 lived in family-type homes, 113 in substitute families, and 1429 with relatives. 287 children returned to the biological family. Children are removed from their biological family only if there is a threat to the health or life of the child. For a child protection specialist, removing a child from a family is an extreme measure that is only taken when all other methods do not work. Preferred placement is with relatives but if this is not possible, then with substitute families. The removal of a child from the family and the deprivation of parental rights are considered extreme measures that is taken by the court and social services. First of all, social workers tell the family about the services that can be provided to the family, about the benefits that the family can receive—social housing, help with household chores, and help families apply for these services and benefits.

Families are also referred for consultations to various specialists who can help parents correct the situation in the family. If necessary, parents are offered the opportunity to learn the skills necessary for taking care of the child. In addition, parents can be associated with various non-profit organizations and volunteers where they can be provided more extensive and informal support. If these methods don't help, parents are not necessarily stripped of their parental rights. For example, courts can restrict a parent's right to make certain decisions about a child's health, but otherwise they retain other rights. In addition, the court may restrict the rights of parents if it is obvious that the abuse of these rights creates a risk for the child.

When removing a child from the family, the child protection specialist must explain to the child, based on his age and intellectual characteristics, what happened and what will happen to him next (where the child moves, for how long, the opportunity to meet with parents and other relatives, etc.)

3.7 Family Reunification Practices

The first task facing child protection services is to assess, plan and support lifelong family relationships. If it is not possible to reunite a child with a biological family, there are the following options:

- Family care-according to the law on social guardianship, is the care of a person in a suitable family, of which he is not a member. Family care for a child is carried out on the basis of a written agreement concluded between the parish or city Council and the person taking care of the child. Family child care is a guardianship service offered to children as an alternative to an orphanage, which, according to research, can be considered a more appropriate form of child care than a foster home. Family care can be short-term or long-term, depending on the child's needs, but the goal is to return the child to his or her family. If adoption is an opportunity for the child to grow up in the family until adulthood, and the legal relationship between the child and the parents continues throughout life, then family care is more temporary and is intended primarily for situations in which the child is temporarily or for a long period, for example, due to the illness of the parent or for another reason, cannot live in his family, but the full withdrawal of parental rights from his parent is not justified. In the case of family care, it is important to maintain, and if necessary, create and improve the relationship between the child and his biological family. This is necessary in order to ensure that the UN Convention on the rights of the child provides for the child's right to know both parents and, if possible, to have their relationship. In order to ensure the safety of the child in the caregiving family, Articles 15 and 251-253 Of the law on social guardianship impose various requirements on the family, including the obligation to undergo training for PRIDE foster parents. A child who is in family care is entitled to all family benefits, as well as to the benefit of a child who is in care or care in the family, which are regulated by Article 9 of the Law on family benefits intended to cover the costs of maintaining a child.
- A foster home is a care facility that provides services to a foster home. The purpose of the foster home service is to provide the child with a family-like living environment to meet his or her basic needs, to create a safe and supportive living environment for him or her, and to prepare the child to cope with his or her daily tasks as an adult, in accordance with his or her abilities. This is a state-funded service whose price and maximum cost per child in a calendar year is set by a

decree Of the government of the Republic. Providers of foster home services are included in the Register of economic activities on the basis of a license for activities. The location of orphanages on the map of Estonia can be found here. The foster home service is regulated by Articles 151-1511 Of the law on social guardianship.

- If both parents of the child do not have the right of representation, or it is impossible to establish the origin of the child, the child is assigned a guardian. The guardian has the right to care for both the child's person and property. The appointment of guardianship creates a limited legal parent-child relationship between the parent and the child. In specific cases, the court may decide on different amounts of relations. Thus, the tasks of the guardian, in addition to the legal representation of the ward, include taking care of the person and property of the ward within the framework of their tasks. The guardian cannot transfer the performance of its tasks to a third party. The guardian should ask and take into account the opinion of the guardian when exercising guardianship, if possible, taking into account the age and level of development of the child. In addition, the guardian is required to manage the child's property with the care of a good guardian, and he is also responsible for damage caused by a culpable violation of his duties. To enter into transactions with high economic risk, the guardian must obtain the consent of the court. The guardian is not obliged to support the child financially. The guardian, as the legal representative of the child, has the right and obligation to request child support from the person who is obliged to do so. The child under guardianship is entitled to all family benefits, as well as to the benefit of a child who is in family care or in a guardianship relationship. The guardian is an individual or, if a suitable individual cannot be found, a legal entity. A legal entity must systematically take steps to find physical guardians for its ward, consult them, and train them. Prior to the appointment of a guardian, the tasks are performed by the parish or city Council at the child's place of residence or, if the child is absent, by the parish or city Council at the child's usual place of residence. If it is necessary to appoint a guardian to protect the interests of the child, but there is no reason to withdraw the parent's parental rights, you can assign special guardianship to perform only those tasks that the parents cannot perform.
- Adoption by other families (parents and relatives do not want or cannot take on the creation of lifelong relationships, the child needs to be connected to the family, which can meet the needs of the child in the protection/culture/status of a family member)

In the interests of children, primarily focuses on and assists the biological family and if all measures are exhausted, parents deprived of parental rights, the possibility of adoption (Table 3.1).

Starting in 2017, Estonia has a unified database of those who want to become adoptive parents and foster families. In Estonia, adoption is based on the interests of the child, the principle of selecting a family for the child, rather than a child for the family. Adoptive and foster families must take a course on how to preserve and

Table 3.1 Adoption procedure: selection of foster families

2017				2018			
Total adoptions	Family kinship	In the new family	International	Total adoptions	Family kinship	In the new family	International
71	37	33	1	85	63	22	0

support the biological family if that is possible. International adoption has been strongly curtailed in the belief that Estonian children should maintain a connection to their home country.

3.8 Best Practices

While the challenges of transforming child protection based on institutional care have been great, the current belief in Estonia is that every child needs a home and family. It is extremely important for a child who for some reason cannot be brought up in his or her own family to be able to grow up in another suitable family—preferably one that is willing to support, love, and care for the child for the rest of their life.

The prevailing model that has been adopted is The PRIDE program, developed in 1990 by specialists from the United States. In Estonia, PRIDE training has been available since the early 2000s. In 2016–2017, the training content was updated to reflect more culturally appropriate content. PRIDE training is based on competencies-it is based on the belief that adoptive parents, guardians, and foster parents must have certain strengths, knowledge, and skills in order to become as good parents as possible to a child who cannot grow up in their own family.

Further Reading

https://www.riigiteataja.ee/index.html
https://www.sm.ee/et
https://www.sm.ee/ru/patronat
https://www.oiguskantsler.ee/sites/default/files/L%C3%95K%20voldik%20RUS_1%C3%B5plik_0.pdf
https://countrymeters.info/ru/Estonia#Child_dependency_ratio
https://www.sm.ee/sites/default/files/content-editors/Lapsed_ja_pered/Asendushooldus/ah_rr_dets_2014.pdf
https://www.sm.ee/sites/default/files/content-editors/Lapsed_ja_pered/Asendushooldus/ah_rr_dets_2014.pdf
https://www.sotsiaalkindlustusamet.ee/
http://andmebaas.stat.ee/

https://ajakiri.lastekaitseliit.ee/ru/2018/01/12/%D0%BC%D0%BD%D0%BE%D0%B3%D0%BE%D0%BC%D0%B5%D1%80%D0%BD%D0%B0%D1%8F-%D1%81%D0%B5%D0%BC%D0%B5%D0%B9%D0%BD%D0%B0%D1%8F-%D1%82%D0%B5%D1%80%D0%B0%D0%BF%D0%B8%D1%8F-%D0%BF%D0%BE%D0%B4%D0%B4%D0%B5/
https://www.tai.ee/et/
https://tarkvanem.ee/ru
UN Department of economic and social Affairs: Population division

Chapter 4
Georgia

Nino Chikhladze, Nata Kazakhashvili, Nino Chkhaberidze, and Nato Pitskhelauri

4.1 The Development of the Children's Rights in Georgia

The collapse of the Soviet Union led to process of re-evaluation that affected the lives of all citizens. The primary social institutions of the Soviet period, the Communist Party and the trade unions had strong and well-developed mechanisms for addressing social needs. The first civil society and non-governmental organizations began to be established in Georgia in the 1990s, soon after Georgia regained independence, bringing new challenges, trends and difficulties. The evolving roles and responsibilities of civil society, as well as the interactions between government and society, have created a new context for the implementation of children's rights and protection in the country.

The rights of the child are guaranteed both by international law and national legislation. Georgia joined the Convention on the Rights of the Child in 1994. The Convention is used in Georgia as a directly applicable law as well as a framework for practice in protecting children. State bodies, local authorities, NGOs and religious organizations, as well as international organizations, participate in the child protection system. UNICEF and EU representatives as well as the World Health Organization, Global Fund and various foreign embassies have participated in the implementation of many important child welfare projects.

On September 27, 2019, the Law on the Rights of the Child was adopted in Georgia, in which almost all issues that integrate the national child protection system are present: social welfare, education, healthcare, safety, and the justice system, other regulations, policies and services to prevent and eliminate risks to child

N. Chikhladze (✉) · N. Kazakhashvili · N. Chkhaberidze · N. Pitskhelauri
Faculty of Medicine, Department of Public Health, Ivane Javakhishvili Tbilisi State University, Tbilisi, Georgia
e-mail: nino.chikhladze@tsu.ge; nata.kazakhashvili@tsu.ge; nino.chkhaberidze@tsu.ge; nato.pitskhelauri@tsu.ge

I. Earner, A. Telitsyna (eds.), *The Development of Child Protection Systems in the Post-Soviet States*, Child Maltreatment 12,
https://doi.org/10.1007/978-3-030-59588-3_4

protection. The national child protection system serves to eliminate all forms of violence against children in the education, health and justice systems, in the family and elsewhere, including physical punishment, cruel, inhuman and degrading treatment of a child, his/her exploitation, child trafficking and harm.

Earlier, the Government of Georgia's Resolution # 762 of April 24, 2012 approved the Action Plan for Child Welfare and Protection 2012–2015. The main goal of the plan was to ensure that all children living in Georgia are protected from violence and neglect and have the opportunity for individual and positive psychosocial development at home or family environment. The program was also aimed at supporting particularly vulnerable children and their families. Responsibilities for the implementation of the measures envisaged in the plan were distributed among the various structural units, namely: Ministry of Internally Displaced Persons from the Occupied Territories, Labour, Health and Social Affairs, Ministry of Education and Science, Local Municipality, Tbilisi City Hall, Ministry of Sport and Youth Affairs, Ministry of Internal Affairs, Ministry of Justice, Ministry of Corrections and Legal Assistance.

According to the Child Welfare and Protection Action Plan, child welfare reform is still ongoing. This reform has more or less affected such areas of social welfare of children as prevention/reintegration and empowerment of families, youth leaving the care system, juvenile justice and psychosocial rehabilitation of victims of violence. Over the past 10 years, several studies have been conducted in Georgia to assess key areas of reform of the child welfare and childcare system (Well-being of Children and Their Families in Georgia, UNICEF, 2013–2014–2015–2016–2017).

In 2012, the Coalition for Child and Youth of Georgia was created. Coalition for Child and Youth is a union of 48 Georgian civil society organizations which work in the field of children and youth. Coalition is based on principles of equality and targets the protection of rights of children and youth and supports development of existing system of child and youth welfare. The main activity of the coalition is the advocacy of rights of children and youth on the local and on international level. The Coalition is member of ChildPact—a regional coalition of child protection NGOs from the Wider Black Sea Area. The coalition currently focuses on advocacy work in four thematic directions and the range of activities include:

- Analysis and needs assessment of current system of child and youth welfare;
- Support the improvement of the child and youth welfare system through the advocacy;
- Support adoption of international standards into the local legislation by initiating legislation changes;
- Support the improvement of the mechanisms of child and youth rights protection;
- Support of society's involvement and awareness rising;
- Monitoring of child and youth rights protection;

On February 18, 2019, a 3-year project was launched within the framework of EU financial support to Georgia for the protection of child rights and wellbeing. A unified coordination mechanism of the country will be establish under the project. The project will establish a unified coordination mechanism of the country—a structure that will unite various ministries as well as NGOs and human rights defenders. The project aims to:

- Promoting quality improvement of family-based alternative services;
- Improving the process of deinstitutionalization;
- Include children's institutions in government regulation;
- Improving of the state system of social workers;
- Improving legislation and practice in the area of child protection policies.

The participation of religious organizations in child protection programs is evidenced by an official partnership established between UNICEF and the State Agency for Religious Affairs of Georgia. The Government of Georgia and UNICEF continue to work with religious leaders to promote and protect children's rights in Georgia. The latest manifestation of the bilateral partnership is the conference dedicated to the 30th anniversary of the UN Convention on the Rights of the Child. The event was held on February 3, 2019 at the National Parliamentary Library of Georgia in Tbilisi. UNICEF has already organized four seminars with the participation of 100 Orthodox Christian priests, Muslim Muftis and Imams, as well as representatives of the Lutheran Church in Georgia.

4.2 Legislation Directed at Protecting Children

According to Georgian legislation, a person under the age of 18 is considered a minor. An adolescent is a child from 10 to 18 years of age. A minor under the age of 7 years (an underage) is deemed not to have legal capacity. His rights are exercised by a guardian or custodian. A minor from the age of 7 to 18 years shall have limited legal capacity. The capacity for rights of a natural person is the ability to have civil rights and duties that arise from the moment of the person's birth.

In accordance with the Civil Code of Georgia and the Law on Citizenship, a child at birth acquires a surname, name and citizenship. The Law on Citizenship of Georgia (1993) defines the issue of citizenship of a child. A child whose both parents are citizens of Georgia at the time of his/her birth is considered a citizen of Georgia regardless of place of birth. Citizenship of a child between the ages of 14 and 18 may be changed only with his/her consent.

A child (minor) has the same rights and freedoms as an adult, with some exceptions (for example, voting rights). Human rights, including the protection of the rights of the child, are guaranteed by Chapter II of the Constitution of Georgia. The Constitution protected the right to life of the child, the right to privacy, freedom of speech, the right to assembly, right to freedom of thought, belief and religion, the right to development, the right to a fair trial, the presumption of innocence, the right to protection against illegal detention, torture and more.

Civil Code of Georgia (1997) provides for two circumstances in which a person is considered to be equivalent to an adult person with full legal capacity: (1) The marriage of a minor who has reached the age of 16; (2) Granting the right to independently manage an enterprise to a minor who has attained the age of 16. According to the legislation of Georgia marriage shall be permitted from the age of 18. The marriage of a minor who has reached the age of 16 shall be permitted with the consent of his/her parents or custodian.

In accordance with article 9 of the Convention on the Rights of the Child, every child must grow up in the family and not leave his/her parents against his/her wishes. This requirement is reflected in the Civil Code of Georgia, which states that "the child has the right to live and grow up in the family." All questions of parenting are decided by mutual consent of parents. In case of disagreement of the parents, the dispute is resolved by a court with the participation of the parents and the minor. The rights of the child are protected even in the event of a divorce of parents. If the child's parents live separately for divorce or for any other reason, they agree with whom the minor child will live.

The law also protects the property rights of children. If necessary, the guardian of the property helps the child with providing such property. If a parent systematically avoids parental responsibility and improperly enjoys parental rights—the child suffers from parent's immoral behavior or parent is a chronic alcoholic or drug addict, parents may be deprived of all rights and obligations by court decision. This can happen both on the initiative of the Guardianship and Custody Authority and at the request of a child aged 14 years and older.

In the case provided for by the legislation of Georgia, a minor who has reached the age of 14 has the right to apply to the court for the protection of his rights and legal interests. In this case, the court appoints a procedural representative and examines the case. The minor has the right to disagree with his plea representative and to defend himself/herself.

According to article 20 of the Convention on the Rights of the Child, even in cases where the child has no parents, he/she is protected by the state. The same is shared by the Georgian legislation. In particular, under Georgian law, if a child is found whose identity as well as whereabouts of parents are unknown, the guardianship and custody authority is obliged to take all steps to establish the identity of the child and his/her parents. If the identity of the child and his or her parents is not established in accordance with the laws of Georgia, the guardianship and custody authority should take measures to care for a child and apply to the court for the recognition of the child as abandoned.

Georgian legislation protects the interests of the child when adopting. Adoption of a child older than 10 years is not allowed without his/her consent. The law strictly protects confidentiality during adoption. According to the Criminal Code, disclosure of adoption secrets, violation of personal or family secrets is punishable.

The rights to protect the health of the child and respect for his/her will in this area is reflected in various legislative acts of Georgia: Law of Georgia on Health Care; Law of Georgia on Patient Rights; Law of Georgia on Organ Transplantation and others. The rights of minor patients are best illustrated by the Law of Georgia on Patient Rights (2000), which gives juvenile patients the same rights as to adults, except of specific cases when due to the patient's age, the patient needs increased attention (for example, to give informed consent for any medical manipulation/intervention).

Protection of the rights of the child is guaranteed by the Law of Georgia on General Education (2005). In accordance with the law pupils have the right to enjoy all rights and freedoms protected and recognized by the school, as well as all school resources on equal terms, without discrimination and in the prescribed manner during school hours or on school grounds. Pupils have the right to know about their rights and freedoms, as well as the grounds for limitation them. The school is obliged to introduce each new pupils their rights and freedoms.

The Law of Georgia on Advertising (1998) protects the rights of a minor. In particular, to protect minors from manipulation due to their credulity and inexperience during the production, placement and dissemination of advertisements, the following are prohibited: (a) convincing minors to persuade their parents and other persons to buy advertised goods; (b) drawing attention of minors to the fact that owning advertised goods will grant them privilege over other minors, and not owning the goods will have the opposite effect; (c) using in advertisements of the text or audio and video information that displays minors in dangerous places and circumstances; etc.

The Law of Georgia "On Protecting Minors From Bad Influences" (2001) provides for protection minors from bad influences related to the consumption and sale of alcohol and tobacco, and to participation in gambling and watching films, consuming and selling printed matter that could harm the mental and/or physical health of the minor, his or her moral and social development. A similar prohibition is contained in the Law of Georgia on Broadcasting (2004), which prohibits the airing of programs that adversely affect the physical, mental and moral development of children and adolescents at a time when they are likely to be seen or heard.

Guarantees for the protection of the labor rights of minors are set forth in the Labor Code of Georgia (2006). Georgian legislation generally provides for resolutions and standards of the International Labor Organization (ILO) and other international organizations.

The minimum age for employment under the Georgian legislation is 16 years. However, the legislation of Georgia does not prohibit the employment of minors under 16. Therefore, the legislator points to the conditions that must be taken into account when employing a minor. Minors under the age of 14 may enter into employment contracts only for sports, art and cultural events, as well as for promotional work.

The Labor Code prohibits the employment of minors with hard, harmful and dangerous work. The Labor Code limits the employment of a minor from 10 p.m. to 6 a.m.

Article 32 of the Convention on the Rights of the Child prohibits the use of child slave labor. Special articles are also provided in the Criminal Code of Georgia—Human trafficking; Trafficking in minors. Law of Georgia On Combating Human Trafficking (2006) protects the rights of children. Georgian legislation is aimed at providing an effective, fair and humane attitude towards adolescents who are in conflict with the law and seeks to establish international standards in national legislation in this area. The Criminal Code of Georgia abounds with the protection of the rights of minors.

4.2.1 Family Environment and Alternative Care

In 2008–2010, significant changes were made to Georgian legislation in order to improve existing child protection rules. According to Article 1197 of the Civil Code of Georgia, the child has the right to live and grow up in a family, and parents have equal rights and duties with respect to their children. The Code lists the rights and responsibilities of parents:

- Parents shall be entitled and obligated to rear their children, to take care of their physical, intellectual, spiritual and social development, and to raise them as decent members of a society, taking into account the best interests of the children.
- Parents/legal representatives of minors must not use child-rearing methods that may cause physical and/or mental suffering of minors.
- Parents shall have the duty to maintain their children.
- Parents may determine with whom and where their child is to live.
- Parents shall be obligated to protect the rights and interests of their minor children, including managing and using children's property.
- Parents shall be entitled and obligated to interact with their children, and determine the rights of third persons with respect to interacting with their children.
- Parents shall be legal representatives of their minor children and shall act for the protection of their rights and interests in relation to third persons, including in a court.
- Parents shall determine all issues of rearing their children by mutual agreement. In the event of disagreement between the parents, a court shall settle the subject with the participation of the parents.

Inadequate fulfillment of rights and duties may serve as a ground for limiting or even depriving these rights and responsibilities. The child has the right to be protected from parents/legal representatives that abuse the minor's rights. When a minor's rights and legitimate interests are breached, including when both or one of the parents fails to fulfil or improperly fulfils the duties related to the upbringing and education of the child, or abuses a parental right, the minor has the right independently apply to guardianship and custodianship authorities or to the court at the age of 14 years. Furthermore, natural and legal persons who are aware of cases of breach of a minor's rights and legitimate interests are obliged to report the fact to guardianship and custodianship authorities.

These processes occur with the participation of social workers. The guardianship and custodial authorities take appropriate measures as required by law and as they receive information, engage social workers in the case. Based on the assessment of the social worker, the court makes a decision. In such cases, the child shall be separated from the parents. In case of deprivation of parental rights of parents, the child is assigned the status of child for adoption.

4.2.2 *Prevention of Separation from Parents*

Georgian legislation recognizes the importance of raising a child in a biological family. Assistance services and material benefits, including day care centers, reintegration assistance, social services, counseling are intended to prevent child abandonment. The country has shelters for pregnant women, mothers with various problems and children under the age of 10 years. Such children receive 24-hour shelter for a period of 1 year if they are at risk of being abandoned or admitted to the institution. In addition, the state program offers services such as daycare services, cash assistance benefits for vulnerable families, and health insurance.

4.3 Day Center

Service of the day center includes:

- Daily 2-time meal (except weekend and holidays), one of which should be three-component dinner;
- Detection and compliance with the academic necessities of the beneficiaries;
- Promotion of development of household and vocational abilities of the beneficiaries;
- Provision of inclusion of the beneficiaries in cultural and sports-recreational activities;
- Teaching of proper time management, efficient communication, making of a choice, participation in the decision-making process and abilities of settlement of conflicts via non-violation ways;
- If needed, organization of outpatient medical and psychological service.

In case of persons with disabilities, the service of the day center additionally includes: organizing/bringing/return of beneficiaries to/from the center; drafting and realization of individual habilitation and/or rehabilitation programs and training of the beneficiaries for inclusive education.

Persons who can apply to the day center are:

- The children of 6–18 years, being under the risk of abandonment, who do not belong to the category of the children with disability status and whose family is registered in the "unified database of the socially vulnerable families", herewith the rating score established by the social-economic assessment of the family upon making the decision on enrollment of the child in the service of the day center shall not exceed 100,000 units, as well as the children of the same age groups, which do not belong to the category of the children with disability status and whose families receive the reintegration allowance. Number of the beneficiaries of this category shall not exceed 550 simultaneously;
- The children of 6–18 year with disability status and the persons with disabilities, whose families are registered in the "unified database of the socially vulnerable families", herewith the rating score established by the social-economic assessment of the family upon making the decision on enrollment in the service of the day center shall not exceed 120,000 points, as well as the children and persons with disabilities, who used the service of the day center in 2009, within the frameworks of appropriate state program. Number of the beneficiaries of this category shall not exceed 758 simultaneously.

4.3.1 Alternative Forms of Care

The Georgian legislation defines the circumstances in which the child is given the status of a child without parental care. The child without parental care is considered person under 18, if:

- His/her parents are recognized by the court as incompetent, missing or dead;
- He/she is an orphan;
- His/her parent (s) is deprived (limited or suspended) of parent's rights and duties in accordance with the rules established by law;
- He/she is recognized as abandoned;
- Staying with the parent (s) or guardian is dangerous for any reason.

If the child is separated from the biological parents, the guardianship and custody authority will consider alternatives for placement so that the child is as close as possible to the family environment. According to the decision of the Guardianship and Custodianship Authority (based on the assessment and conclusion of the social worker), depending on the situation, the following may occur:

- The child shall be granted the status of prospective adoptee;
- The child shall be received guardianship/custodianship;
- The child shall be provided with services (adoptive family/foster care, small family-type house, orphanage), where his interests are maximally protected.

On August 26, 2009, the Minister of Internally Displaced Persons from the Occupied Territories, Labor, Health and Social Affairs of Georgia approved "The Standards of Child Care" (Order N281/n).

The standards for the care of children with disabilities were approved by the Minister of Internally Displaced Persons from the Occupied Territories, Labor, Health and Social Affairs of Georgia on April 8, 2011 by order N01-13/N. Their goal is to identify quality indicators for services for children with disabilities. The standards were established with the support of UNICEF.

4.3.2 Guardianship and Custodianship

Guardianship and custodianship are established for the upbringing a minor and protecting the personal and property rights, and interests of the minor who is left without parental care because:

1. His/her parents have died;
2. His/her parents have been deprived of parental rights;
3. Their parental rights have been suspended or restricted;
4. They have been declared missing;
5. The child has been declared abandoned.

Guardianship shall be established for a child under the age of seven. Custodianship shall be established for a minor from the age of seven to the age of 18. The central and local guardianship and custodianship authorities are the Ministry of Internally Displaced Persons from the Occupied Territories, Labour, Health and Social Affairs of Georgia and/or an authorized agency, as well as their territorial bodies. Guardianship and custodianship may be established over a child when:

1. A court notifies a guardianship and custodianship authority about limiting or depriving parental rights and duties of both parents of the child;
2. The parental rights and duties have been suspended;
3. Both parents of the child have died;
4. The guardian appointed for the child has died or has been deprived of his/her functions;
5. The court has declared the child abandoned;
6. The parent has been declared missing.

Guardianship and custodianship authorities shall appoint a guardian or a custodian for discharging the duties of a guardian or a custodian. A guardian or a custodian may be appointed only with their consent. A guardian or a custodian may be appointed on the basis of a notarized document (the Will) as instructed by the deceased parents. In addition, a guardian or a custodian shall be selected by taking into account his/her personal qualities, the ability to perform assigned duties, the reciprocal relationship existing between him/her and the ward, the interests of the ward.

A guardian/custodian is obliged to care for the maintenance of the ward, create the necessary living conditions for him/her, provide care and medical treatment and protect his/her rights and interests. A guardian and a custodian are obligated to live together with a minor in a ward. In individual cases, a custodian and a ward may live apart with the permission of the guardianship and custodianship authority. A guardian is the legal representative of a ward, and enters into the necessary transactions in the name and interests of the ward.

If guardians or custodians improperly perform their duties, a guardianship and custodianship authority shall remove or relieve them of their duties. If a guardian (custodian) uses guardianship (custodianship) for mercenary ends or leaves a ward without supervision or necessary assistance, he/she shall be held liable according to established procedures.

Guardianship shall be terminated by decision of the guardianship and custodianship authority if:

1. A ward dies;
2. A minor ward reaches the age of seven;
3. Parental rights and duties have been restored to the parent of a minor ward who has not reached the age of seven.

A guardianship and custodianship authority shall supervise the activity of a guardian/custodian. If a guardianship and custodianship authority ascertains that a guardian/custodian fails to perform/unduly perform the duties defined for him/her under court decision and/or the legislation of Georgia, the guardianship and custodianship authority shall prepare a negative report and act as follows:

- it helps a guardian/custodian with the help of a social worker to better understand and perform his/her duties;
- it relieves a guardian/custodian of his/her duties;
- based on the performance of actions of a guardian/custodian, it acts in accordance with the rules established by the Code of Administrative Offences of Georgia and the criminal legislation of Georgia.

4.3.3 Foster Care and Adoption

Since the regaining independence of Georgia in the early 90s of the last century, the issue of caring children without care has become increasingly acute. During this period, there has been a significant increase in the contingent of children's homes and orphanages. The structure of the causes of child placement in orphanages has changed. If during Soviet times in orphanages were children of prisoners, orphans or children born with congenital anomalies, then in the early 1990s, children grew up in orphanages because of poor economic conditions and poverty. In 1993–2000, various foreign organizations began to adopt Georgian children outside of Georgia. The issue of adoption of children abroad has been criticized by the public. The media often covered this issue in an extremely negative context. The Government of Georgia adopted law on adoption in 1997. Since then, numerous changes have been made to the law, although the law still did not meet international standards, so work on the new law was resumed and adopted several times with new amendments.

The law did not provide for the individual needs and best interests of the child.

On December 18, 2009, the Parliament of Georgia adopted a new Law on Adoption and Foster Care. The purpose of the law was to ensure the proper functioning of the adoption and foster care system, to promote the realization of a child's right. New regulations are designed to make the system transparent and prevent corruption in the field of adoption. Changes in the legislation have addressed issues such as adoption order, child rejection, adoption of children over 10 years of age and foster care. The Law distinguishes foster care and adoption.

Foster care—provision of upbringing of children in the family environment under the agreement concluded by and between the Government and foster family. Foster care implies placing a child in a pre-studied and selected family on the basis of a bilateral agreement between the State and the foster family. During this time, the biological family has the opportunity to have constant contact with the child, and in their absence the child is released from 18 years old and does not depend on the adoptive family. Foster care has been operating as an independent sub-program since 2013.

Foster care may be provided to:

- The children deprived of care, who cannot be returned to their biological families or adopted;
- Leaving a child to parent/guardian/custodian is harmful for child and therefore the parent/guardian/custodian applies to the body of guardianship and custody;
- Right of parent/parents to decide, whom the child shall live with, is limited and the child must be placed outside of his/her family;
- Parent/parents is/are deprived of or have limited parental rights and obligations and the child must be placed outside of his/her family.

Foster care for a child may be provided by:

- A citizen of Georgia;
- A person without citizenship residing in Georgia on a permanent basis;
- A citizen of foreign state residing in Georgia on a permanent basis;

Except the persons:

- Recognized as disabled or with limited capabilities by the court;
- With limited, retained or deprived parental or guardianship/custody rights;
- Which are unable to bring up a child for health condition (according to the list of the diseases approved by the Ministry of Internally Displaced Persons from the Occupied Territories, Labour, Health and Social Affairs of Georgia);
- Who or whose family member(s) is convicted for serious or especially serious crime and has not expunged previous convictions;
- Parent/guardian/custodian of a foster child, to whom the obligation of maintenance of this child is applied;
- Whom the right of foster care is deprived.

Foster care of a child, who has already reached 10 years, is available only with his/her consent. Separation of sister and brother is not admitted unless this corresponds to their interests. Age difference between the foster child and the foster mother/father must not be less than 15 years.

The state of the foster child shall be checked by the social worker: 4 times per month—during the first month, and in following months—at least once a month. If needed, the frequency of visits may increase.

The following persons under the age of 18 shall be subject to foster care:

1. An orphan;
2. A child whose parent(s) has (have) been declared missing or dead by a court;
3. A child whose parent(s) has (have) been deprived or suspended of parental rights, or whose parental rights have been restricted.
4. A foster child, who was placed in foster care upon the attainment of the age of 18, who has attained the age of 18 and is a pupil of a general education institution/school, a student of a vocational education institution, or a student of a higher education institution, may be placed in foster care until the completion of studies, but no longer upon the attainment of the age of 21.

Financial provision of foster mother/father is carried out as follows and by following amount:

- For healthy child placed in relative foster care—GEL 200 per month;
- For healthy child placed in non-relative foster care—GEL 450 per month;
- For a child with disabilities placed in relative foster care—GEL 300 per month;
- For a child with disabilities placed in non-relative foster care—GEL 600 per month;
- For urgent foster care (including a child with disabilities)—GEL 600 per month

4.3.4 Adoption

Adoption of a child means the permanent transfer of child to the family by a court decision. Adoption changes the status of the child permanently. He/she becomes the bearer of the name of the adoptive parents and the heir to their property. In this case, all kinds of relationships with the biological family are terminated.

For the adoption of a child aged 10 or over, his/her informed written consent shall be necessary, and in the case of a child under the age of 10, his/her opinion shall be considered, taking into account his/her degree of maturity. Siblings (a sister and a brother, sisters and/or brothers) may not be separated except when this is in their best interests.

The decision on the foster family is taken based on the data on the needs of the child and the foster family, in accordance with the following principles:

1. The desire of the adoptive guardian about the age, gender and health status of the child;
2. Placement of children in appropriate ethnic, religious and cultural conditions;

3. The number of children in foster families is not more than seven;
4. Consent of a child over the age of 10;
5. Placing siblings together.

According to the Civil Code of Georgia: Adoption shall be permitted only for the welfare and in the best interests of a minor child, provided it is expected that a parent-child relationship will develop between the adoptive parent and the adopted child. A social worker who fully appreciates the child and the adoptive parent is himself involved in the adoption process. Depending on ethnic, religious, cultural, or personal factors, social worker checks whether an adopted child and adoptive parent get along well.

The final decision on adoption is made by the court. The process of international adoption is managed by the Ministry of Internal Affairs of Georgia. Persons permanently residing in Georgia may adopt a child both in Georgia and abroad. Persons permanently residing abroad may adopt a child permanently residing in Georgia under the procedures established Law.

A child, who has been granted the status of prospective adoptee shall be subject to adoption. A child shall be granted the status of prospective adoptee by a decision of the local guardianship and custodianship authority, on the basis of which the prospective adoptee shall be registered in the Registry. The status of prospective adoptee shall be granted to a child:

1. whose parent(s) was (were) declared missing by a court;
2. who is an orphan;
3. who is declared an abandoned child by a court;
4. whose parent(s) was (were) deprived of parental rights;
5. whose legal representatives all give their consent with regard to his/her placement for adoption under the procedures established by the Minister of Internally Displaced Persons from the Occupied Territories, Labour, Health and Social Affairs of Georgia.

A child shall be de-registered only in the case of his/her adoption, death, change of the status of prospective adoptee, or in the case of the attainment of full legal age.

Adoption of the child requires the consent of the parent (s) or other legal representative. Adoption without the consent of a parent(s) shall be permitted, when:

1. a parent(s) is (are) deprived of parental rights by a court;
2. a parent(s) is (are) declared missing by a court;
3. a parent(s) is (are) dead;
4. a child is declared abandoned by a court.

Adoption of a child of the age of 10 or over requires his/her written informed consent. In the case of a child under the age of 10, his/her opinion shall be considered, taking into account his/her degree of maturity. When placing a child with special needs for adoption, adequate assistance shall be rendered in order to enable him/her to express his/her own will.

A child shall be recognized as abandoned if:

(a) he/she is a foundling and within 6 weeks after his/her discovery, the identity of the child and/or the identity of his/her parent(s) could not be determined;
(b) he/she is a foundling and the identity of the child and/or the identity of parent (s) were determined, but he/she (they) avoid(s) exercising parental rights and fulfilling parental duties;
(c) the parent (s) of the child (s) have, by their own action or inaction, indicated their intention to abandon the child and/or they avoid exercising parental rights and fulfilling parental duties, or if the duration of a 24-hour state guardianship over the child exceeds 3 months.

Before a child is declared as abandoned, the local guardianship and custodianship authority makes a decision on the temporary placement of the child and ensure the protection of the rights and legitimate interests of the child and is his/her legal representative.

The following persons have priority right to adopt a prospective adoptee:

1. an adoptive parent, who intends to adopt the child of his/her spouse;
2. an adoptive parent, who is the relative of a prospective adoptee;
3. an adoptive parent, who has already adopted the sibling of a prospective adoptee;
4. a foster parent, under whose foster care a foster child has been placed for the last 6 months.

Who cannot be adoptive parent:

- person who has been deprived of parental rights or had previously adopted a child, or had been a guardian/custodian of a minor, or had provided foster care;
- person whose parental rights and duties were restricted in accordance with the procedures provided for by the legislation of Georgia due to their failure to exercise his/her parental rights and the non-fulfilment or improper fulfilment of his/her parental duties;
- person who cannot fulfil his/her parental duties properly due to health status (based on the list of diseases approved by the Minister of Internally Displaced Persons from the Occupied Territories, Labour, Health and Social Affairs of Georgia);
- person whose family's social status does not exceed the standards established by the State for the placement of a child in foster care, except for a person provided for by Article 15 of this Law, who has the priority right to adoption;
- person who was convicted of a serious or grave crime by a court, of a crime provided for by Chapter XXIV of the Criminal Code of Georgia, and whose conviction has not been expunged or removed in accordance with the rules established by the legislation of Georgia, except for a crime provided for by the articles of the Criminal Code of Georgia specified in sub-paragraph (f) of this paragraph, when a person may not be an adoptive parent, regardless of whether or not his/her conviction has been expunged or removed;

- person who has been convicted of a crime provided for by Articles 109 and 112, Article 126(11) and Article 126(2)(d), Article 1261(2)(a), Article 137, Article 138, Article 139, Article 140, Article 141, Article 1422, Article 1431, Article 1432, Article 1441, Article 1442, Article 1443, Articles 171 and 172, Article 1721, Article 253, Article 2551 and Article 2552 of the Criminal Code of Georgia, regardless of whether or not his/her conviction has been expunged or removed.

The age difference between an adoptive parent and a prospective adoptee shall not be less than 16 years and not more 49 years (if prospective adoptee is under the age of 10). A person who intends to adopt a child in Georgia and/or from a foreign country shall complete the mandatory training courses, which are aimed to give a person who intends to adopt a child the skills that are necessary for the development of a child.

4.4 International Adoption

International adoption in Georgia is in accordance with the requirements of the The Hague Convention on Protection of Children and Co-operation in Respect of Intercountry Adoption (Hague Adoption Convention) and the UN Convention. The relations of Georgia with a state that is not a party to the Hague Convention shall be determined on the basis of bilateral and multilateral treaties. The issue of international adoption in Georgia is governed by the Law of Georgia on Adoption and Foster Care.

Adoption of a child from Georgia in foreign countries is available in the cases, when it is impossible to return a child to the biological family or his/her adoption by a citizen of Georgia or/and a person without citizenship, permanently residing in Georgia.

When the adoptive parent(s) of a prospective adoptee permanently residing in Georgia cannot be found in Georgia, the central authority shall initiate the procedure for the international adoption of the child. If a child is not adopted in Georgia within 8 months after he/she obtains the status of a prospective adoptee, and at the same time it is established that international adoption meets the best interests of the child, the central authority prepares an opinion on the prospective adoptee on its own initiative, and submits it to the competent body. An opinion shall include information on the identity, origin, social environment and family history of the child, the medical history of the child and his/her family, the special needs (if any) of the child, and on granting the status of a prospective adoptee to the child. A person (s) permanently residing abroad who intends (intend) to adopt a child in Georgia shall duly file an application with a competent body in the field of international adoption in a receiving state.

If a competent body of a receiving state determines that a person (persons) permanently residing abroad, who intend to adopt a child meet the established requirements, and is (are) ready to adopt the child, the competent body of a receiving country sends an opinion to the central authority. The opinion shall include information on the identity of the person who intend to adopt a child, his/her (their) origin, social environment, existence/absence of conflict with law, medical history, necessary skills for adopting a child. The central authority determines the compatibility of a prospective adoptee permanently residing in Georgia and of adoptive parents permanently residing abroad. When determining compatibility, the ethnic, religious or cultural affiliations of a child is taken into account.

A citizen of foreign state willing to adopt a child must submit following documents to the central body of the Social Service Agency:

- An application of adoption of a child;
- Consent of the spouse, if a child is adopted by one of the spouses;
- Copy of the identification document (ID card, passport, residence certificate);
- Copy of the marriage certificate (if any);
- Reference on health state;
- Reference of medical-drug abuse examination;
- Reference on previous convictions;
- Examination of adopting family carried out by the authorized person working on the affairs of adoption of foreign citizen;
- Permit on adoption issued by the authorized organ of foreign state;
- Other documents (in case of request of the Agency).

4.4.1 Reintegration

Reintegration aims to return the children from the orphanages to their biological families. In case of reintegration, social functioning of family is raised, strengthened and the risk of return of a child in the institution is decreased to minimum.

Reintegration is subordinated by a child, placed in the orphanage, small family-type home or foster care, who returns to the biologic family and is provided with the financial assistance, as well as other types of social assistances oriented on strengthening of family.

If the parent(s) want(s) to return the child to the biological family, he/she(they) shell apply to the regional department of the Social Service Agency (according to the place of residence), with personal application on return of the child.

Availability of returning the child is shown on the basis of primary and complete assessment of the family and the child (25 day). In case of positive solution, the regional board of guardianship and custody considers the assessment report together with the recommendation (on return to the family) and makes the conclusive decision on return of the child to the family.

On return of the child to the biological family, the state pays reintegration allowance to the parents by amount of GEL 90—in case of healthy child and GEL 130—in case of the child with disabilities. Besides the reintegrated child shall be provided with health insurance and, if needed, day center service and food voucher. As well as both the child and the parent are provided with an opportunity of vocational retraining and subsequent employment.

The family of the reintegrated child shall cooperate with the social agent, who provides control over assessment of the child's state. The biological parents shall carry out the measures specified in the individual development plan drafted by the social agent.

4.4.2 De-institutionalization

Orphanages in Georgia have not existed for several years. In 2005, the Government of Georgia declared deinstitutionalization of children as a priority. As part of the reform of the childcare system, the Georgian government closed 44 large childcare facilities and reintegrated 1316 homeless children. The 'Child Protection and Welfare Promotion' project has been underway for 3 years within the framework of EU financial support. The goal of the program was to reduce the number of large childcare facilities and to introduce and expand alternative, family-based child care services. Large children's homes in Georgia have been replaced by small family-type homes. Today there are only two orphanages in Georgia: one in Tbilisi and the other in Kojori—where up to 90 children with disabilities are raised.

Small family-type home is an environment imminent to biological family, where children will be able to get care and appropriate service during 24 hours. Small family-type home may be accommodated by:

- 6–8 years old children deprived of care, who are not able to return to biological families or adopted, including the educational institutions of children and the residents of orphanages;
- Persons subordinated to foster care.

In small family-type home, a child may be provided with following services:

- 24-hour service;
- At least 3-times per day meal, one of which must be three-component dinner;
- Provision with clothes according to age, gender and season and the things necessary for personal hygiene;
- Development of individual plan of child service and provision of its implementation and periodic re-examination;
- Teaching of daily, household abilities (self-care, involvement in household activities, etc.);
- Assistance to development of professional and vocational abilities, considering their interests, inclinations and capabilities;
- Assistance to improvement of their academic achievements and proper and targeted organization of their free time;
- Inclusion in cultural-educational and sports-recreational events;

- If needed, organization of psychological service;
- Provision of dynamic surveillance of a child in primary health institutions and, if needed, provision of initial medical assistance, as well as organization of outpatient and inpatient medical service specified or not specified by the state programs;
- Provision of upbringing of a child in conditions maximally close to the family environment, through periodic visits of the social workers and appropriate surveillance of state and development of the child.

Within the period of no more than 1 month after submission of the application for the placement to the small family-type home and the appropriate documents to the Agency, a social worker shall make the report on expediency of placement of a person in the specialized institution.

The regional council makes the decision on placement of a person in small family-type home. In case of positive decision, the child will be placed in small family-type home.

The materialized voucher is used for reimbursement of the cost of service of the small family-type home, which is defined for financing of the rendered service during no more than 12 months and consists of the coupons of appropriate months.

Amount of daily financing per voucher coupon defined for reimbursement of the cost of service in small family-type home totals GEL 15 since March 1, 2011.

A beneficiary placed in small family-type home, shall enjoy the right to accept the service from the same provider in the month, when he/she becomes 18 years old, from whom he/she received the service in previous months.

A voucher defined for reimbursement of the cost of service in small family-type home is issued on the basis of appropriate decision of the regional council.

In small family-type homes, in addition to providing full nutrition, education and health care for children, much attention is paid to identifying and developing their inclinations, interests, outstanding skills, proper organization of leisure time, and interaction with biological families (if this is not contrary to the child's interests). Children of small family-type homes spend 12 days a year at various resorts in Georgia.

4.4.3 Protecting the Rights of Children with Disabilities

Georgia acceded to the UN Convention on the Rights of the Child in 1994, which states that "States Parties recognize that a mentally or physically disabled child should enjoy a full and decent life, in conditions which ensure dignity, promote self-reliance and facilitate the child's active participation in the community" (Article 23). This means that the country has taken a serious moral and political responsibility to create equal conditions for this category of people and the rest of the population in Georgia.

State care for children in Georgia falls within the competence of several institutions. Many NGOs work professionally on child-related problems. Many international organizations also provide great support to children. On 14 June 1995 the Parliament of Georgia adopted the Law on Social Protection of Persons with Disabilities, which defines the basis for the state policy towards persons with disabilities and is intended to ensure equal enjoyment of rights by persons with disabilities, as well as to create favourable conditions for these persons to live full lives and participate in the economic and political activities of the society.

The State provides social protection to persons with disabilities and create necessary conditions for their individual development, and realisation of their creative and production capabilities, also additional guarantees in order for them to exercise their rights and legal interests. The law requires that persons with disabilities to be provided with medical, professional and social rehabilitation, education and vocational training, social assistance, adequate working conditions, the introduction of and development of relevant sports. The state provides persons with disabilities with the necessary conditions for education and professional training. In particular, educational institutions, together with healthcare and social security authorities, provide preschool and out-of-school education to children with disabilities in order to create favourable opportunities, to provide appropriate rehabilitation assistance to them; also provides secondary specialized education and higher education according to their individual rehabilitation program. Persons with disabilities receive general secondary and specialized higher education at general education institutions, or if necessary, at appropriate special educational institutions. Educational classes are also organized for children who are receiving treatment in inpatient or rehabilitation institutions.

Persons with disabilities receive social assistance in the form of financial support (pensions, allowances, etc.), as well as in the form of technical and other means, wheelchairs, prosthetic and orthopaedic appliances, sound amplification devices and signalling system. Persons with disabilities are provided by various means according to their individual rehabilitation program, free of charge or on concessionary terms.

4.4.4 Rehabilitation of Children

Since 2019, in Georgia has been operating the subprogram for children with disabilities—Rehabilitation of children. The interdisciplinary team of the specialists draft annual plan of rehabilitation of children, which provides following services:

- Physical therapy;
- Occupational therapy;
- Speech and language therapy;
- Neurological examination of a child;
- Psychological assistance to a child (psychological testing);
- As well as psychological assistance to a parent or a legal representative.

The beneficiaries of following categories may apply to the service of the subprogram—Rehabilitation of children:

- Children of 3 years and more with disabilities, having cerebral palsy, primary disorders of muscles, residual occurrences of inflammatory or vascular diseases of central nervous system, epilepsy and injury of the nerves of shoulder, as well as belt of shoulder;
- Children less than 3 years with spinal muscular atrophy and related syndromes, muscular dystrophy, congenital myopathy, primary disorders of muscles, cerebral palsy, hemiparesis and tetraplegia;
- Persons of 18 years with bone-joint disease, accepting the service "with component of rehabilitation of children with bone-joint diseases" as of December, 2011.

In order to get the service of the subprogram—Rehabilitation of children, the legal representative of the child shall apply to the service-provider organization in Tbilisi, Batumi or Kutaisi. The application must be appended by following documents:

- A copy of the identification document (ID card of citizen or passport) of the legal representative;
- A copy of the certificate of legal representation of the person;
- A copy of the birth certificate (ID card or passport);
- A reference on health status (medical documentation form No. IV-100/A);
- A copy of the certificate of disability status of a person, if a person is a child with disabilities.

In order to reimburse the expenses of the service of the subprogram—Rehabilitation of children, two kind of immaterialized vouchers are used:

1. A voucher appropriate to 20-day course, with reimbursement limit of GEL 554;
2. A voucher appropriate to 10-day course, with reimbursement limit of GEL 372.

The vouchers are funded after the appropriate course is over till no later than the end of the subsequent month. Herewith, the mandatory condition of financing is to submit the reporting information on the service rendered by the appropriate provider within the frameworks of the completed course and signed by the legal representative of the beneficiary to the Agency. The form of submission of the information is defined by the Agency.

Financing of the service is carried out as follows:

- The service rendered by the voucher within the frameworks of the subprogram to the children, who are the members of the families registered in the "unified database of the socially vulnerable families", whose rating score does not exceed 70,000 units, shall be funded by 100% of the appropriate limit;
- The service rendered by the voucher within the frameworks of the subprogram to the children, who are the members of the families registered in the "unified database of the socially vulnerable families", whose rating score is from 70,001 up to 100,001, shall be funded by 90% of the appropriate limit;

– The service rendered by the voucher to the beneficiaries of the subprogram shall be funded by 75% of the appropriate limit.

4.4.5 *Early Child Development*

The subprogram—Early child development aims to develop the social, cognitive, self-care and communication abilities for integration of the persons with mental and physical retardation into the society.

The service of early child development, considering the individual needs of the child, shall include at least nine services of various specialists per month.

The subprogram—Early child development—may be applied by:

– The children of 0–3 years with mental or physical retardation (including Down's syndrome, cerebral palsy, etc.);
– The children of 7 years, being the beneficiaries of early child development program with mental or physical disorders stipulated by the program of 2011, as of December, 2011.

In order to get the service, the parent or the legal representative of the child shall apply to the regional branch of the Social Service Agency and submit following documents:

– An application;
– A copy of identification document (passport, ID card) of the parent or the guardian;
– A certificate of legal representation;
– A birth certificate of the child and its copy;
– A reference to health condition of the child (medical documentation form No. IV-100/A).

Within the period of 1 month after submission of these documents to the Agency, the regional board shall make the decision on selection of the beneficiary and on rendering of the service to him/her. The voucher shall be issued to the legal representative of the beneficiary no later than 10th day of the following month.

The beneficiaries participating in the early child development subprogram are funded by the materialized vouchers, consisting of the coupons of appropriate months. Limit of financing of the voucher totals GEL 135 per month.

4.5 Protection of Child from Violence

The purpose of child protection referral procedures is to protect children from all forms of violence within and outside the family.

The Georgian law defines the following forms of violence:

- Physical violence;
- Sexual assault;
- Psychological violence;
- Economic violence;
- Coercion;
- Neglect.

According to the Civil Code of Georgia (family law) “parents/legal representatives of minors must not use such child-rearing methods that may cause physical and/or mental suffering of minors”. The Law on Early and Preschool Education prohibits any violence against children. The General Education Act prohibits school violence, physical and/or verbal abuse of a pupil or any other person. The Code of Administrative Offenses establishes financial sanctions for failure to perform the upbringing and education of a minor by a parent or his/her substitute. The police are responsible for detecting the violation and fining the person. Financial sanctions will also be imposed on professionals who do not fulfill the obligation to disclose child abuse to the relevant government authorities.

The Law of Georgia on the Prevention of Domestic Violence, Protection and Assistance to Victims of Domestic Violence provides that a child shall be separated from the abusive parent, other legal representative or any other abuser based on police restraining order or a social worker decision.

The Administrative Procedure Code sets out the rules of procedure for applying to the court in relation to a child abuse case, limiting parental authority, and making and appealing a decision to separate a child from a parent. The victim, as well as his/her family member, and, in the case of a minor, as well as the guardianship and guardianship authority, may apply to the court. According to the law, at all stages of administrative proceedings, including interrogation of a minor, “the best interests of the minor in his/her age and level of development” must be taken into account. The court makes a reasoned decision to recall or refuse to recall a minor on the basis of internal conviction. This decision must be transmitted to the parties within 24 hours of receipt.

Obligation of detection of facts of a child violence is imposed to every institution, being into relation with a child, including: school, medical institution, country doctor, special institution of children, the Social Service Agency, district service or patrol police. However, the application may be made by any citizen.

One of the following factors may become the sign on a child violence:

- Signs of injury on the body of the child (bruises, new wounds, new scratches, new sores, complicated walk, swollen parts of body, fractures);
- Suspicious behavior of a child (the child is excited, depressed, has fears, is not willing to go to school, goes to school irregularly, does not study, is neglected, is not willing to go home, has radically changed character, cannot explain the reasons of trauma).

The Georgian authorities recognized the problem of domestic violence as one of the top priorities in the country and the Law on Prevention of Domestic Violence, Protection and Assistance to Victims of Domestic Violence (Law of Georgia on

Violence Against Women and/or Elimination of Domestic Violence, Protection and Support of Victims of Violence) was adopted in 2006. This Law defines the set of actions that characterize violence in the public or private life, legal and organizational grounds for detecting and eliminating domestic violence, as well as guarantees for social and legal protection and support for victims of violence. This Law shall also apply to the relations that contribute to violating constitutional rights and freedoms of a minor through negligence and/or physical, psychological, economic, and sexual violence or coercion.

In case of violence towards a minor, the minor shall be separated from the abusive parent (parents), another legal representative or any other abuser on the basis of a restraining order issued by an authorized police officer. Separation of a minor from a parent(s) shall be the last resort to be used only in cases when all other, less stringent measures (including talking and warning) have been used, and the measures were unable to bring the intended effect, or when in the current situation it is clear that application of a less stringent measure cannot ensure protection of the minor's life and health. The opinion of a minor as to where to accommodate him/her must be considered taking into account the age and the level of development of the minor, and in any case, the decision must be taken in consideration of the best interests of the minor.

The court shall determine by its decision the terms of visiting the minor by the abusive parent. The abusive parent may be allowed to visit the minor only when all security measures have been taken with respect to him/her, which may include the place of visit of the minor, time of visit, frequency, duration, and the person who is responsible for the fulfilment of security requirements/measures.

In the case determined by the legislation of Georgia, from the age of 14, a minor may, apply to a court for the protection of his/her rights and legitimate interests. In such a case the court shall assign a procedural representative and hear the case. A minor claimant may disagree with his/her procedural representative and defend himself/herself. The court shall involve a guardianship and custodianship body in such cases.

4.5.1 Economic Exploitation, Including Child Labor

According to the Labor Code of Georgia, the legal capacity of a natural person comes from the age of 16 with the consent of his/her legal representative or guardianship/custodianship authority, if the employment relationship does not conflict with the interests of the minor, it does not prejudice his/her moral, physical and mental development and does not limit the right to and access to compulsory elementary and basic education. The Labor Code of Georgia prohibits the employment of minors if this contract involves the performance of difficult, harmful and dangerous work.

According to Georgian law, it is prohibited:

- Adolescent work at night (22:00 to 06:00);
- Adolescent employment in the gambling business;
- Adolescent employment in the erotic and pornographic industries;
- Adolescent employment in the production, transportation and sale of pharmaceuticals or toxic substances.

Although protecting children from exploitation is one of the country's top priorities, there are still many gaps in child exploitation data.

4.6 Administration of Juvenile Justice

Juvenile justice is one of the top priority areas for the Government of Georgia. Its reform is part of a general reform of the criminal justice system in Georgia. The juvenile justice strategy was developed by a specially authorized working group. This strategy and action plan are aimed at preventing juvenile delinquency, ensuring fair trial, promoting alternative forms of criminal prosecution and providing education and reintegration or rehabilitation schemes for children in conflict with the law.

According to Article 80 of the Criminal Code of Georgia, the minimum age of criminal responsibility is 14 years. Accordingly, a person between the ages of 14 and 18 is considered a juvenile offender.

Sources

Civil Code of Georgia, 1997
Child Rights Code of Georgia, 2019
Law of Georgia on Adoption and Foster Care, 2017
Law of Georgia on Violence Against Woman and/or Elimination of Domestic Violence, Protection and Support of Victims of Violence, 2006
Law of Georgia on Health Care, 1997
Law of Georgia on Social Protection of Persons with Disabilities, 1995
Law of Georgia on Patient Rights, 2000
Law of Georgia on Early and Preschool Education, 2015
Law of Georgia on General Education, 2005
Law of Georgia on Protecting Minors From Bad Influences, 2001
Law of Georgia on Broadcasting, 2004
Labour Code of Georgia, 2010
Law of Georgia on Advertising, 1998
The Law on Citizenship of Georgia, 1993
Law of Georgia On Combating Human Trafficking, 2006
Criminal Code of Georgia, 1999
Georgia Multiple Indicator Cluster Survey, National Statistics Office of Georgia, 2018
Convention on the Rights of the Child (Adopted and opened for signature, ratification and accession by General Assembly resolution 44/25 of 20 November 1989)
A National Study on Parenting Adolescents and Parenting Support Programmes in Georgia, UNICEF, 2018

Access to Justice for Children in Georgia, UNICEF, 2017
The Wellbeing of Children and their Families in Georgia, UNICEF, 2018
Monitoring of Child Care System – Effectiveness of Alternative Care Special Report, Public Defender (Ombudsman) of Georgia, 2018
Challenges of maternal and child health in Georgia, Transparency International Georgia, 2016
Perinatal Health Report of Georgia, NCDC, 2016
Social Service Agency of Georgia, http://ssa.gov.ge/
Ministry of Internally Displaced Persons From the Occupied Territories, Labour, Health and Social Affairs of Georgia., https://www.moh.gov.ge/
Public Defender (Ombudsman) of Georgia, http://www.ombudsman.ge/
National Centre For Disease Control AND Public Health of Georgia., https://www.ncdc.ge/
Concluding observations on the fourth periodic report of Georgia, OHCHR, 2017
Child Welfare System in Georgia – Recommendations for System Improvement and Future Development Strategies, Salome Namicheishvili, 2015

Chapter 5
Kazakhstan

Aigerim Mussabalinova

5.1 Background

Kazakhstan by territory is the largest state in the Central Asian region that gained independence from the Soviet Union in 1991. As in other post-Soviet nations, a child protection system in Kazakhstan remains similar to that which was inherited from the Soviet Union. It has a centralised political structure with progressive modernisation policies in many spheres, although in some spheres such reforms are yet to begin.[1] The hope for further reforms and positive changes is identified in the Conception of the Gender and Family Policy (2016) that embraced matters of child protection and care. In spite of the number of pieces of legislation related to children's welfare in Kazakhstan, there is no one comprehensive child protection policy that regulates child protection and child care.[2] There are several triggers for the development of child care and child protection in Kazakhstan, including the "Strategy Kazakhstan-2050: new political course of the established state" and the UN Sustainable Development Goals. It is 'the largest economy in central Asia, and one of the fastest growing, benefiting from oil wealth as well as a diversifying and

[1]Beazley Ivor, Downes Ronnie and Nicol Scherie, Budgeting in Kazakhstan. A roadmap for continued budgetary governance reform (Public Governance Directorate, Senior Budget Officials, OECD 2019) 6.

[2]The UN Committee on the Rights of the Child in its Concluding observation in 2015 'recommends that the State party prepare a comprehensive policy for implementing the rights of children . . .'. It also recommended to Kazakhstan 'to develop an action plan based on that policy that includes establishing efficient mechanisms for its implementation, supported by sufficient human, technical and financial resources.' See Concluding observations on the fourth periodic report of Kazakhstan, CRC/C/KAZ/CO/4 (30 October 2015).

A. Mussabalinova (✉)
School of Law, Sociology and Politics, University of Sussex, Brighton, UK
e-mail: am942@sussex.ac.uk

I. Earner, A. Telitsyna (eds.), *The Development of Child Protection Systems in the Post-Soviet States*, Child Maltreatment 12,
https://doi.org/10.1007/978-3-030-59588-3_5

liberalised economy'.[3] The biggest challenge for Kazakhstani development is the high level of corruption. According to Transparency International's 2019 edition of the Corruption Perceptions Index Kazakhstan is ranked 113 out of 180 countries that evidence high perceived levels of public section corruption, according to experts and business people.[4]

Evidence for specific concerns in the area of child welfare are highlighted by the 2020 Best Countries to Raise Kids ranking: Kazakhstan was ranked 73rd out of 73 states. In spite of achievements in economics, children in Kazakhstan do not fare well according to the ranking's measures of Kazakhstan's 'human rights, being considered family friendly, its environment for gender equality, being seen as happy, having income equality, being safe, and having well-developed public education and well-developed health care systems'.[5] According to UNICEF, almost every third child aged 3–9 in Kazakhstan is experiencing violence.[6] At the same time, Kazakhstan, compared with other Eastern Europe and Central Asian states has one of the highest suicides rates amongst children and adolescents.[7]

According to the official statistics, at the beginning of 2016 the population of Kazakhstan was 17,753,200, of whom 5,460,449 (30.7%) were children aged 0–17.[8] Notably, the population of Kazakhstan is growing (from 17,753,200 in 2016 to 18,595,443 in 2019) due to the birth rate (21.77 per 1000) versus the lower rate of death (7.14 per 1000). While the majority of the population are Kazakh (63.1%) and Russian (23.7%) Kazakhstan is home to 125 nations and ethnic groups.[9] The main religion is Islam (70%) while many other religions are also represented.

---

[3]Beazley Ivor, Downes Ronnie and Nicol Scherie, Budgeting in Kazakhstan. A roadmap for continued budgetary governance reform (Public Governance Directorate, Senior Budget Officials, OECD 2019) 6.

[4]Transparency International, 'Corruption Perceptions Index 2019', https://www.transparency.org/cpi2019. Accessed 5 February 2020.

[5]U.S. News & World Report L.P., 'Best Countries for Raising Kids. Nordic nations may be the best place to raise children, according to the Best Countries report', accessed 10 February 2020; Tengrinews.kz 'Kazakhstan ranks last in the ranking of the best countries for raising children' (16 January 2020), accessed 10 February 2020.

[6]UNICEF, Annual report UNICEF in Kazakhstan, 2018 (December 2018).

[7]UNICEF, Annual report UNICEF in Kazakhstan, 2018 (December 2018).

[8]Ministry of Education and Science of the Republic of Kazakhstan Committee for the Protection of Rights Children, SANGE Research Center, Dzhandosova Zh C, Sharipbaeva A E, Kudasheva T V, Baitugelova N Yu, Smagulova Sh K, Dzhandosova F S, Baitugelova Z E, Kolmogorova E A, Sharipbaeva K M, Zhappar A T, Serikbaeva S Sh, and Isagalieva A A, Report on the situation of children in the Republic of Kazakhstan in 2016 (Ministry of Education and Science of Republic of Kazakhstan 2016) 201.

[9]Kukanova G Zh, *Dissemination of data based on the results of the National Population Census of the Republic of Kazakhstan 2009* (The Statistics Agency of the Republic of Kazakhstan 2012); A A Smailova, A Zh Ashuev, G Zh Kukanova, E N Musabek, Yu K Shokamanov, N E Alkuatova. N A Mukhtarova, E Zh Alykpasheva, S S Abdukarimov, S T Nukutov, A R Ikambaeva, Sh A Iskakova, and L N Sergazieva, Analytical report. "Results of the National Population Census of the Republic of Kazakhstan 2009" (Agency of the Republic of Kazakhstan on Statistics, LLP Investment and Industrial Corporation "AstanaBlankIzdat" 2011) 20; Zhanat Tukpiev, '125 nations in one: what

As of 31 July 2019, the number of children deprived of parental care was 24,873, of whom 17,335 are under the care of relatives on custody, only 2269 (less than 10%) were placed in foster families, and whilst a further 5269 lived in institutions such as orphanages, baby homes and student accommodation.[10] As of 1 January 2019, there were 86,956 children (aged 0–18) with disabilities (Dzhandosova Zh C, Sharipbaeva AE, Kudasheva TV, Nikolaeva OV, Baitugelova N Yu, Dzhandosova FS, Smagulova Sh K and others, Report on the situation of children in the Republic of Kazakhstan in 2018 (Committee for the Protection of Children's Rights of Ministry of Education and Science of Republic of Kazakhstan, 2019) 153). In the same period of time, the infant mortality rate was 8.03 per 1000 (versus 16.59 in 2010).[11]

Kazakhstan according to its Constitution is a secular and unitary state with 14 regions.[12] The leading industries of the state are mining of natural resources and agriculture. GDP per capita in 2018 was 11,187 US dollar while living wage was 78.5 US dollar (per month) and average income was 270.2 US dollar (per month). Therefore, Kazakhstan is one of the ex-Soviet developing state with more or less stable economic growth, but also with a range of issues in the social sphere, including the realms of child protection and child care.

5.2 Legislation

The legislation and policies of Kazakhstan relating to child protection are complex, constantly changing and multi-layered. Although for the reader from the post-Soviet region, it might seem understandable how the Kazakhstani child protection system operates due to common history and possibly similar mechanisms for child protection, it is not easy to follow the law and understand the legal framework of the system for ordinary reader from beyond the post Soviet states. I argue that Kazakhstani legislation regulates spheres like education, health etc. so that children's matters might be regulated by a range of pieces of legislation on different subjects. It will be argued that legislation is formulated on the basis of the roles and competence

---

makes the Kazakhstani model of social harmony unique' Kazpravda.kz (01 May 2018). Accessed 20 July 2018.

[10]The Committee for the Protection of Children's Rights, *Main results in the field of children's rights protection for the first half of 2019 and priorities for activities for the second half of 2019* (Ministry of Education and Science of the Republic of Kazakhstan 2019).

[11]Ministry of National Economy of the Republic of Kazakhstan Statistics committee, 'The main socio-economic indicators of the Republic of Kazakhstan' https://stat.gov.kz/official/dynamic Accessed 8 February 2020.

[12]Nazgul Assylbekova and Anuarbek Kakabayev, 'Kazakhstan' in Penelope Welbourne and John Dixon (eds), *Child Protection and Child Welfare: A Global Appraisal of Cultures, Policy and Practice* (Jessica Kingsley Publishers 2013).

of relevant institutions and agencies and not on the basis of the best interests of affected children.

Kazakhstan ratified the United Nation Convention on the Rights of the Child (UNCRC) in 1994. In addition to this key international treaty, Kazakhstan is the state party of the following international treaties and protocols related to children:

1. International Labour Organization (ILO) Convention on the Prohibition and Immediate Action for the Eradication of worst forms of child labor
2. Convention on the Elimination of All Forms of Racial Discrimination
3. ILO Maternity Convention
4. Optional Protocol on the sale of children, children prostitution and child pornography
5. Optional Protocol on the involvement of children in the armed conflicts
6. Convention for the Suppression of the Traffic in Persons and of the Exploitation of Prostitution by third parties
7. International Convention on Civil and Political Rights
8. International Convention on Economic, Social and Cultural Rights
9. Protocol to Prevent and Combat Trafficking in Persons, Especially women and children, and punishment for her
10. Convention on the Protection of Children and Cooperation with regard to Foreigners adoptions
11. Convention on the Rights of Persons with Disabilities
12. Convention against Discrimination in Education
13. Convention on the International Procedure for the Collection of Alimony for Children and other forms of family support and the Protocol on the Law Applicable to maintenance obligations
14. Convention on the Civil Aspects of International Abduction children.

However, being a member of international treaties does not mean that the practice will be in compliance with international standards. The latter is apparent in Kazakhstan where the legislation has been criticized for being purely formal and inconsistent meaning that children do not enjoy their rights. (Ademi Bidaishiyeva, Kalamkas K Nadirova, Saltanat Kuldinova, Nurlan Apakhayev, Zhanna A Khamzina, and Yermek A Buribayev, 'Improving quality of legal regulation for social rights of family and child within new social course in the Republic of Kazakhstan' (2018) 21 Journal of Legal, Ethical and Regulatory Issues 1).

At the national level, the key acts that govern child protection are The Code on Marriage (Matrimony) and Family (CMMF), the laws On the Rights of the Child in the Republic of Kazakhstan (LRCRK), On Social, Medical, Pedagogical, and Correctional Support for Children with Disabilities, On Juvenile Crime Prevention and Prevention of Child Neglect and Homelessness, On Special Social Services.

The policies related to children are not allocated in the special document and mentioned in the Kazakhstan-2050 Strategy, the Kazakhstan 2030: Concept for Social Development, and the Conception of the Gender and Family Policy (2016). There have been a number of time-limited state programmes focusing on particular issues such as for example, state programmes on the prevention of infant mortality, prevention of suicide among children and the prevention of child abuse. Each of the listed state programmes was implemented with the assistance of UNICEF Kazakhstan and has achieved an improvement in then statistics, but this approach is not sustainable. That is because no programme tackles the lack of budget and the absence of action.

It might be concluded that Kazakhstan has the basis for a positive legal framework for child protection, one where international treaties set up the standards, and national legislation reflects such standards and policies to promote child protection. In reality, the legislation of Kazakhstan tends to be inconsistent, purely formal and complex with many examples of subordinate pieces of legislation that contradict the key legislation or do not help in identifying the legal decision-making process.[13]

There are several instances described later in this chapter that reflect the issues of Kazakhstani law raised above. The main concern is that subordinate legislation has a greater role since it regulates the mechanism of child care and child protection in practices, and this legislation is far removed from the international standards of child protection. It lacks reference to the UNCRC principles and is, on the contrary, adapted to the existing resources remaining from the Soviet Union child protection era. The absence of child-oriented policy during the 30 years since Kazakhstan obtained its independence demonstrates that child protection is not a priority of state development. The improvements that have been made by the state are fragmented since they are the results of critiques at the international level.[14] For example, the deinstitutionalization of children happened due to critiques of the UN Committee on the Rights of the Child.[15] However, the actions of the state is not underpinned with any plan or policy of the state and has had negative outcomes for children from the institutions.[16]

> ...the lack of a realistic assessment of the motivation of foster carers and guardians, and ignorance of the age characteristics of children, has led to the return of children to orphanages. According to statistics, in Kazakhstan, out of 1107 children transferred to care and patronage (small foster families) in 2015, 211 (19%) were returned to institutions. In 2016, 188 (26%) of the 734 children transferred were returned to institutions. <u>Almost every fourth child</u> is experiencing secondary orphanhood.[17]

[13]Ademi Bidaishiyeva, Kalamkas K Nadirova, Saltanat Kuldinova, Nurlan Apakhayev, Zhanna A Khamzina, and Yermek A Buribayev, 'Improving quality of legal regulation for social rights of family and child within new social course in the Republic of Kazakhstan' (2018) 21 Journal of Legal, Ethical and Regulatory Issues 1.

[14]United Nations Committee on the rights of the Child, 'Concluding observations on the fourth periodic report of Kazakhstan' (30 October 2015) UNCRC/C/KAZ/CO/4, paras 11-13; The United Nations Committee on the Rights of the Child, 'List of issues in relation to the fourth periodic report of Kazakhstan' (10 March 2015) UN Doc UNCRC/C/Kaz/Q/4, para 10.

[15]Ibid.

[16]The Commissioner for Human Rights in Kazakhstan, *Report on the activities of the Commissioner for Human Rights in the Republic of Kazakhstan for 2017* (Astana 2018) 77.

[17]Ibid.

This and other issues of the system will be discussed in the next section on how the system operates in practice.

5.3 Child Care and Child Protection in Kazakhstan

In spite of almost three decades since Kazakhstan obtained its independence in 1991 and its ratification of the UN Convention of the Rights of the Child in 1994, the way Kazakhstan protects its children and provides care has not changed much. In particular, all referrals related to child protection and child care are considered within the 'guardianship department' of the local authority. Hamilton and Watkins (2011) in their report for UNICEF 2011 described the system as 'not child centred' because it is passive and fragmented between several bodies.[18] However, since this report, the Department of Child Protection, which up to that point did not offer children other services than the authority of guardianship, was merged with authority of guardianship—*organy opeki e popechitelstva (the authority of guardinship)* in 2014.[19] Hence, at the local level child welfare and child protection fall primarily within the competence of three state bodies: the guardianship authority, the police minors department and the juvenile commission (see Fig. 5.1). At the national level, the Ministry of Education and Science, the Ministry of Healthcare, the Ministry of Labour and Social Protection and the Ministry of Internal Affairs all hold responsibilities in the regulation of child protection. Child protection is the subject of different state policies depending on the priority of the relevant ministry such as education and health. In spite of the growing expenditure of Kazakhstan on education, health and social protection, the current budgeting scheme has been criticised for lacking a children's rights perspective, indicators and a controlling system.[20] Overall, I argue that Kazakhstani children's interests are not what drives the policy makers and others in the state. Since the budget and policies are sector and agency oriented, the priority and indicators such as education and health are driving the state bodies involved in child protection.

What is child protection according to Kazakhstani law? Since the UNCRC is a part of Kazakhstani legal framework, it might be defined as suggested in Article 19 of this convention, namely:

> States Parties shall take all appropriate legislative, administrative, social and educational measures to protect the child from all forms of physical or mental violence, injury or abuse,

---

[18]Carolyn Hamilton and Jonathan Watkins, *Modelling for Integrated Child Protection System in Kazakhstan* (UNICEF 2011).

[19]The Decree of the Government of the Republic of Kazakhstan On Certain Issues of Staff Limits for Ministries, Other Central and Local Executive Bodies and the Abolition of Some State Institutions 2013; Tengrinews.kz, 'Departments for the protection of children's rights abolished in Kazakhstan' (15 of February 2014) <https://tengrinews.kz/kazakhstan_news/upravleniya-po-zaschite-prav-detey-uprazdnili-v-kazahstane-250495/> accessed 25 September 2018.

[20]UNICEF, *Situation analysis of children in Kazakhstan* (UNICEF 2019) 15.

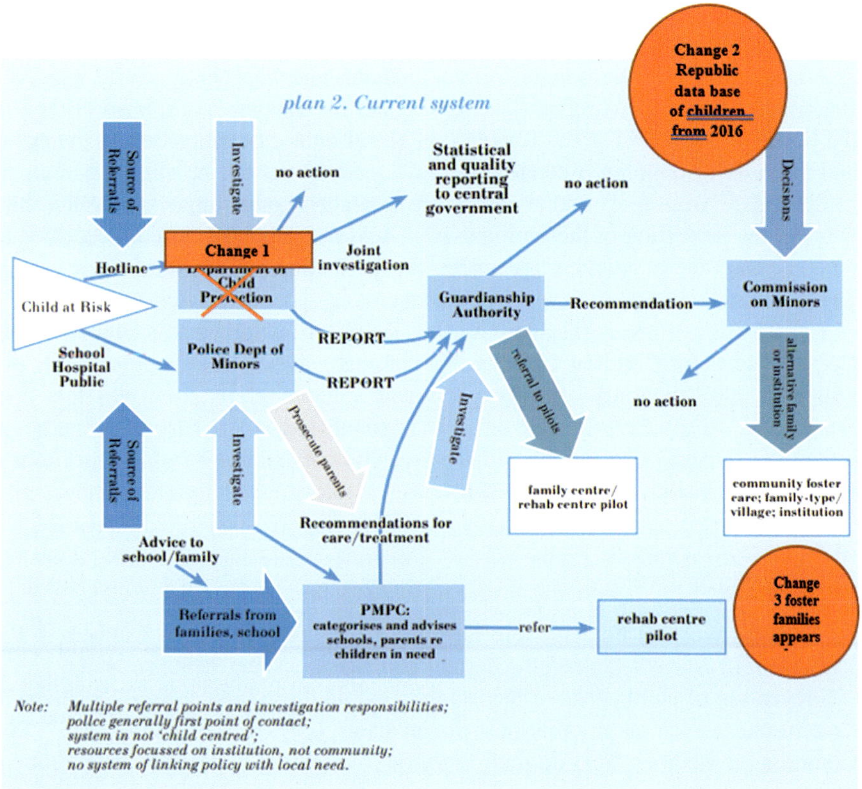

Fig. 5.1 Child protection system in Kazakhstan (Aigerim Mussabalinova, The Right of the Child to be Raised in the Family: Reflection on Decision-Making Processes in Child Placement in Kazakhstan in the Light of English Experience (PhD thesis, University of Sussex, coming 2020) 103; Carolyn Hamilton and Jonathan Watkins, Modelling for Integrated Child Protection System in Kazakhstan (UNICEF 2011))

> neglect or negligent treatment, maltreatment or exploitation, including sexual abuse, while in the care of parent(s), legal guardian(s) or any other person who has the care of the child.

According to national law, in particular article 67 (3) of the Code on Marriage (Matrimony) and Family child protection implies the following,

> The civil servants of state bodies and organizations and other citizens who have knowledge of danger to a child's life or health, violation of his (her) rights or legal interests, shall be obliged to report this to a body carrying out the functions of trusteeship or guardianship at the actual local area of a child. Upon the receipt of this information, a body, carrying out the

> functions of trusteeship or guardianship shall be obliged to use reasonable efforts in the defence of the rights and legal interests of the child.[21]

It is not clear what 'reasonable efforts' includes and what 'body, carrying out the functions of trusteeship or guardianship' implies. According to article 43 of the law the Rights of the Child in the Republic of Kazakhstan, the protection of the rights and interests of children protected by law is carried out by the child's parents or caregivers, or, in case of children in the care of health or other organisations the child is under the protection of these organisation, and in relation to children deprived of parental care these children are under the protection of the local authority of guardianship—*organy opeki e popechitelstva*.[22]

From April 2016 Kazakhstan established the post of Kazakhstan's Human Rights Commissioner for Children's Rights. Such a post was suggested by the UN Committee in 2002 but only after 14 years and a reminder in 2015 was this post established.[23] However, the post remains nominal (formal). It has no leverage and influence to change the situation with the protection of children's rights, especially at the system (legislative and political) level.

> The institution of the Kazakhstan's Human Rights Commissioner for Children's Rights is established by the President of the Republic of Kazakhstan and carries out its activities on a voluntary basis. . .[24]

The first two post holders were members of the two different chambers in the Parliament of Kazakhstan and the current commissioner represents an NGO.

Prevention of child abuse or neglect falls within the competence of the Juvenile Commission which, as in other post-Soviet states, plays a gatekeeping role.[25] The Commission members also do their work on a voluntary basis or as an additional function in addition to their main job as the deputy *Akim* (Mayor) of the corresponding administrative-territorial unit; a public service manager from internal affairs, education, culture, health, justice; the authorized body for employment, guardianship and trusteeship; public and other organizations interested in preventing crime, neglect and homelessness among minors.[26] The problem is that this commission (like the Kazakhstan's Human Rights Commissioner for Children's Rights)

---

[21]The Code of the Republic of Kazakhstan on Marriage (Matrimony) and Family (2011), art 67.

[22]The Law of the Republic of Kazakhstan The Rights of a Child in the Republic of Kazakhstan (2002), art 43.

[23]United Nations Committee on the rights of the Child, 'General Comment No. 2' (15 November 2002) CRC/GC/2002/2; United Nations Committee on the rights of the Child, 'Concluding observations on the fourth periodic report of Kazakhstan' (30 October 2015) UNCRC/C/KAZ/CO/4, paras 16–17.

[24]The Law of the Republic of Kazakhstan The Rights of a Child in the Republic of Kazakhstan (2002), art 7–1.

[25]Andy Bilson, *The Development of gate-keeping functions in Central and Eastern Europe and the CIS: Lessons from Bulgaria, Kazakhstan and Ukraine* (University of Central Lancashire and UNICEF 2010) 46–47; Assylbekova and Kakabayev (2013).

[26]The Law of the Republic of Kazakhstan On the Prevention of Juvenile Delinquency and the Prevention of Child Neglect and Homelessness 2004, art 9 (5).

does not have resources so that it relies mostly on the local authority of guardianship—*organy opeki e popechitelstva*.[27] For example, this commission relies on the guardianship authority to provide support to children in difficult life situations.[28] The Ministry of Education and Science of Kazakhstan in its meeting on 15 February 2019 acknowledged the inefficiency of the work of this commission, and in some region the lack of any meetings of the local Juvenile Commission during 2018.[29]

A declaration of intent is not the same as implementation and real protection. In 2019 there were 2115 crimes committed against children.[30] Meanwhile, Kazakhstan has high rates of suicide among minors. For example, in 2018—178 children committed suicide and a further 329 suicide attempts were recorded. The above statistics vary between different reports and the problems might be bigger in the light of statistics from UNICEF indicating that 17.3% of children under 1 year old experience physical punishment and 75% of adults assume that it is normal to administer physical punishment to children.[31] Hence, awareness or understanding among adults of children's rights is very low.

Extracts from the Legislation Regarding Protection Measures
The law concerning the Rights of the Child in the Republic of Kazakhstan declares the requirement of protection for the child from:

1. Negative impact of social environment, information, propaganda and agitation;
2. Negative impact of alcohol products and tobacco products,
3. Narcotic drugs, psychotropic substances, their analogues, potent or toxic substances, prostitution;
4. Involving a child in the manufacture, advertising, public demonstration or
5. Distribution, as well as selling to a child, print, film or video materials, images, other objects or materials of a pornographic nature and (or) erotic content that are harmful to the child's health and development;
6. Involvement of the child in military operations, armed conflicts, the creation of children's paramilitary groups;

(continued)

[27]Mussabalinova (2020) Chap. 4, Sect. 4.3.

[28]The Law of the Republic of Kazakhstan on the Prevention of Juvenile Delinquency and the Prevention of Child Neglect and Homelessness 2004, art 9 (6).

[29]Edugovkz, 'The extended board meeting of the Ministry of Education and Science of Kazakhstan' (online translation, 15 February 2019) <http://parent.kz/2Ebn9uQ> accessed on 15 of February 2019.

[30]The Committee on Legal Statistics and Special Accounting General Prosecutor's Office of the Republic of Kazakhstan, Statistic of crimes on minors, December 2019, <http://infopublic.pravstat.kz/crime/crime-stat/underage.html> accessed 10 February 2020.

[31]UNICEF, Annual report UNICEF in Kazakhstan, 2018 (December 2018) 9.

7. Illegal movement, abduction of children, trafficking in them, regardless of the goals, forms and methods of execution.

In regards to the function of the authority of guardianship, according to the Rules on the Operation State Functions in Custody and Guardianship approved by the Government in 2012, it includes:

- Participation in the court when considering cases related to children;
- The resolution of issues of assignment or change of the surname, or other names of minors;
- The initiation of claims for the deprivation or restriction of parents of their parental rights, for the cancellation of an adoption or for the invalidation of an adoption;
- Representing children deprived of parental care; identification of children deprived of parental care and children in need; protection of the property of children in care, and
- Resolving disagreements between parents on issues related to the upbringing and education of children.[32]

An analysis of the protection measures in Kazakhstan demonstrates that the system relies on existing limited resources which are not effective. Hamilton and Watkins (2011) in their report for UNICEF, Kazakhstan in 2011, emphasise the passive role of the state in child protection provision.

> The system waits for children to present themselves rather than undertaking active identification of children. For instance, children are mostly presented to the Guardianship Authority by parents, seeking assistance mainly because of poverty, family breakdown, family death or inadequacy. Services tend to be offered on the basis of the financial need of the family rather than the needs of the child.[33]

Therefore, due to limited resources, the existing system does not provide preventive measures and offers the limited services to those who present themselves or emerge within the system as the result 'of poverty, family breakdown, family death or inadequacy'. There is social protection assistance for children and their families, but the size of benefits is very small while only a quarter of the families in the poorer rural areas were able to access such benefits due to 'poor outreach and service delivery that do not seek the most marginalised population'.[34]

---

[32] The Rules on Operation State Functions in Custody and Guardianship that approved by the Government (2012).

[33] Hamilton and Watkins (2011) 8.

[34] UNICEF, A Situation Analysis of Children in Kazakhstan (2019) 5.

> Although 46 per cent of the population live in rural areas and have higher poverty rates, only about a quarter of rural households receive social assistance transfers, compared to over 40 per cent in the large cities of Nur-Sultan and Almaty. Therefore, many children in rural households live in poverty, unsupported by social assistance. (UNICEF, A Situation Analysis of Children in Kazakhstan, 2019).

Legrand expressed his concerns that existing child protection systems in all post-soviet regions do not deal with prevention and do not provide support services to families.[35] The lack of such services according to Legrand (2015) is responsible for the number of children in care. Without services and resources children rights are undermined and remain on the paper.[36] This problem is often raised in documents provided by the UN Committee on the rights of the child.[37] The current legislation of Kazakhstan implies state protection for children's rights and interests only when the child is in a care setting, including hospitals and institutions for children deprived of parental care.[38] The existing care system for children deprived of parental care relies more on residential care than alternative family-type care. In addition, the child protection is lacking on preventive measures and assistance for the family in difficult life circumstances. Due to the 'campaign' of the politicians on reducing number of children in institution, the number of institutions and children in them has decreased significantly during the last 10 years, from 2010 to 2018, but the mechanism of such decrease is unclear.[39] The practice of the officials are not child–oriented because their main goal is to report on decreasing the number of institutions for children deprived of parental care. In particular, children are not prepared before they move, and while some might be placed in foster families, many are just moved to another orphanages. As it was noticed earlier in this chapter, almost every fourth child is returned to the system (See Sect. 5.2; Diagrams 5.1, 5.2 and 5.3.).

The research that was conducted during 2016–2019 in regards to the child's right to be raised in the family demonstrated that children in Kazakhstan who were

[35]Jean-Claude Legrand, 'Child care system reforms in Eastern and Central Europe and Central Asia: Why there is a need to focus on children below three years' (2015) 15 Irish Journal of Applied Social Studies 2.

[36]Ibid; Onora O'Neill, 'Children's rights and children's lives' (1988) 98 Ethics 44.

[37]United Nations Committee on the rights of the Child, 'General Comment No.5' (27 November 2003) UNCRC/GC/2003/5, paras 6-8; United Nations Committee on the rights of the Child, 'Concluding observations on the fourth periodic report of Kazakhstan' (30 October 2015) UNCRC/C/KAZ/CO/4, paras 11-13.

[38]The Code on Marriage (Matrimony) and Family (2011), art 116 and The Rights of a Child in the Republic of Kazakhstan (2002), art 29 (5).

[39]Aigerim Mussabalinova, The Right of the Child to be Raised in the Family: Reflection on Decision-Making Processes in Child Placement in Kazakhstan in the Light of English Experience (PhD thesis, University of Sussex, coming 2020) Chap. 4, Sect. 4.5.

Diagram 5.1 The number of institutions for children deprived of parental care (The Committee for the Protection of Children's Rights of Ministry of Education and Science of the Republic of Kazakhstan, Основные итоги в сфере охраны прав детей за 1 полугодие 2018 года и приоритеты деятельности до конца 2018 года (The Committee for the Protection of Children's Rights, Main results in the field of children's rights protection for 2018 and priorities for activities for 2019 (Ministry of Education and Science of the Republic of Kazakhstan 2018) 5); Ministry of Education and Science of the Republic of Kazakhstan, Report on the situation of children in the Republic of Kazakhstan (Ministry of Education and Science of Republic of Kazakhstan 2011) 43)

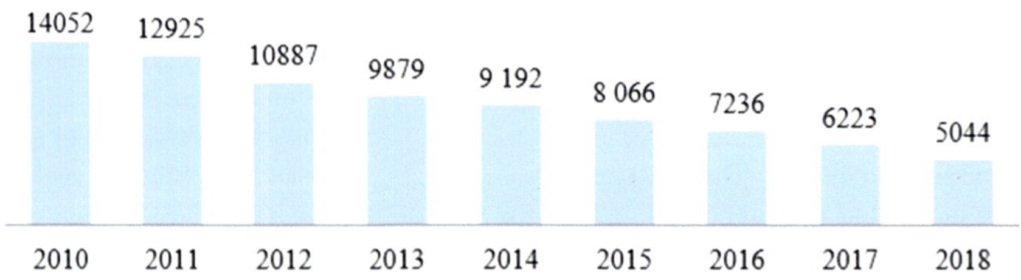

Diagram 5.2 Children left without parental care in institutions, 2018 (Dzhandosova Zh C, Sharipbaeva A E, Kudasheva T V, Nikolaeva O V, Baitugelova N Yu, Dzhandosova F S, Smagulova Sh K and others, Report on the situation of children in the Republic of Kazakhstan in 2018 (Committee for the Protection of Children's Rights of Ministry of Education and Science of Republic of Kazakhstan, 2019) 150)

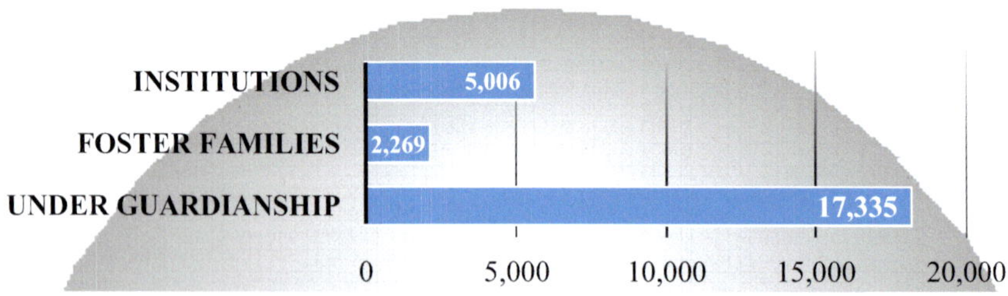

Diagram 5.3 The number of children deprived of parental care, 2019 (The Committee for the Protection of Children's Rights, Main results in the field of children's rights protection for the first half of 2019 and priorities for activities for the second half of 2019 (Ministry of Education and Science of the Republic of Kazakhstan 2019) 4)

deprived of parental care are placed directly in institutions for children.[40] The exception to this common practice is the cases where the child has a relative who wants to take the child and become the guardian. The latter was the common practice among Kazakh nomads prior to the Soviet Union era when there were no institutions and children remained within the tribe of their father.[41]

5.3.1 Institutional Care

As I have previously descibed in my doctoral research findings, in law, there are a different institutions that cater for protection of different categories of children (depending on their age, health condition and the reasons they are placed in care (see Table 5.1)).

The large institutional care system that was inherited from the Soviet era is what the state offers to children deprived of parental care. In my doctoral research, I argue that Kazakhstan provides for alternative care within family settings only in cases where it can easily be found (such as in the extended family of the child) (Aigerim Mussabalinova, The Right of the Child to be Raised in the Family: Reflection on Decision-Making Processes in Child Placement in Kazakhstan in the Light of English Experience (PhD thesis, University of Sussex, coming 2020, Chap. 4). That study also provided an analysis of the practice of child care where there is no such family member who is ready to take care of the child deprived of parental care. In practice, if there is no family member who is ready to take the child, this child directly placed temporarily in institutions such as shelters or the adaptation centers for minorities. After this temporal placement, the child might be placed in foster family (if such is available) or transferred to orphanage. This happens due to the inconsistency of both key law and subordinate legislation. In addition, the reason of the described practice is the lack of resources and services and the underdevelopment of family-based care. For example, this is how some of the respondents in my research described the childcare system in Kazakhstan:

> Kazakhstan certainly pays great attention to this target group of children, namely children left without parental care, and now every effort is made to ensure that as few children as possible are in residential institutions. Unfortunately, however, institutionalization still remains one of the forms of placement, because the long-standing legislation and the employees themselves have not yet learnt how to avoid the system of residential institutions before the child enters an alternative family... (Olga, NGO, 09 March 2018)

The procedures of child care is different from what is suggested and declared in the key legislation of Kazakhstan. In particular, subordinate legislation and some of the provisions of key legislation are contradictory. Article 116 and 117 of the CMMF and Article 29 (paragraph 1) of the LRCRK suggest that as part of state protection of

[40] Mussabalinova (2020) Chap. 4.

[41] Mussabalinova (2020) Chap. 3.

Table 5.1 List of the institutions for children deprived of parental care, description of eligibility criteria of resident children (Aigerim Mussabalinova, The Right of the Child to be Raised in the Family: Reflection on Decision-Making Processes in Child Placement in Kazakhstan in the Light of English Experience (PhD thesis, University of Sussex, coming 2020, Chap. 4))

Name of institution	Description of children eligible for placement in institution
1. The baby home	Orphaned children and children being left without custody of parents, from birth to 3 years. Special departments shall be opened in baby homes for the temporary accommodation of children[a]
2. The specialized children's homes	Children with psychological or physical development disabilities from birth to 4 years old
3. Boarding school organizations (orphanages)	Orphaned children and children left without custody of parents, aged from 3 to 18 years[b]
4. Education boarding school of general type	Orphaned children, children left without custody of parents, as well as children from needy and large families aged from 6 to 18 years that do not have medical needs requiring care in specialist organisations[c]
5. Boarding house for children with learning disabilities	Children being in need of care, medical, personal care and social and educational/vocational training aged from 4 to 18 years[d]
6. Children's village of family type	Orphaned children and children left without custody of parents aged up to 18 years
7. Youth houses	Orphaned children and children left without custody of parents aged from 16 to 23years[e]
8. Youth houses functioning as a separate legal entity on the basis of a decision by local executive bodies*	Foster children from children's villages and graduates of children's homes, boarding schools for orphaned children and children left without custody of parents aged from 16 to 23, with the exception of persons having psychoneurological diseases
Adaptation centres for minors	The Centre accepts: (1) neglected and homeless children pending identification of their parents or other legal representatives; (2) children left without parental care, if they are not available in a timely manner, and also removed from their parents (or one of them) or other persons in the care of whom they were in immediate threat of their life and health; (3) minors sent to special educational organizations; (4) children in a difficult life situation, due to cruel treatment, which has led to behavioural issues and social deprivation[f]
9. Organisations to provide assistance created in accordance with the Law of the Republic of Kazakhstan on preventive measures with regard to domestic violence	Children being in a difficult life situation due to abusive treatment leading to behavioural issues and social deprivation[g]

(continued)

Table 5.1 (continued)

Name of institution	Description of children eligible for placement in institution
10. Shelters	For orphans and children left without parental care, providing temporary residence pending future living arrangements. The period of stay of children in the shelter is not more than 6 months[h]
11. Orphanages of family type	For orphans and children left without parental care[i]
12. Centre for supporting children in difficult life situations	(1) children from disadvantaged families; (2) children who find themselves in unfavourable family conditions, threatening their health and development, children who have suffered from cruel treatment; (3) orphans and children left without parental care. Aged from 3 to 18 The length of stay of children in difficult life situations, indicated in paragraphs 1) and 2) is not more than 6 months[j]

[a]The Regulations on the activities of the health organization for orphans, children left without parental care from birth to 3 years old, with mental and physical development defects from birth to 4 years, carrying out psychological and pedagogical support for families with the risk of abandoning the child, approved by the order of the Minister health Republic of Kazakhstan 2017, para 2

[b]The Standard rules for the activities of types of educational organizations for orphans and children left without parental care, approved by the order of the Minister of Education and Science of the Republic of Kazakhstan 2013, Appendix 1. Standard rules for the activities of orphanages, paras 16 and 18. According to para 18 of the rules, orphanages can take children from birth to 18 years old, but according to practice children under 3 years old (in some cases 4 years old) are placed in the Baby Homes

[c]Ibid, Appendix 3. Standard rules for the activities of boarding schools for orphans and children without parental care, para 7

[d]Ibid, Appendix 2. Standard rules for the activities of orphanages for children with special educational needs, para 20

[e]Ibid. The main goal of the Youth House is to help children from children's villages, graduates of orphanages, boarding schools for orphans and children left without parental care (persons undergoing social adaptation) to integrate into society according to their desire, in particular, in the labour market

[f]The Standard rules for the activities of types of educational organizations for orphans and children left without parental care, approved by the order of the Minister of Education and Science of the Republic of Kazakhstan 2013, Appendix 6. Standard Rules for the Activities of Adaptation Centres for Minors, para 8

[g]The Standard for the provision of special social services victims of domestic violence, approved by the order of the Minister Health and Social Development of the Republic of Kazakhstan 2016, paras 26-27

[h]The Standard rules for the activities of types of educational organizations for orphans and children left without parental care, approved by the order of the Minister of Education and science of the Republic of Kazakhstan 2013, Appendix 4. Standard Rules for the Activities of Shelters, paras 14-18

[i]Ibid, Appendix 5. Standard Rules for the Activities of Orphanages of Family type, para 17

[j]The Standard rules for the activities of types of educational organizations for orphans and children left without parental care, approved by the order of the Minister of Education and science of the Republic of Kazakhstan 2013, Appendix 7. Standard Rules for the Activities of Centres for supporting children in difficult life situations, para 3

children deprived of parental care, the child should be placed in family and in its absence in institution. In fact, placement of the child in family-based care is not possible unless such family is related to the child. That is because, children might be placed in the family only if they are selected by alternative families from a database with all information about children deprived of parental care.[42] This database is a relatively new tool for placement of children in the family and was introduced on 1st of January 2017.[43] It operates likewise online shopping but in which potential families choose a child instead of products to buy.[44] The data in this database appear only the child is placed in institution so that institutional setting are not avoidable.[45] Initially, children above 4 years old are placed in temporal setting such as the Adaptation Centres for minors (or Shelter for children) and after 6 (in the Adaptation Centres for minors) or 3 months (in Shelter for children) children are moving to the orphanages.[46] Historically, the majority of children and institutions for children deprived of parental care are in the North and East of Kazakhstan (see the Map 5.1). This phenomenon is explained by the historical characteristics of these regions (such as forced migration, existing of Soviet labor camps and the mixed ethnically population of the region).[47]

5.3.2 *Family-Based Care*

Family-based care for children deprived of parental care in Kazakhstan is primarily provided by relatives who become the guardians of such children (almost 70% of children deprived of parental care are under the custody of their relatives). Foster care and adoption for the rest, however, are not popular forms of child placement. There are several reasons for this tendency. This includes the custom of nomads to look after their relatives' children according to customary law, (but not necessarily the children of non-relatives). At the same time, there is such contradictable reason

[42]Mussabalinova (2020) Chap. 4.

[43]The Law of the Republic of Kazakhstan On Amendments and Additions to Some Legislative Acts of the Republic of Kazakhstan on the Protection of the Rights of the Child 2016, art 1 (1) (18), art 2 (1); The Rules for the Formation and Use of the Republican Data Bank of Orphans, Children Left Without Parental Care, and People Who Want to Take Children to Their Families approved by the Order of the Minister of Education and Science of the Republic of Kazakhstan dated November 16, 2016 (registered with the Ministry of Justice of the Republic of Kazakhstan on January 11, 2017).

[44]The Rules for the Transfer of Children Who are Citizens of the Republic of Kazakhstan, for Adoption, approved by Resolution of the Government of the Republic of Kazakhstan 2012, para 20; the Regulation on Foster Care (patronage), approved by the Order of the Minister of Education and Science of the Republic of Kazakhstan 2015, paras 11, 13.

[45]Mussabalinova (2020) Chap. 4.

[46]Ibid.

[47]Ibid.

Map 5.1 The number of children placed in institutions by region 2017 (The Committee for the Protection of Children's Rights of Ministry of Education and Science of the Republic of Kazakhstan, 'Information on orphans and children left without parental care for 2017', <http://www.balakkk.kz/ru/node/15756> accessed 10 February 2018. To note: (1) the data was analysed and transferred to the map from the available information of the Committee for the Protection of Children's Rights of Kazakhstan; (2) on 19 June 2018 the South Kazakhstani oblast was renamed as the Turkestan oblast according to the Decree of the President of the Republic of Kazakhstan: On some issues of the administrative-territorial structure of the Republic of Kazakhstan)

as the inherited from the Soviet Union stereotypes and social exclusion practice of children deprived of parental care.[48] In addition, the institutionalisation of children is explained by the high level of corruption, complexity and inconsistency of decision-making processes and legislation, the low level of awareness of the rights and interests of the child at all levels, and the lack of social services support pre- and post adoption or fostering.[49]

Fostering in Kazakhstan was introduced with the new law regulating family matters in 2012 (The CMMF on December 26, 2011 replaced The Law of the Republic of Kazakhstan About marriage and family 1998 and introduced the foster family (patronage) in Kazakhstan for the first time). In particular, according to the new Code on Marriage (Matrimony) and Family that replaced the law on Marriage and Family in 2012, the foster family was referred to as 'patronage', but in 2016 in addition to 'patronage' the Code added new forms of family-based foster family and guest family care. Practitioners and society do not understand differences between 'patronage' and foster family and apply them as a cover for what are in effect 'hidden

[48]Mussabalinova (2020) Chaps. 3–5.

[49]Ibid Chap. 7.

adoptions' since adoption is a longer and more complicated process.[50] In fact the differences between these two forms of child placements are that for 'patronage' it is allowed to take up to three children (the exception is group of siblings bigger than three),[51] while for foster families it is compulsory to take between three and ten children.[52] Moreover, the legal status of children in 'patronage' might be still not sorted while foster families take only children whose status is already known (when the parents' rights have been revoked, or children are orphans).

Adoption is the most corrupt of the practices within child protection due to the demand for newborn babies and the existing stereotypes against older children from institutions.[53] The (corrupt) charge made by officials to arrange for the adoption of a baby ranges between 2000 USD and 25,000 USD.[54]

According to the statistics of 2013 provided by the prosecutors:

- there were 25 crimes related to child trafficking (the child might be sold whilst in the institutions, more often though in maternity hospitals),[55]
- during 2012–2013, 457 children were adopted by persons who were not registered as candidates for adoption avoiding the legal procedures,[56]
- at the same time due to the fault of the guardianship authority, which excluded 1858 orphans from the database with no reason, children were deprived of the opportunity to be adopted.[57]

Since 2012, Kazakhstani law has encouraged a clear preference for domestic adoption although international adoptions are still possible and exist. In particular, Kazakhstan ratified The Hague Convention on the Intercountry Adoption of Children in 2012 and amended its national subordinate legislation that governs the procedures of adoption. In particular according to the Rules for the Transfer of

---

[50] Ibid Chaps. 4 and 5.

[51] The Regulation on Foster Care (patronage) approved by the Order of the Minister of Education and Science of the Republic of Kazakhstan dated January 16, 2015, para 5.

[52] The Regulation on Foster Care approved by the Order of the Minister of Education and Science of the Republic of Kazakhstan of October 7, 2016, para 2.

[53] Mussabalinova (2020) Chap. 5.

[54] Ibid Chap. 5, Sect. 5.3.

[55] Mygorod.kz, 'Illegal activity of Baby houses in Kazakhstan' (13 June 2017) accessed 20 September 2018; Informburo 31, 'Why trafficking of children is still flourishing in Kazakhstan?', <https://www.youtube.com/watch?v=9jrGdK1rJgg> accessed 01 August 2018; TV Channel KTK, 'A resident of Almaty region sold a newborn for $3000' (17 of March 2013) <https://www.ktk.kz/ru/news/video/2013/06/17/23137/> accessed 01 August 2018. Trafficking of children is explained by the high level of corruption, the existing of demand, poverty and the lack of understanding of what is better for children.

[56] Mussabalinova (2020) Chap. 4, Sect. 4.4 that explains the legal procedures for family-based placement and adoption.

[57] Ibid.

Children who are Citizens of the Republic of Kazakhstan for Adoption (March 30, 2012), adoption of the child-resident of Kazakhstan by foreigners is possible only after three months from the date of registration of the child in the database and if there are no relatives to take the child regardless of their citizenship and place of residence and if there is no citizen of the Republic of Kazakhstan who wants to adopt the child.[58]

5.4 Good Practice

One of the good practices in regard to child protection, demonstrating a measure of state compliance with the UNCRC, is that there exist alternative independent reports by UNICEF, the general observations of the UN Committee on the Rights of the Children and reports by the Human Rights Ombudsmen. These reports provide information on the situation of children in Kazakhstan that cover both positive and negative phenomena in equal measure while national reports tend to report the achievements first whilst downplaying the problems. Due to the alternative reports with their evidence of problems, such issues as the institutionalisation of children, high level of suicides and violence among minors were brought to light. However, the state did not develop any special policies to overcome these problems since, as noted in one of the UNICEF reports, the social sphere in Kazakhstan is allocated a lower budget than the OECD average.[59] One of the problems highlighted is related to the deinstitutionalisation of children which is covered by the policy on gender and family and as mentioned in the first plan on the implementation of this policy, the government did not allocate any budget for the planned activities related to the deinstitutionalisation of children. As a result, the number of institutions and children in them is decreasing, but there is no concomitant provision of services or resources to deal with the fallout of this policy. The private projects of the NGOs outlined below show that extra services and resources are needed, otherwise there is risk of the return of children to institutions (in 2015–2016—19–26% of children were returned by ill-prepared families to the institutions[60]).

There are at least three projects that provide services to families and children in need in ways which in other circumstances might be carried out by the state.

The first project was named ‘The Child Must live in in a Family’. This project was initiated following the civil forum in Almaty in February 2013 with the same title. More than 10 NGOs and experts collaborated on this project after the forum signing

[58]The Rules for the Transfer of Children Who are Citizens of the Republic of Kazakhstan, for Adoption, approved by Resolution of the Government of the Republic of Kazakhstan (2012).

[59]UNICEF, *Situation analysis of children in Kazakhstan* (UNICEF 2019) 15.

[60]The Commissioner for Human Rights in Kazakhstan, *Report on the activities of the Commissioner for Human Rights in the Republic of Kazakhstan for 2017* (Astana 2018) 77.

the memorandum of co-operation, including the author as a volunteer lawyer.[61] Since 2013, the activities of these NGOs, mostly run by Sholpan Baibolova and her NGO 'Family Academy' have thrown the spotlight on the problem of institutionalised children. Representing civil society in the working groups of the lower chamber of the Parliament of Kazakhstan, the author and Sholpan lobbied for the deinstitutionalisation of children, the development of family-based care and family support. Two pilot projects on the transformation of orphanages in Almaty into Family Support Centres revealed the low level of interest and financial investment on the part of the local authority as well as resistance to the changes amongst the personnel in the orphanages.[62] The latter is explained by the lack of a state policy on deinstitutionalisation, or resources, or a plan for gradual transformation of the institutions, and the absence of relevant training and the unclear future of the workers in the orphanages who were terrified of being unemployed.[63]

Family Support Centre are being piloted at the moment in different ways in Kazakhstan. The Gender and Family policy declared the need of Family Support Centres while due to restricted competence of the Ministry of Education and Science of Kazakhstan that is in charge only for children, according to the standards these centres were called as Support Centres for the Children in Difficult Life Situations. As the result there different numbers of such centers work as the structure of the orphanages or Adaptation Centres.

The second project that also started in 2013 is run by the NGO '*Ана Үй*' (translated as Home for Mother). This project focused on the prevention of newborn child abandonment by the mothers across the country. Due to the provision timely support and services to women in difficult life situations, over a period of five years (from 2013 to 2018) this project helped 3654 mothers and prevented the abandonment of their newborn children. Social services provided by this NGO include accommodation, psychological and legal counselling and support in overcoming the difficulties of their circumstances.[64] Following this project, starting from 2018, '*Ана Үй*' in collaboration with the government, in particular the Ministry of Education and Science of Kazakhstan, continued the activities of the NGO 'Family Academy' on family-based placements. In their website, this project is called the national adoption centre that provides services to the potential families who are considering adopting a child from the institutions. These services include pre-placement assistance and training for the potential caregivers (adopters).[65]

---

[61]Memorandum between members (experts) of the Social movement 'The Child Must Live in a Family" on mutual understanding and cooperation (Almaty city, 16 August 2013). Working as practising lawyer at the time, I was also a signatory to this memorandum (as a volunteer).

[62]Mussabalinova (2020) Chap. 5.

[63]Ibid.

[64]Home for Mother Foundation, 'About the project' <http://www.dom-mamy.kz/dom-mamy/o-proekte/> accessed 09 October 2019.

[65]Home for Mother Foundation, 'About the project' https://januia.kz/o-proekte/ accessed 25 February 2020.

What makes different of the activities of different pilots is that NGOs practiced their work on the way they think it is right so that there was not any standards on the training for the potential caregivers and still this practice remains unclear. In 2015 the social movement 'The Child Must live in in a Family' developed practical guidance on the training for potential caregivers based on international practice and psychological theories (attachment and trauma), but this material was not implemented or considered by the Ministry of Education and Science. Therefore, it might be concluded that until there is an order from the President, the recommendation of international organisation such as UNICEF or the UNCRC or OESD, the Ministry of Education and Science will only pay lip service to good practice. The funders of the NGO '*Ана Үй*' are powerful and wealthy and decided to extend their practice by creating the national agency of adoption covering also the placement of children in foster families and the families of relatives. On 28 November 2018, their work was brought to the attention of the First President of Kazakhstan Nursultan Nazarbayev and permission was sought to do work using their own resources.[66] According to the latest amendments to the Code on Family and Marriage, a national agency of adoption along these lines will appear in Kazakhstan on 1 July 2020. The rush to accept the amendments can be explained by strong lobbying by the "wealthy and powerful", who received approval from the First President Nursultan Nazarbayev '*Elbacy*' (translated from Kazakh as leader or head of nation).[67] However, a number of NGOs and deputies of the lower chamber of the Parliament expressed their worries that this idea requires more rigorous study as it concerns the interests of children whose protection falls within the competence of the state. At the same time, in accordance with the instructions of *Elbacy*, the pilot project for the national adoption agency was launched in August 2019, however, at the time of writing of this chapter, the official results of the piloting in open sources was not available as well as in the reports of the Ministry of Education and Science. In addition, the appearance of national adoption agency does not address the raised issue of the lack in the system preventive measures and family oriented services. These include prior preparation of children for adoption and foster placements, subsequent assistance to families and children who are adopted or fostered, and work with original families that will promote the reunion of children with their parents where possible (more than 80% of children in care in Kazakhstan are 'social orphans' – they have living parents.[68] Therefore, the ongoing changes in the system

[66]Tamara Abubakarov and Amina Malakshinova, 'Nazarbayev supported the idea of creating the first Kazakhstani agency for the adoption of children' *Informburo.kz* (28 November 2018) <https://informburo.kz/novosti/nazarbaev-podderzhal-ideyu-sozdaniya-pervogo-kazahstanskogo-agentstva-po-usynovleniyu-detey.html> accessed 28 November 2018.

[67]The Constitutional Law of the Republic of Kazakhstan About the First President of the Republic of Kazakhstan—Elbacy (2000).

[68]Zh C Dzhandosova, A E Sharipbaeva, T V Kudasheva, O V Nikolaeva, N Yu Baitugelova, F S Dzhandosova, Sh K Smagulova and others, *Report on the situation of children in the Republic of Kazakhstan in 2018* (Committee for the Protection of Children's Rights of Ministry of Education and Science of Republic of Kazakhstan, 2019) 135.

are far from meeting interests of the child and compliance with the UNCRC and the UN Guidelines for the Alternative Care of Children.

While, the government is grappling with the issues such as which ministry will deal with families, and how to reduce the number of children in institutions and the number of families in need, the third project is just working with children from orphanages who are about to leave institutions and continue on into their adult life. The project is called '*Nastavniki*' (translated as Mentors). It was started in 2014 in Almaty by the 'Family Academy', and was established in 2015 in Astana (Nur-Sultan) financed through the private fund 'DARA' and now operates in eight big cities in Kazakhstan: Almaty, Nur-Sultan, Karaganda, Pavlodar, Uralsk, Aktau, Shymkent and Semey.[69] Being a member of this project in Astana in 2015, I can argue that this project introduced the services that required for development alternative family-type care and the procedures how children should be involved in the process of their placement into the alternative family-type care. In particular, before this project in Kazakhstan, nobody provided prior training for adults outside institutions who might become alternative (foster) families and nobody gave children the power of choice as is the case with potential mentors. Yes, this project concerns mentoring, not placements for children, but the approach to child placement should at least be similar to what is practiced in this project. This includes training being given to alternative families, the availability of both pre- and post placement assistance and the involvement of children in their placement decisions. The result of the project in the end of 2019 were that 104 children found mentors who they chose and their choice was matched with the choice of the mentors.[70] This is very different to the current situation in which children are selected by methods similar to online shopping (see Sect. 5.3). It is significant that there were 1057 applications from potential mentors from whom only 333 decided to pass trainings and only 104 of the original 1057 candidates became mentors.[71] There are different reasons for leaving the project, including conscious decision to leave because of entire understanding of the commitments and rejection of the candidate by the team of the project based on the assessed decision in favour of the interests of the children. This approach shows the child-centred approach so that it would be beneficial for the state to learn how to treat children in the centre and to find them family taking in account children's view and interests.

[69]Dara Charity Foundation, 'Mentors', https://dara.kz/proekty/nastavniki/ accessed 14 February 2020.

[70]Message from the director of Fund DARA—Ainur Aimursina to author with the Presentation related to the project 'Nastatvniki' (14 February 2020).

[71]Ibid.

5.5 Recommendations

The PhD research that I conducted from 2016 to 2019 exploring the decision-making processes in Kazakhstan and England, concluded that Kazakhstan needs to improve its child protection system.[72] At the same time, it concluded that the principles of UNCRC should guide Kazakhstan in further development of the treatment of children. This would require not only amended legislation, but also significant changes in practices and in attitudes and approaches within the broader society.[73]

5.5.1 *Child-Centred Approach*

The state approach to the child protection in contemporary Kazakhstan reminds us of fire station that is ready to put out a fire, but where there is nothing done to stop one starting in the first place. The state relies on the existing resources budgeting them from what is left or no more than usual.

UNICEF in their 2010 report noted that Kazakhstani child protection with its limited service 'does not meet the standards set out in the UN Guidelines on Alternative Care'.[74] According to the annual report of 2018, UNICEF stated that social work in Kazakhstan is not well established, arguing that,[75] England, on the other hand, operates a child centred approach in framing and regulating its practice and standards:

> A child centred approach means keeping the child in focus when making decisions about their lives and working in partnership with them and their families.[76]

This approach corresponds with the UNCRC and UN Guidelines on Alternative Care so that Kazakhstani policy-makers must review their approach and make it more child-centred. Mainly, the system should work for children to be heard and participate in the decision-making processes related to them. This kind of work assumes working with the family since the family is the key environment for child development if there is no abuse and neglect so separation from the family should be the last resort.[77]

---

[72]Mussabalinova (2020) Chaps. 7 and 8.

[73]Ibid.

[74]Hamilton and Watkins (2011).

[75]The main challenges remain in definitions of social services workforce, numbers, caseload of social workers in sectors, absence of national strategy and a single coordinating agency. (UNICEF, Annual report UNICEF in Kazakhstan, 2018 (December 2018) 27).

[76]HM Government, Working Together to Safeguard Children A guide to inter-agency working to safeguard and promote the welfare of children (London, July 2018), para 10.

[77]Mussabalinova (2020) Chap. 2.

Social (contextual) aspect of the state, including shame, is what stops and at the same time contributes to good practice. Unwillingness to accept the problems, reflect on them and build the policy which might be understood also as fear to lose job. The latter is explained due to the practice of Kazakhstani politics to change the Ministers or the entire Government, while the problem is dealt with, like in the fire analogy, by urgent but not sustained actions. This is what happened in March 2019 when initially the entire Government was fired as the result of social tension following the death of five sisters in one family in difficult circumstances in Astana (currently Nur-Sultan) when parents were at work during the night.[78] According to several initiatives of the Ministry of Labour and Social Protection of the Population of the Republic of Kazakhstan, there is understanding and good strategy of future development of social sphere that include trainings of staff, social assistance and inter-agency collaboration.[79] The problem is that children in need are separated from the family (in providing the services) while family (family needs) as a unit is not assisted by the state. Meanwhile, the majority of children who need social protection under the competence of the Ministry of Education and Science and the local authority which both have other priorities. The fragmented, isolated, and poorly planned work of the latter remains the main concern. Consequently, children in need of care and protection are at risk since they are victims of structural violence and neglected by the state. Therefore, a central governmental body is needed to develop and to control the child-centred approach and related policy and to coordinate the work between different agencies in order to ensure the implementation of this approach in practice.

5.5.2 *In Law and In Practice*

The legal framework needs to be revised to comply with the UNCRC and other international treaties. For example, the principles of the UNCRC should be reflected clearly in each legal act that concerns a child, including subordinate legislation.

Well-written policies on the inclusion and deinstitutionalisation of children should include detailed and gradual (consistent) plans for the changes. At the same time, the staff should be actively involved in the process of transformation. Such

[78]Taskinbayev Renat, 'Kazakhstani grief. Five girls -sisters were carried out on their last journey' Tengrinews.kz (5 of February 2019), accessed 5 February 2019; Zhadra Zhulmuhametova, 'Mothers of many children gathered spontaneously in Astana and Almaty. What do they want to change?' Informburo.kz (7 of February 2019) accessed 7 of February 2019; The Decree of the President of the Republic of Kazakhstan dated March 23, 2019 On renaming the city of Astana—the capital of the Republic of Kazakhstan to the city of Nur-Sultan—the capital of the Republic of Kazakhstan. The name of the capital was changed on 23rd March 2019 after to the forename of the first president of Kazakhstan Nursultan Nazarbayev (resigned on 19 of March 2019).

[79]Ministry of Labour and Social Protection of Population of the Republic of Kazakhstan, 'Draft of the concept for further modernization of social services', accessed 20 October 2018.

involvement should be supported by relevant trainings and support to instil motivation of the personnel to work for the best interests of the child.

5.5.3 *In Society*

The policies of inclusion and deinstitutionalisation should reach the mentality of ordinary people through the media and work within the community. In particular, the state should raise awareness in the population in regards to children's rights, the significance of the family for child development, improving parental skills and inclusion of all children at all levels (school, home, hospital and others). Although there are families that might take a leading role in presenting good examples, there are well-known structural obstacles. These include the level of corruption within the stakeholders of institutions for children deprived of parental care and their resistance to deinstitutionalisation. However, taking into account the fact that Kazakhstan is a state with an authoritarian regime, an order from the president of the state could change the practice. Therefore, though society might start providing alternative care, in order to widen and embed alternative care, the state needs to take action and to provide supportive social services to families in need.

5.6 Conclusion

In spite of declarations that children and their wellbeing are important, the child protection system in Kazakhstan remains one of the lowest priorities of the state and perpetuates the Soviet era child protection system in practical terms. At present, due to the state's neglect of the sphere of child protection, positive changes have come from the bottom up, based on NGOs' actions and resources. As a result, Kazakhstan fails to comply with the UNCRC in terms of its commitment to ensuring the implementation of children rights in practice. At the same time, the lack of a long-term approach to child care and child protection might rebound on the state with the emergence of a generation of traumatised adults that will prevent Kazakhstan achieving its ambition to take its place amongst developed states. According to Cantwell, the changes on child care in the post-Soviet region is a matter of political will and/or pressure from international institutions such as UNICEF or OHCHR.[80] There is strong potential for better implementation of children's rights and child protection measures in Kazakhstan in the short-term. The activities of civil society and numerous international triggers will also contribute to such developments. But

---

[80]Nigel Cantwell, 'The human rights of children in the context of formal alternative care' in Wouter Vandenhole, Ellen Desmet, Didier Reynaert, Sara Lembrechts (eds), Routledge international handbook of children's rights studies (Routledge 2015); Mussabalinova (2020) Chap. 2.

political will is also required for effective reforms in the field of child protection. Kazakhstan is a unitary state in which power is exercised vertically so that actions in the regions depend on what is established and ordered by the central authorities. My recommendations to the policy makers of Kazakhstan are those which I made in my doctoral thesis (Aigerim Mussabalinova, The Right of the Child to be Raised in the Family: Reflection on Decision-Making Processes in Child Placement in Kazakhstan in the Light of English Experience (PhD thesis, University of Sussex, coming 2020, Chap. 8). They require a range of actions by the state. There must also be regular training for personnel that work with families and for foster and adoptive families.

Chapter 6
Kyrgystan

Ashimova Chinara

6.1 Introduction: Kyrgyzstan Short review

The Kyrgyz Republic is located in the mountainous regions of Central Asia. The largest ethnic group are the Kyrgyz, formerly nomadic, who were settled into collectivized agriculture during the Soviet period from 1926 to 1991. Kyrgyzstan gained independence on August 31, 1991. The majority of the population lives in the river valleys and along the lakes in the north. Urban populations, which constitute only 1/3 of the total population are also largely non-ethnic Kyrgyz. While demographic data shows that the majority of the Kyrgyz population are young (30% are under the age of 15 years) Kyrgyzstan continues to lose population because of migration.

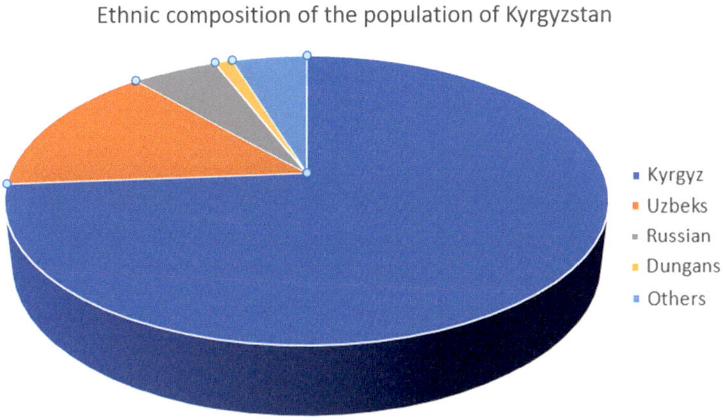

Drawing 1 Distribution of population by age groups

A. Chinara (✉)
Kyrgz State University, Bishkek, Kyrgyzstan

I. Earner, A. Telitsyna (eds.), *The Development of Child Protection Systems in the Post-Soviet States*, Child Maltreatment 12,
https://doi.org/10.1007/978-3-030-59588-3_6

The number of European ethnic groups is decreasing from year to year, while the number of Asian population is growing dynamically.

As of early 2019, the population of Kyrgyzstan had the following age distribution:

	Under 15 years of age	Aged 15 to 65 years old	Under 15 years of age
Absolute value (pers.)	1,842,803 (men's: 939,593/women: 903,210)	4,118,737 (men: 2,017,163/women: 2,101,637)	333,047 (men's: 128661/women: 204,385)
Specific weight (%)	29.3	65.4	5.3

Source: These tables are based on the latest publications of the UN Department of Statistics in the field of demographic and social statistics

Religion in Kyrgyzstan

The main religion is Islam, which is practiced by about 88% of the population, while more than 11% identify with Christianity.

Religion	Number of followers	Percentage of total population
Islam	5,620,191	88.0
Christianity	734,457	11.5
Non-religious and atheists	25,546	0.4
Folk beliefs	6387	0.1

Source: The Pew Research Center. The Global Religious Landscape

According to the National Statistical Committee of the Kyrgyz Republic, in 2018, 22.4% of the population were poor, of which 68% were residents of rural areas. Poverty increased markedly in the 1990s following the collapse of the Soviet Union due to a decline in manufacturing and loss of trade. Kyrgyzstan is now a member of the Eurasian Economic Union along with Kazahkstan, Russia, Belarus and Armenia.

6.2 History of Civil Law in Kyrgyztan

It is important to consider the history of the development of laws in Kyrgyzstan in order to understand how this history continues to inform the present. Laws that governed civil matters were based on a variety of structures including the 'adat' (a form of conventional law as determined in a court of 'aksakals' or elders), sharia law based on the teachings of the Koran, and Russian feudal law. "Udachnoe" laws, governing family relations, included the status of each family member, the status of men and women, regulated the status of children and their rights and obligations depending on gender and age. These laws also established such institutions as the guardianship of children, and secured a system of mutual responsibility of relatives for children left without parents. Children—"baldar" in the Kyrgyz family were expected to unquestioningly obey their elders. This determined the right of children to take part of the family property, and the obligations of the head of the family to provide it to children. The division of property among children was one of the complex elements of the 'adat'. In traditional Kyrgyz families, close relatives on the mother's side (usually uncles) were obliged to take over the upbringing and financially help their nephews. 'Adat', in fact, was an extensive system of social norms, the basis of which were the local customs of predominantly non-Islamic origin. Most of these customs were formed in the conditions of the existence of tribal relations and pagan beliefs.

The future formation and development of social protection of children in Kyrgyzstan needs to be intimately connected to the concepts of mutual assistance in the cultural and historical heritage of the Kyrgyz people. Folk epics, fairy tales, proverbs and sayings embody the most important moral norms and principles, humane and gracious ideals that served to settle people's relationships and were their beliefs. For centuries, customs and traditions that provide social protection for children have been formed and developed.

The nomadic Kyrgyz family functioned within the community, which assumed most of the functions of the public and at the same time regulated the sphere of family relations. There was no separation of private and public in the nomadic way of life. The diversity of positions and the stability of ties, based on the nomadic way of life itself, the formation of a special system of information transmission and continuity of actions, which was interpreted as membership, including children (Long 1998). This was also evident in the practice of raising children, who were responsible not only for the immediate family, but for the entire community. Tribal relations were the most important protective mechanism for the preservation of the people, identity and socialization of the individual and led to the development of ideas of social protection of children in Kyrgyz society. The child, like every human being, was protected by the traditional structures to which he belonged. These structures included, first of all, the family, the community, the family, which traditionally helped their members, including children. Social protection was provided in various forms of assistance: religious, communal and traditional, the essence and elements of which have survived to the present day.

6.3 Features of Child Protection in the Soviet Period

In the Kyrgyz Republic of the Soviet Union, orphanages, or institutional care of children, began to appear in the mid-1930s. The first residents were children of "enemies of the people", "basmachs" who were sent to orphanages if their parents were executed or sent to the Gulag. In the 1940s, children from other republics of the Soviet Union whose parents died during the great Patriotic war or as a result of famine were sent to orphanages. In many of the former republics of the Soviet Union orphanages were gradually closed down as demand decreased and alternative forms of out-of-home care were implemented. This has not been the experience in Kyrgystan where orphanages and boarding schools continue to operate. According to international standards, orphanages and boarding schools are classified as closed institutions. Human rights activists equate them to prisons. With the significant changes associated with the transition to a market economy, child protection issues remain in the spotlight.

6.4 Modern Child Protection System

Protection of the rights of the child is one of the priorities of the domestic policies of the Kyrgyzstan. This is confirmed by the international human rights obligations that Kyrgyzstan undertook to fulfil after becoming a full member of the United Nations (2 March 1992). Since 1994, Kyrgyzstan has acceded to 13 international agreements on the protection of human rights and freedoms. Kyrgyzstan joined the UN Convention on the Rights of Persons with Disabilities, adopted on December 13, 2006 and signed on September 21, 2011, the law on ratification was adopted on February 7, 2019. At the same time as the Convention, the optional Protocol was adopted and entered into force.

The government of the Kyrgyzstan has taken measures to improve the situation of children and families in difficult situations. The Department for Family and Child Support and the Ministry of Labor and Social Development are responsible for child protection, including guardianship, national and international adoption of orphans and children left without parental care. These agencies are also tasked with the creation of a system of foster families, ensuring social guarantees; and organization of the creation and development of a network of social services that provide services to socially vulnerable categories of citizens, families and children in difficult situations. However, because of the history of mutual assistance and reliance on conventional norms, the reliance on government intervention into family matters remains minimal.

Under current civil code definitions, the concept of "child at risk" is synonymous with the concept of "children in difficult situations". These are children who are left without parental care, children with disabilities, children in conflict with the law, who are victims of violence or crime, children living in low-income families, working children, street children, children in conflict zones and emergency situations, whose life activity is violated as a result of the circumstances, as well as children who cannot overcome these circumstances independently or with the help of their family.

6.5 Promising Practices

Since the ratification of the UN Convention on the Rights of the Child in 1994, the Kyrgyzstan has taken measures to develop the system of child protection, as well as justice for children in conflict with the law (juvenile justice), harmonization of national legislation with international standards, and prevention of juvenile delinquency.

The most characteristic trend in the development of the Kyrgyz system of social protection of children is the transition from the Soviet system of social security for all children, i.e. their maximum coverage of social benefits mainly at the expense of the state, to the targeted system of social protection of specific children in the most unfavorable situation.

Every year, questions about meeting the needs of children are heard at Government meetings. The initial report on the implementation of the Convention on the rights of the child (CRC) was prepared in accordance with the requirement of article 44 of the CRC in 1997. An alternative report was prepared and sent to the UN Committee on the rights of the child by a number of non-governmental organizations. The 24th session of the Committee considered the initial report of Kyrgyzstan on 24 may 2000. Subsequently, the Government received The concluding observations of the Committee and, in close cooperation with UNICEF, is developing an action plan and mechanism for further implementation of children's rights in Kyrgyzstan.

Note that the modern system of social protection of children in Kyrgyzstan, due to the transition of the country from the Soviet system to the new socio-economic relations, is still at the stage of formation. Kyrgyzstan has a fragmented system of social protection for children. In the rural areas the predominant forum for resolution of family problems is located in to council of elders (adat) and sharia law. Conflicts arise when Prosecutor's offices at the state and local level try to perform their tasks and in cases requiring immediate intervention aimed at protecting the rights of children, deprivation of parental rights, or the removal of children from parents who abuse or neglect their children. 'Bride kidnapping' (ala kachuu), a practice of taking a young woman by force to become a wife, has gained international notoriety. Outlawed in 2013, the practice nevertheless persists in rural areas and is often sanctioned by the council of elders. The legal framework for working with children, which would fully regulate the mechanism for implementing child protection in the country, needs a comprehensive study, identifying shortcomings, identifying current problems and improving legal support. Raising the status of the child is realized through a solid legislative framework, which strengthens the specific rights of children and the responsibilities of parents, the state and society.

6.6 Challenges

The challenges facing Kyrgyzstan in implementing child protection systems are many. Experts are still discussing the possibilities and limits of applying international norms, especially in countries whose social development differs significantly from the Western path. The national model of social protection that is being formed in Kyrgyzstan can be effective only if its distinctive features and national and cultural traditions are preserved. Actors who protect children's rights must rely on historical and spiritual heritage and use national and cultural levers to overcome social difficulties. At the same time, the ideological guidelines of Kyrgyz thinkers can be a kind of spiritual basis for the formation of the Kyrgyz model of all social work.

Important is the activation and inclusion of the informal level for the protection of children's rights and the entire public in the development of the promotion of children's rights and interests through charity, mutual assistance, integration of the population, the development of social responsibility to the new generation, a sense of civil duty and mobilization of all forces for optimal and timely solutions to civil problems.

A shocking figure—in the Kyrgyz orphanages, children without parents consist no more than 3%. The remaining 97% are social orphans with living parents. Namely: children who were left without parental care, or their parents were deprived of their parental rights, children from families in difficult situations, children of migrant workers.

The system of domestic orphanages and boarding schools produces people with atrophied skills, with limited thinking. The syndrome of hospitalism is formed. They develop a learned helplessness. When we employ graduates of orphanages, they can't do a certain amount of work. Because we did not see a living example of how to work every day in adolescence. It is difficult for orphans to socialize and adapt to real life outside the orphanage or boarding school. Many graduates of orphanages have developed an addiction syndrome. With such a psychology, it is difficult for them to go to work or study. Added to these problems is the fact that orphanage graduates enter adulthood without a livelihood.

There are no official statistics on the fate of orphanage graduates. Since state institutions, like the orphanages and boarding schools themselves, are not monitored and are not interested in how the life of their wards after graduation is developing.

Children do not know their rights and, moreover, do not know how to protect them. This leads to the fact that they protect them by any known means other than legal ones. The society and its adult part have an objective task to deal with the formation of legal awareness in children from an early age. To solve this problem, a system of state support and prevention should be created, which would explain the child's rights and obligations at an accessible level.

Parents believe that if a child is more than 11–12 years old, then he must learn to do something, learn to earn. The main reason lies in the socio-economic situation of the family itself. For example, single mothers believe that the child should help the family. But there are also some parents who give the child part of their responsibilities at an early age. They consider it the norm that a child should be responsible for something and work. This work deprives children of the opportunity to go to school.

The state does not sufficiently inform the population about the marriage legislation, the minimum age of marriage, the responsibility for conducting marriage religious rites, as well as the negative consequences of early marriage. Therefore, it is very important to strengthen the information campaign on all these issues.

There is no equal access to education for children with disabilities. In Kyrgyzstan, only 14% of children with disabilities are enrolled in schools. There is also a need for a standard of education for people with intellectual disabilities to adapt basic general education programs, as well as to amend the law "on education" to include standards for children with intellectual disabilities.

The main drawbacks in the child protection sector are the high turnover/outflow of stakeholders from child protection at all levels, as well as the lack of skills and knowledge of social workers and professionals due to the lack of appropriate training and retraining programs. In addition, social services lack a systematic approach to addressing the root causes of child separation or abandonment, and lack support and understanding at the highest level of the need to develop alternative and community-based family support services.

There is no specialization of judges and prosecutors in the field of juvenile justice. Also, law enforcement officers are not trained to conduct an investigation and interrogation, taking into account the interests of the child. Although children suspected of criminal offences are legally entitled to free legal assistance, the provision of qualified and timely legal and social protection for these children remains low.

Further Reading

Denisenko MB (2011) Population of Kyrgyzstan at the beginning of the XXI century. Bishkek

Family code of the Kyrgyz Republic

Family code of the Kyrgyz Republic

Government Of The Kyrgyz Republic

Identification and social support of families and children in difficult life situations. Modules of training courses for social professionals. Bishkek 2017

Ishmuratova ND (2017) Criminal law of Kyrgyz by the norms of ADAT and Sharia. J Innov Sci

Labor code of the Kyrgyz Republic No. 106 of 4 August 2004

Law "on protection and protection from family violence" 2017

Law of the Kyrgyz Republic "on education" of 30 April 2003 No. 92

Law of the Kyrgyz Republic "on measures to prevent harm to the health of children, their physical, intellectual, mental, spiritual and moral development in the Kyrgyz Republic" dated 21 July 2015 No. 185

Law of the Kyrgyz REPUBLIC "on the basics of social services in the Kyrgyz Republic" of December 19, 2001 N 111

Mateeva KM (2015) Theoretical approaches to the study of customary law. Bull KRSU

"National study on child poverty and inequality in the Kyrgyz Republic". Bishkek. 2009

Regulation of the Commission for children (PPCR No. 878 of 24 December 2015)

Resolution of the government of the Kyrgyz REPUBLIC "on approval of the Regulations on the procedure for the transfer of children for adoption to citizens of the Kyrgyz Republic and foreign citizens, as well as the List of diseases in the presence of which a person can not be an adoptive parent, guardian (Trustee) and foster parent" dated October 27, 2015 No. 733

Resolution of the government of the Kyrgyz REPUBLIC "on approval of the Model regulations on the Commission for children" dated December 24, 2015 No. 878

Resolution of the government of the Kyrgyz REPUBLIC "on approval Of the regulations on accreditation of entities providing services to children in difficult situations" dated March 23, 2015 No. 140

Resolution of the government of the Kyrgyz REPUBLIC "on approval of the Regulations on the procedure for identifying children and families in difficult situations" dated June 22, 2015 No. 391

Resolution of the government of the Kyrgyz REPUBLIC "on foster (foster) family" dated October 1, 2012 No. 670

Resolution of the government of the Kyrgyz REPUBLIC "on issues of guardianship and guardianship" dated September 24, 2013 No. 522

Resolution Of the government of the Kyrgyz Republic "on issues of social standards in the sphere of social services for families and children, as well as institutions providing social services to children in difficult situations" dated October 9, 2012 N 691

Resolution Of the government of the Kyrgyz Republic "on issues of social standards in the sphere of social services for families and children, as well as institutions providing social services to children in difficult situations" dated October 9, 2012 N 691

Resolution of the government of the Kyrgyz REPUBLIC "on the procedure for the formation and use of the state data Bank on children left without parental care" dated March 2, 2010 No. 125

Special report of Akyikatchy (obudsman) of the Kyrgyz Republic. VIOLENCE AGAINST CHILDREN IN the KYRGYZ REPUBLIC (Administration of justice: legislation and practice). Bishkek 2017

The CODE of the KYRGYZ REPUBLIC ON CHILDREN dated July 10, 2012 No. 100 (as amended by the Laws of the Kyrgyz Republic dated 27.04.2017 No. 64, 30.03.2018 No. 33, 24.04.2019 No. 56) was Adopted by the Jogorku Kenesh of the Kyrgyz Republic on May 31, 2012

The current state of the sustainable development goals: adaptation of indicators of the sustainable development Goals to the indicators of the sustainable development Strategy of the Kyrgyz Republic for 2018–2040 and the "Unity. Trust. to create a unified monitoring and reporting system". Bishkek 2019

The law of the Kyrgyz REPUBLIC "on guaranteed state minimum social standards"

Thisbecause J. CH (2013) Regulation of marriage and family relations of Kyrgyz people under customary law: thesis ... PhD in law: 12.00.01. Bishkek

Chapter 7
Latvia

Ilona Kronberga and Arta Jalili Idrissi

This chapter explores the development of the rights of the child in Latvia and how the principle of the 'best interests of the child' is understood and implemented within the Latvian legal system and practice. The first part of this chapter aims to contextualise the socio-economic situation of Latvia with a particular focus on the welfare of children and young people. The latter part of the chapter delves into the legal and practical application of the rights of the child, and how the principle of the best interests of the child has been interpreted and applied in the Latvian context. While acknowledging the shortcomings of the established system, this chapter highlights the developments that have strengthened and safeguarded the rights based approach towards children and young people in the country.

7.1 General Context

The Republic of Latvia is a country in the Baltic region of Northern Europe and is the second smallest nation of the three Baltic countries.[1] At the beginning of 2019, the population of Latvia was 1.92 million, which is 14,400 less than a year earlier a decline of 0.7% in the year. Since gaining independence, Latvia has experienced a population decline—the population decreased by 750,000 between 1990 and 2019.

[1]Since its independence, Latvia has been referred to as one of the Baltic states together with Estonia and Lithuania. It is bordered by Estonia to the north, Lithuania to the south, Russia to the east, Belarus to the southeast, and shares a sea border with Sweden to the west. Latvia is a parliamentary republic.

I. Kronberga · A. Jalili Idrissi (✉)
Staffordshire University, Stoke-on-Trent, UK
e-mail: arta.jaliliidrissi@staffs.ac.uk

I. Earner, A. Telitsyna (eds.), *The Development of Child Protection Systems in the Post-Soviet States*, Child Maltreatment 12,
https://doi.org/10.1007/978-3-030-59588-3_7

In 2018 Latvia reported the largest relative decrease in population (7.5 per 1000 persons) among the EU-28 countries (Central Statistical Bureau of Latvia 2019a). This trend is due to a negative rate of natural population change and a negative rate of net migration. However, in recent years, a growth in the number of children has been observed. In 2019 children and young people comprised 359,000 or 18.7% of the total population, which is an increase of 1.4 percentage points since 2014.

In 2018/2019, school and higher education institutions had 322.2 thousand students, of which 207.9 thousand students were aged 17 and younger. At the beginning of school year 2017/2018, 96.6 thousand children participated in pre-school education, which is the highest number in recent years (Central Statistical Bureau of Latvia 2019b).

The health of children and adolescents is one of the key health care priorities in the country. The latest data show that in 2017 90.9% of the households assessed the health of their children (aged 15 and younger) as good or very good, 8% described it as fair, and only 1.2% as bad. Breakdown by age shows that the largest share of high health ratings—good or very good—among children aged 3 and younger—94.2%, while the lowest share among adolescents (aged 11–15).

Economic growth in Latvia continues at a pace that is above the EU average. Between 2011 and 2018, GDP grew at an average annual rate of 3.5%. In 2017–2018 the growth rate accelerated. GDP grew by 3.8% and 4.6% respectively. The acceleration of growth was facilitated by the improvement of the situation in the external environment, more intensive absorption of the EU structural funds, and the increase of employment and wages (The Ministry of Economics 2019). Despite this, in 2017 23.3% of Latvia's population (446,000) was at risk of poverty (Central Statistical Bureau of Latvia 2019c). The official EU figures show that in 2018 23% of households with children in Latvia were single-parent households (the EU average is 15%) (Eurostat 2019a) and due to Latvia's minimum provisions for social welfare (see Vanhuysse 2009; Bohle and Greskovits 2012) more than one third of these type of households are at risk of poverty. In 2017 lone parents were the second largest group after lone elderly people at risk of poverty (32.6%) and while two-parent families with three or more children were the fourth largest group (20.7%) (Central Statistical Bureau of Latvia 2019c).[2]

Inequality and income disparity has been a growing issue since the collapse of the Soviet Union in the early 90s. The Gini index, which measures the fairness of income distribution, has consistently remained high for Latvia. During the mid-2000s Latvia had the highest income disparities across the 30 European countries (Lappi-Seppälä 2011) and this trend has continued. Also in 2017 Latvia's Gini index was one of the highest among the EU countries (Eurostat 2019b). Despite achieving the highest rate of real GDP per capita in 2018 (12,180 €) (Eurostat 2019c) the social divisions and income disparities remain high and the share of people at risk

[2]The at-risk-of-poverty threshold was 367 euros per month for one-person household and 770 euros for two-parent families with two up to 14 years old children (Central Statistical Bureau of Latvia 2019c).

of poverty is growing. In 2018 every fifth inhabitant in Latvia was at risk of poverty (Latvian Public Broadcasting 2018). The socio-economic insecurities have led to the situation where emigration from Latvia has become 'the new normal' (Hazans 2016, p. 314) and for many families it means at least one parent living and working abroad. This situation poses one of the challenges to the practical application of the principle of the best interests of the child due to the conflict between providing financial security and a child having the emotional support of both parents.

7.2 What Does the Principle of the Best Interests of the Child Entail?

The principle of the best interests of the child stems from Article 3 of the Convention on the Rights of the Child 1989 (UNCRC), which states that all activities concerning children, whether they are public or private, or dealing with social welfare matters or other legal issues, the child's best interests must be a primary consideration. As suggested by Scraton and Haydon (2002, p. 317) 'the UNCRC established a framework of principles and minimum standards for legislation, policy and practice concerning children and young people'. States which have acceded to the UNCRC are obliged to provide every child with the protection and care necessary for their well-being. The well-being of the child can be achieved through activities that are based on the principles of the protection of children's rights. This implies that it is the duty of the state to ensure that parents, guardians, municipal authorities and other agents involved in the protection of children's rights observe the rights and principles promulgated by the UNCRC (see Gray 2019). To this end, as Latvia has been a state which is party to the UNCRC since 1992, it has had to develop and adopt legal norms consistent with the principles of the protection of the rights of the child, ensuring effective and professional institutional solutions and uniform application of the law, irrespective of the field of application. At the same time, quality requirements for the protection of children's rights have become a nationwide priority, which means institutions must meet national quality standards and these quality standards require regular monitoring.

The principle of the best interests of the child in Latvia is implemented at three levels of law enforcement:

(a) substantive rights—the right of the child to the best interests of the child, considering the diversity of the child's interests in a given situation, and the guarantee that this right will always be exercised if a similar situation recurs;
(b) the fundamental principle of interpretation of a rule of law: where a rule of law can be used for more than one interpretation, the interpretation which best serves the best interests of the child must be chosen. The rights contained in the UNCRC and its Optional Protocols provide such a framework for interpretation;
(c) procedural rules—whenever a decision is to be taken that affects a specific child, a specific group of children or children in general, the decision-making process

must include an assessment of the impact of possible decisions (positive or negative).

Procedural safeguards are needed to assess and determine the best interests of the child. In addition, the grounds for the decision must show that the rights are clearly taken into account. The decision must be weighed up in such a way that it is possible to explain exactly how the decision respects the rights and the best interests of the child; on what criteria the decision is based and how the best interests of the child are weighed against other considerations, and whether they are broad policy issues affecting groups of children or individual cases.[3]

An objective assessment of the child's needs is a tool to ensure that the best interests of the child are safeguarded. This requirement of the UNCRC shall apply whether the decision is in the public or private sector. The best interests of the child include the fundamental values of the UNCRC. It should also be pointed out that the concept of the best interests of the child is not new, but was included in the Declaration of the Rights of the Child (1959), incorporated in the Convention on the Elimination of All Forms of Discrimination against Women (1981) and within the frame of other international instruments and standards issued by the United Nations. The concept of the best interests of the child aims to ensure the full and effective protection of all the rights enshrined in the UNCRC, namely the holistic development of the child. Therefore, the principle of the best interests of the child is also present in the governing parts of the UNCRC, including—article 9: separation from parents; article 10: family reunification; article 18: parental responsibilities; article 20: deprivation of family environment and alternative care; article 21: adoption; article 37(c) and other situations involving the application of the rights of the child. The decision on the best interests of the child cannot take precedence over the obligation to respect all the rights of the child under the UNCRC, as there is no hierarchy of rights in the Convention—all rights are equally important. In order to fully apply the principle of the best interests of the child, a rights-based approach must be developed involving all actors in the protection of children's rights to ensure the comprehensive (holistic) physical, psychological, moral and mental integrity of the child. Thus, the implementation of the principle of the best interests of the child within the framework of the rights of the child creates a precedent of mutual respect, or a practical model of behaviour. Everyone deserves respect and rights—this approach is at the heart of Latvian system of protection of children's rights.

Among other objectives, the National Development Plan of Latvia 2014–2020, aims at ensuring that children live in a family-oriented or family-like environment (The Saeima 2012). The legal framework is geared to providing for children family or parental care. Section 26, Paragraph 1 of the Law on the Protection of the Children's Rights defines family as the natural environment for the development and growth of a child, and every child has the inalienable right to grow up in a

[3]See also General comment No. 14 (UN Committee on the Rights of the Child 2013), which provides an in-depth explanation of the principle of the best interests of the child and how this should be taken as a primary consideration (art. 3, para. 1).

family. If no parental (family) care is available to the child, they are transferred to out-of-family care (i.e., guardian, foster family or child-care institution). The child is in out-of-family care until it reaches the age of majority, which in Latvia is 18 years of age, or until the moment they can return to their parents or become adopted. In 2019, 352,562 children lived in families, while 6438 minors were in out-of-home care. Of all children in out-of-home care 68% were under guardianship, 20% in foster families, but 12% under long-term social care and social rehabilitation institutions (Central Statistical Bureau of Latvia 2019b).

Child well-being is measured in three main levels: at European Union level, by collecting data from all Member States (see for example, the European Union Agency for Fundamental Rights 2020); at Member State level (see the Ministry of Welfare 2018); and at the level of individual research projects (see Latvian Child Welfare Network 2017). As a result, the area of child welfare is regularly analysed in the Common European Area of Law by the European Union Agency for Fundamental Rights (and others); at national level, annual monitoring of the rights and well-being of children is carried out by both the Ministry of Welfare and the Ombudsman's Office. In parallel with the above mentioned research on the protection of children's rights, a number of non-governmental organisations regularly publish their findings and recommendations.

The policy of protecting children's rights is developed by the Latvian Government, under the auspices of the Ministry of Welfare. A special institution, the State Inspectorate for the Protection of the Rights of the Child, is responsible for the implementation of the Children's Rights Protection Policy. The umbrella regulation on the legal protection of children is the Law on the Protection of the Children's Rights (1998). The Law on the Protection of the Children's Rights defines the functions and tasks of the state and municipal institutions in the process of protection of the rights of the child. The Law on the Protection of the Children's Rights stipulates that protection of the rights of the child is an integral part of state policy and the local governments shall organise and monitor the protection of the rights of the child throughout Latvia. The purpose of this law is to guarantee the human rights of the child, considering the child's age and maturity. This law determines the rights and obligations of children and young people as well as establishing liabilities of parents and other natural persons and legal persons in ensuring the rights of the child. It also determines the system for the protection of the rights of the child and the legal principles regarding its operation.

According to the law in Latvia the following persons or entities should be involved in children's rights protection: parents (adopters), foster family and guardians of a child; educational, cultural, health care and childcare institutions; state and local government institutions; public organisations and other natural or legal persons whose activities are related to the provision of support and assistance to children; and employers. All the above—are assigned by law the tasks for the protection of the rights of the child, while the state administration institutions and local governments have established their areas of responsibility. In each of these areas of responsibility, policy planning documents and legal frameworks are developed. For example, the following policy guidelines have been developed: Guidelines for the prevention of child crime and the protection of children against crime; National Identity, Civil Society and Integration Policy Guidelines; Guidelines on preventing trafficking in human beings; Education Development Guidelines; Public Health Guidelines and other policy development documents.

7.3 How the Best Interests of the Child Are Determined and Relationship Between the Best Interests of the Child and the Principle of Participation

As explained above, the best interests of the child are a right, a principle and a process based on weighing up the best interests of the child in each situation. Assessing and defining the best interests of the child with a view to deciding or applying a measure to the child is necessary:

(a) to understand, in the overall context of the facts of a situation, which are the most important elements in assessing the best interests and then weighting each against all the others;
(b) in order to achieve this goal, it is necessary to follow a process to provide the child with both a legal guarantee and the due process of law. Assessing the best interests of the child means assessing and balancing all the elements needed for making a decision in each situation with regard to a particular child or a group of children. This is done by the decision maker (specialist) and the professionals at their disposal, preferably a multidisciplinary team, with the participation of the child. The degree of participation of a child in the decision-making process in Latvia takes into consideration the child's age and maturity. The assessment of the best interests of the child follows a formal process with strong procedural guarantees.

There are several elements that are considered in the process of assessing the best interests of the child in order to ensure fundamental rights, namely:

- *Views of the child and right to be heard.* Article 12 of the UNCRC establishes the right of the child to express their views and to be heard in relation to any decision taken in respect of their rights. Under the UNCRC there is no reason to believe that a decision is in the best interests of the child if it is taken without hearing the child's views which should be in accordance with the child's age and maturity;
- *Identity (characteristics) of the child.* The UNCRC stipulates that children shall not be regarded as a homogeneous group because they differ in sex, age, nationality, culture and other characteristics. For example, religious and cultural identities require consideration when choosing a foster family for a child;
- *Maintaining family environment and relationships.* The best interests of the child shall be assessed in the light of the possible separation of the child from the parents. Bearing in mind that the family is not only the basic unit of society, but also the child's natural environment, the UNCRC states that the concept of family

must be interpreted in the broadest sense (Article 5 of the UNCRC). Preventing family separation and maintaining family unity are important components of the child protection system and are based on the right set out in Article 9 of the UNCRC, which states that *a child shall not be separated from his or her parents against his or her will, unless* [...] *such separation is necessary in the best interests of the child,* for example if the child is treated in a cruel manner by the parents. Separation of a child from the family can have serious consequences, so such decisions should only be taken as a last resort;

- *Childcare, protection and safety*. Care and protection are to be understood in the broadest sense without giving these concepts an initially negative connotation. Children's well-being in the broad sense includes their material, physical, educational and emotional needs as well as attachment and security needs. Emotional care (bonding) is a basic need of children; if parents or other primary caregivers do not meet the child's emotional needs, action should be taken to develop the child's secure attachment. Children need to form emotional bonds with people who care for them from a very early age, and such attachment, if enough, should be maintained over time to provide the child with a stable environment. It is this stable emotional bond as a factor of positive protection that protects the child from low self-esteem;
- *Feeling of protection (or such a situation)*. This element protects not only the best interests of the child but also other important fundamental rights. For example: if a child has been the victim of violence, is an asylum seeker or lives on the street. The best interests of the child in such specific situations may differ, as the personal situation has a great influence. Therefore, an individual approach should be taken when assessing their personal circumstances;
- *The right of the child to health*. Assessing the child's health is central to determining the best interests. However, where there are multiple options for improving health or where the outcome of treatment is uncertain, the benefits of all possible treatments should be weighed against all possible risks, and the child's views should also be considered, taking into account his or her age and maturity. In this context, children should be provided with the appropriate information so that they understand the situation and all relevant aspects of their interests;
- *Children's right to education*. It is in the child's best interests to have free access to quality education, including early childhood education (pre-school education), non-formal education and related activities. In all decisions and actions relating to a child or group of children, the best interests of the child or children regarding education shall be considered. Promoting education, or improving education for more children, requires educators to have the knowledge and skills to put the best interests of the child into practice, as well as a child-friendly environment and appropriate teaching and learning methods.

In the process of assessing the best interests of a child, the elements to be evaluated will vary in practice and the content of each element will vary from case to case. For this reason, it is particularly important to adopt an inclusive or holistic approach. When assessing the various elements and their content, the purpose of this evaluation must not be forgotten. When assessing interests, it should be borne in mind that the child's abilities will change. Therefore, decision makers should consider measures that can be reviewed or adjusted accordingly, rather than making definitive and irreversible decisions. This requires not only assessing the physical, emotional, educational and other needs at the time of the decision, but also considering and analysing the possible child development scenarios, both in the short and the long term. Thus, decisions are based on the continuity and stability of the child's present and future circumstances.

This decision-making process extends to all area of law. For example, if the child has committed a criminal offense and is involved in criminal proceedings; if the child has committed minor offenses and is being held administratively liable; if the child has been the victim of a criminal offense or domestic or non-domestic violence; if the child is a witness; if the child is involved in the divorce of parents; as well as if the child is in the process of adoption. Based on the above, several new initiatives have recently been adopted in Latvia to stimulate the practical application of the best interests of the child. This chapter will highlight two particular examples: the inter-institutional cooperation platforms (Cooperation groups) and children's homes.

7.4 Importance of Inter-institutional and Multidisciplinary Cooperation in the Best Interests of the Child

7.4.1 Cooperation Groups in Municipalities

In 2017, a special working group was set up to assess whether all responsible institutions working in the field of the protection of children's rights are actively cooperating and acting in the best interests of children. The analysis showed that the regulatory framework already provides for the responsible institutions such as: the Orphan's Court, the local social services, the municipal police or the state police, education and child care institutions, medical institutions and other institutions in contact with children to cooperate with each other in order to protect children's rights and best interests. However:

(a) the obligation to cooperate in a multidisciplinary environment is not always understood and implemented in a uniform and targeted manner;
(b) not all institutions involved in the process of protecting children's rights understood the responsibilities of the other institutions,
(c) there can be overlapping tasks, which agencies fail to address.

On September 12, 2017 a new legal framework[4] was introduced, based on which a platform for cooperation of specialists and institutions of various fields in the

[4]See Provisions on inter-institutional cooperation in the protection of the rights of the child (2017).

protection of children's rights was created. The legal framework foresees the establishment of Cooperation groups in each municipality, which includes representatives of different professions working with children within their sector.

The Cooperation group were allocated the following duties:

(a) to deal with the individual cases of the alleged violation of the rights of the child, where rapid action and cooperation between several institutions are needed and where the situation cannot be resolved with the involvement of a single institution or has not been resolved on a long-term basis;
(b) to analyse the situation in the field of the protection of children's rights and make proposals to the municipality for the development of a county or city children rights protection program, including measures needed for improving the inter-institutional cooperation system and co-ordinated inter-institutional cooperation;
(c) to make proposals to the Ministry of Welfare for the improvement of legal acts and the possible cooperation in the field of protection of children's rights. The Ministry of Welfare directs these proposals to the Children's Cooperation Council for consideration;
(d) to inform the public of current issues relating to the protection of children's rights.

In the second half of 2019, a study was conducted to establish if the inter-institutional cooperation mechanism and the Cooperation groups are working effectively and are promoting the best interests of the child. The study concludes that the Cooperation groups have been successful since their inception and they have a great potential for future development. It was also noted that the inter-institutional cooperation platform has contributed to the improvement of the system of protection of the rights of children living in Latvia (Kronberga et al. 2019).

Inter-institutional and multidisciplinary cooperation for the protection of the rights of the child is established for the countries of the European Union by Guidelines of the Committee of Ministers of the Council of Europe on child friendly justice. Paragraphs 16-18 of the Guidelines state that close co-operation between different professionals should be encouraged in order to obtain a comprehensive understanding of the child, and an assessment of his or her legal, psychological, social, emotional, physical and cognitive situation. Considering that different institutions and professionals are involved in the decision-making process, the best practices and methods of cooperation between specialists and institutions are presumed.[5]

Several projects have also been implemented in Latvia, in which various models of inter-institutional cooperation have been implemented (see Kronberga and Sīle 2015). Inter-institutional cooperation is essential as one local authority usually involves several agencies and professionals of different backgrounds and skills. For example, social workers are trained to carry out assessments and care planning

[5]See also United Nations Office of the High Commissioner for Human Rights, Recommended Principles and Guidelines on Human Rights and Human Trafficking (2010).

in a child-centred manner, with due regard for the rights and needs of the child; law enforcement officials are competent to conduct investigations and safety assessments, and to work in civil and criminal matters; Immigration authorities have access to information on the countries of origin of the persons, including children, and to focus their assessment on the general situation of the child in the country of origin. Therefore, it is essential to strengthen cooperation between these institutions to ensure that all rights of the child are duly addressed and that those rights are interdependent and indivisible (Wenke and Heiberg 2015).

Inter-institutional and multidisciplinary cooperation are two separate but goal-oriented concepts. Namely, these are two levels of cooperation, where the development of joint activities takes place at the level of inter-institutional cooperation. The cooperation strategies, visions and the conceptual solutions of individual issues are developed. At the same time at the level of multidisciplinary cooperation, the case (situation) of a child is handled. Thus, the framework of inter-institutional cooperation for the protection of children's rights in Latvia is planned both at the national, regional and municipal levels, while multidisciplinary cooperation takes place between specialists from different fields within the planned framework.

Inter-institutional and multidisciplinary collaboration is a platform that allows for the most effective and comprehensive decision-making in the best interests of the child. It contributes towards the identification of the elements to be assessed and the evaluation process itself. On a practical level, this involves finding out the answers to the questions, or measurable elements that include each of the most fundamental rights of the child—the child's opinion and views to be heard (participation), personal characteristics, family situation, child's safety, health and education needs are assessed. In practice, this means that every decision that is taken in any area of law (civil, criminal, administrative, or otherwise) must ensure that the child receives information, understands and is heard according to his or her age and maturity.[6]

7.4.2 Child's Home Project

Children's home projects in Latvia are still in the process of being implemented by the non-governmental organisation "Centrs Dardedze",[7] which is experienced in the field of protection of children's rights. Child's home is a Nordic interdisciplinary model for working with child sexual abuse victims ("all under one roof"). The Lanzarote Committee recommends the "Children's House" as an effective solution for inter-institutional cooperation among the member states of the Council of Europe.

---

[6]See also: The best interests of the child—A dialogue between theory and practice (The Council of Europe 2016).

[7]See The pilot project children's house (Centrs Dardedze 2020).

To implement the recommendations of the Committee, Latvia has developed a plan for the protection of minors from crimes of morality and sexual integrity (The Plan for the Protection of Minors against Morals and Sexual Offenses 2019–2020).[8] In order to facilitate the effective implementation of the Lanzarote Convention, it was decided to: (a) develop cooperation between the various persons acting in the name of or on behalf of children in criminal proceedings; and (b) provide additional support for child victims; and (c) organise interviews with child victims in a child-friendly environment—away from premises normally used for investigations or inquiries (such as police stations, hospitals or court rooms) and by following best practice to provide such locations throughout the national territory. A problem was identified that there was a lack of specially equipped facilities and technical support in cases where a child was victims of sexual abuse and needed to be interviewed. The national and international law require that juvenile victims and witnesses should be interviewed, where appropriate, in specially adapted premises and, where appropriate, in the presence of a psychologist. In order to facilitate the effective implementation of the Lanzarote Convention, the Lanzarote Committee has indicated that, in order to better support children and improve the quality of the data collected, the Member States should consider introducing data collection systems with specialised centers. For example, orphanages would have integrated comprehensive control points, which would be created as a safe place for those who have suffered child abuse.

Thus, in cases where the child has been the victim of sexual abuse, as well as in other difficult cases where the child has been abused or neglected, the work with the child victim (obtaining information from the child, questioning, medical examination, psychological support for the child and family, rehabilitation, child protection) will take place within the interdisciplinary and inter-institutional cooperation model of the Children's Home in premises specially designed or adapted for this purpose.

In order to develop the implementation of the "Children's House" model in the regions of Latvia and to improve the knowledge of specialists working with children who have suffered from sexual abuse, "Centrs Dardedze" in cooperation with the Ministry of Welfare has participated in two projects supported by the European Commission. Within the framework of the BADEV project, the Center Dardedze has worked with partners from Estonia and Poland to promote the development of integrated child protection systems and to improve work with child victims of sexual abuse, offering inter-institutional cooperation as a possible solution and ensuring the best interests of the child.

As a result of the project, it is planned to implement the Children's Home model in four regions of Latvia. The work is to be carried out jointly with four crisis centres in all regions of Latvia. The project will enhance cooperation practices with the State

[8]The plan includes measures in line with the Recommendations of the Council of Europe Convention on the Protection of Children against Sexual Exploitation and Sexual Abuse (2015), on the Protection of Child Victims of Sexual Abuse, which is known also as the Lanzarote Convention.

Police and social services, as well as exploring how to improve the "Children's Home" collaboration scheme in future.

In conclusion, Latvia has taken significant steps towards implementing the UNCRC and ensuring the basic rights for all children in Latvia, particularly the rights to education, safety and security. The national Law on the Protection of the Children's Rights (1998) and other legislative measures, which have emerged from it, established the main mechanisms for the protection of the rights of the child in the country and provided a blueprint for the practical application of these rights. However, there are still many issues at the practical level—local municipalities may work together to implement the legal rights and child protection measures but there is not always a sufficient level of training and funding available. Therefore, strenghthening inter-institutional cooperation and sharing best practice is of paramount importance. One of the future focuses is the protection of children from crime and a creation of a specialised support mechanism for those children who have been victims of crime, especially from sexual exploitation. For this reason there is a need to develop and improve the functioning of the Child's home and similar institutions, which can provide a vital support for those in need.

References

Bohle, D., & Greskovits, B. (2012). *Capitalist diversity on Europe's periphery*. London: Cornell University Press.

Central Statistical Bureau of Latvia. (2019a). *Demography 2019*. Accessed October 28, 2019, from https://www.csb.gov.lv/lv/statistika/statistikas-temas/iedzivotaji/iedzivotaju-skaits/meklet-tema/387-demografija-2019

Central Statistical Bureau of Latvia. (2019b). *Children in Latvia*. Accessed October 29, 2019, from https://www.csb.gov.lv/lv/statistika/statistikas-temas/iedzivotaji/iedzivotaju-raditaji/meklet-tema/382-berni-latvija-2019

Central Statistical Bureau of Latvia. (2019c). *23.3% of Latvia population at risk of poverty*. Accessed December 17, 2019, from https://www.csb.gov.lv/en/statistics/statistics-by-theme/social-conditions/poverty/search-in-theme/2530-monetary-poverty-and-income-inequality

Centrs Dardedze. (2020). *Pilotprojekts "Bērna māja"* [The pilot project children's house]. Accessed December 20, 2019, from http://www.centrsdardedze.lv/lv/projekti-1/noslegtie-projekti/pilotprojekts-berna-maja-1

European Union Agency for Fundamental Rights. (2020). *Ending child poverty: Valuing children's best interests*. Accessed December 20, 2019, from https://fra.europa.eu/en/news/2019/ending-child-poverty-valuing-childrens-best-interests

Eurostat. (2019a). *Births and fertility: Over 5 million births in EU in 2017*. Accessed November 26, 2019, from https://ec.europa.eu/eurostat/documents/2995521/9648811/3-12032019-AP-EN.pdf/412879ef-3993-44f5-8276-38b482c766d8

Eurostat. (2019b). *Gini coefficient of equivalised disposable income – EU-SILC survey*. Accessed June 3, 2019, from http://appsso.eurostat.ec.europa.eu

Eurostat. (2019c). *Real GDP per capita*. Accessed December 17, 2019, from https://ec.europa.eu/eurostat/databrowser/view/sdg_08_10/default/table?lang=en

Gray, P. (2019). Rights-based and "children and young people first" approaches to youth justice. In P. Ugwudike, P. Raynor, & F. McNeill (Eds.), *The Routledge companion to rehabilitative work on criminal justice*. London: Routledge.

Guidelines of the Committee of Ministers of the Council of Europe on child friendly justice. (2010).
Hazans, M. (2016). Migration experience of the Baltic countries in the context of economic crisis. In M. Kahanec & K. F. Zimmermann (Eds.), *Labor migration, EU enlargement, and the great recession* (pp. 297–344). Berlin: Springer.
Kronberga, I., & Sīle, S. (2015). *Meklējot labāko Eiropas praksi jauniešu noziedzības novēršanai* [Searching for best practice in Europe for the reduction of youth offending]. Accessed October 30, 2019, from http://providus.lv/article_files/2890/original/keeping_lv.pdf?1427962796
Kronberga, I., Sīle, S., Litvins, G., & Zavackis, A. (2019). *An inter-institutional cooperation in the field of the protection of children's rights*. Latvijas Tiesnešu mācību centrs, Riga. Accessed January 7, 2020, from https://ltmc.lv/lv/publicets-petijums-par-starpinstituciju-sadarbibu-bernu-tiesibu-aizsardziba
Lappi-Seppälä, T. (2011). Explaining imprisonment in Europe. *European Journal of Criminology, 8*(4), 303–328. https://doi.org/10.1177/1477370811411459.
Latvian Child Welfare Network. (2017). *Well-being and welfare of children in Baltic countries: Study report and recommendations*. Accessed January 10, 2020, from http://www.bernulabklajiba.lv/wp-content/uploads/2017/06/Children-Well-Being-in-Baltic-Countries_Report_2017_final.pdf
Latvian Public Broadcasting. (2018). *1 in 5 Latvians 'at risk of poverty'*. Accessed November 26, 2019, from https://eng.lsm.lv/article/society/society/1-in-5-latvians-at-risk-of-poverty.a264753/
Provisions on interinstitutional cooperation in the protection of the rights of the child. (2017). Cabinet Regulation No. 545 of 12 Sept 2017.
Recommended Principles and Guidelines on Human Rights and Human Trafficking. (2010).
Scraton, P., & Haydon, D. (2002). Challenging the criminalisation of children and young people: Securing a rights-based agenda. In J. Muncie, G. Hughes, & E. McLaughlin (Eds.), *Youth justice: Critical readings* (pp. 311–328). London: Sage.
The Convention on the Elimination of All Forms of Discrimination against Women Adopted. (1981).
The Convention on the Rights of the Child. (1989).
The Council of Europe. (2016). *The best interests of the child – A dialogue between theory and practice*. Accessed October 20, 2019, from http://ejuz.lv/eucouncil
The Declaration of the Rights of the Child. (1959).
The Law on the Protection of the Children's Rights. (1998).
The Ministry of Economics. (2019). *Macroeconomic review of Latvia*. Accessed January 2, 2020, from https://www.em.gov.lv/en/economic_development/ekonomiska_situacija/macroeconomic_review_of_latvia/
The Ministry of Welfare. (2018). *Annual reports on the situation of children in Latvia*. Accessed January 10, 2020, from, http://www.lm.gov.lv/lv/15147-nozares-politika/berni-un-gimene/publikacijas-petijumi-un-statistika/publikacijas
The Saeima. (2012). *The National Development Plan of Latvia 2014 – 2020*. Accessed January 10, 2020, from https://rio.jrc.ec.europa.eu/en/library/national-development-plan-latvia-2014-2020
UN Committee on the Rights of the Child. (2013). General comment No. 14.
Vanhuysse, P. (2009). Power, order and the politics of social policy in Central and Eastern Europe. In A. Cerami & P. Vanhuysse (Eds.), *Post-communist welfare pathways: Theorising social policy transformations in central and Eastern Europe* (pp. 53–70). Basingstoke: Palgrave Macmillan.
Wenke, D., & Heiberg, T. (2015). *Guidelines: Promoting the human rights and the best interests of the child in transnational child protection cases*. The Council of the Baltic Sea States Secretariat, Stockholm. Accessed October 30, 2019, from https://www.cbss.org/wp-content/uploads/2013/01/Guidelines_-_promoting_the_Human_Rights_and_the_Best_Interest_of_the_Child_in_Transnational_Child_Protection_Cases.pdf

Chapter 8
Moldova

Domnika Ginu

8.1 Republic of Moldova: General Information

The Republic of Moldova is a small country located in the South-East of Europe bordered by Romania and the Ukraine. Historically, the territory was ceded to the Russian Empire in 1812 and known as Bessarabia; after a brief period of independence Moldova became a republic of the Soviet Union in 1924. On August 27, 1991 Moldova declared independence. The state structure is a parliamentary republic. Moldova has trade agreements with the European Union.

Moldova has a very young population, children represent 19% of the total population. However, because of a poor economy, the population of Moldova has decreased by 14% between 2004 and 2018. Labor migration is very common among residents of both urban and rural areas. This affects the level of well-being of the family, as well as the quality of the child's upbringing. As a result, the number of children living separately from their parents is 43,039 (7%). At the same time, the number of children at risk is also high—7996. The number of children raised in single-parent families is also growing. The share of such families was 6.9% in 2018. It is important to emphasize that during 2018, there were 73 day centers at the community level in the Republic, which served 2666 children from risk groups and 462 children with disabilities.

D. Ginu (✉)
Ion Creanga State Pedagogical University, Chişinău, Moldova
e-mail: Domnica.Ginu@wearelumos.org

I. Earner, A. Telitsyna (eds.), *The Development of Child Protection Systems in the Post-Soviet States*, Child Maltreatment 12,
https://doi.org/10.1007/978-3-030-59588-3_8

8.2 Modern Child Protection System

The United Nations Convention of the Rights of the Child was ratified in the Republic of Moldova in December 1990. According to the Family Code,[1] in the Republic of Moldova, family relations are regulated in accordance with the principles of monogamy, voluntary marriage of a man and a woman, equality of spouses in the family, mutual moral and material support, preservation of marital fidelity, priority of raising children in the family, care for the maintenance and upbringing of minors and disabled family members, protection of their rights and interests, resolution of intra-family problems by mutual consent, inadmissibility of arbitrary interference in family affairs, unhindered access to judicial protection of the rights and interests of family members. It is important to emphasize that raising children in the family, as well as taking care of the maintenance and upbringing of minors, are among the main principles of family law.

8.2.1 Definition of a Child or Youth at Risk

According to article eight of the Law on special protection of children at risk and children separated from their parents, in the Republic of Moldova, the concept of a risk group applies to the following categories of children[2]:

- Children exposed to violence;
- Neglect of children;
- Children roam, beg, and engage in prostitution;
- Children are deprived of parental care and supervision due to the lack of such care at their place of residence for unknown reasons;
- Both parents (the only parent) died;
- Children live on the street, have run away or been expelled from their homes;
- The parents refused to fulfill their responsibilities for raising and caring for the child;
- Children abandoned by their parents;
- The parents were declared incapacitated by a court decision.

It is important to note that out of the total number of children separated from their parents, children whose both or only parent is abroad are placed in a separate category. Unfortunately, this phenomenon has recently become so widespread in Moldova that the number of children in this situation has become statistically important. The number of people who annually become labor migrants in the countries of the near and far abroad is steadily growing. The degree of dependence

[1]Family Code Of The Republic Of Moldova.

[2]Law №. 140 of 14.06.2013 on special protection of children at risk and children separated from their parents.

of the domestic economy on transfers from abroad is very high, in addition, a whole generation of children is actually separated from their families, are brought up in the families of friends or relatives, and sometimes are in the care of the state. There are several categories of young people at risk in the Republic of Moldova: graduates of residential institutions, orphans, young people with disabilities, young people with deviant behavior, HIV-infected. The vulnerability of this group of young people lies in their limited ability to assert themselves and integrate into society. The current health and social protection system offers a range of services. In 12 health-improving youth centers located in some regions of the Republic, young people are provided with free medical information and consultation services. And since the existing centers meet the requirements of a narrow group of people, it became necessary to expand and improve this range of services according to the identified needs for complex and high-quality services. (PP No. 1006 of 10-12-2014 on approval of the national youth sector development strategy 2020 and the action Plan for its implementation.)

8.3 The Legal Framework in the Field of Child Protection and Protection from Distress

The normative framework for the protection of children is based on the international obligations of the Republic of Moldova, as well as on national policies and laws:

- UN Convention on the rights of the child, in force in Moldova since 1993
- UN Convention on the rights of persons with disabilities, in force in Moldova since 2010
- Moldovan Constitution
- Family Code Of The Republic Of Moldova
- Civil Code Of The Republic Of Moldova
- Law on local public administration
- Law on social assistance
- Law on the legal regime of adoption
- Law on social services
- Law on special protection of children at risk and children separated from their parents
- Regulations governing the organization and functioning of services and social servants

National standards relating to the rights of the child are set out in the following documents:

- National child protection Strategy for 2014–2020 (2014)
- National strategy and action Plan for reforming the residential child care system for 2007–2012 (2007)

- National Strategy for promoting inclusion of persons with disabilities (2010–2013)
- Inclusive education development program for the period 2011–2020 (2014)
- Action plan for implementing the child protection Strategy for 2014–2020 (2016)

It should be noted that since children cannot claim their rights on their own and cannot influence state decision-making, the state must find special mechanisms for their protection.

8.4 Significance of the UN Convention on the Rights of the Child for the Development of the Child Protection System

The fact that children are born with the fundamental freedoms and rights inherent in every human being is the main thesis of the United Nations Convention on the rights of the child. The Convention, adopted on November 20, 1989, emphasized the peak development of public organizations, solidarity and cooperation between governments. To date, all but two countries in the world have agreed to accept the standards set forth by this Treaty, as well as the care and protection of each child, as priorities for the state and government. Of course, there are other international treaties and agreements designed to protect the rights of the child, but the Convention is unique for a number of reasons. First, it provides children not only with their civil and social rights, but also with political, economic and cultural rights. Second, it is universal, applied all over the world, thus obliging governments, even in poor countries, to take measures to protect the rights of the child. Third, it is clearly stated, namely, that all rights, without exception, are important, inseparable, interrelated and United for all. It is no secret that the development of children in a supportive environment is a prerequisite for the future of the entire community. Another factor that dictated the need to develop a Convention is that children are more vulnerable to the difficulties of life than adults, and, as a result, more in need of protection. In addition, children have neither the right to vote nor political influence, and their economic opportunities are extremely limited. Unfortunately, they are more likely to be abused and exploited, and their desires and needs are often ignored.

Thus, Moldova has assumed the responsibility to protect children from all forms of discrimination, to provide social protection and conditions for full mental and physical development. In addition, in early 1998, the government decided to establish a National Council for the Protection of Children's Rights. This Council consists of representatives of ministries that are responsible for various aspects of children's life, health and education. Five years later, in 2003, the government adopted the national strategy for the protection of the child and family, which ensures the development and implementation of the state policy in the field of social protection of the child and family at the national and local level. Strategies to protect the rights of the child and the family were adopted for the period from 2007 to 2012, as well as from 2014 to 2020.

8.5 Principles of Social Policy and Legislation in the Field of Child Protection

The Ministry of Health, Labour and Social Protection of the Republic of Moldova is the leading Ministry in the field of social protection and enforcement of children's rights.

First-level guardianship bodies include mayors (mayors) of villages (communes), cities (municipalities), and local social assistants. The second-level guardianship bodies are the district/municipal councils that perform the functions of guardianship and guardianship bodies, namely the social security and family protection departments. The main activity of the guardianship authorities is to take all necessary measures to provide assistance and support to children and their families in order to prevent the separation of the child from the family or, if necessary, to integrate/reintegrate it into the family.

8.6 Creating a Child Protection System

The national strategy "Education for all" is aimed at realizing the right of all children, without exception, to education. In addition, the strategy sets a number of tasks for the government, including reducing inequality and eliminating differences between children from poor and middle-income families, between rural and urban populations, between children with special educational needs and ordinary children, between children placed in various institutions and children living in families. This document includes, among other things, informing the public about the problems associated with the education of children with special educational needs, as well as improving the legislative and regulatory framework for the consolidation of school funds of local communities, focusing on children from poor families, orphans, homeless children, and refugee children.

In the period from 1996 to 2006, there were a number of other events that became significant for the development of the child protection system in the Republic of Moldova. For example, various events were organized to raise public awareness and protect the rights and civil interests of socially vulnerable children. It is important to note that international organizations and development partners such as the Soros Foundation, UNICEF, UNESCO, the Council of Europe and others have played a very important role in the development of the child protection system. At about the same time, a number of other changes are taking place in Moldova aimed at promoting reform, and the first steps towards deinstitutionalization are being taken. For example, the first departments for the protection of children's rights were established, children were placed in foster care for the first time, and boarding schools were evaluated. In the pilot mode, a system for reorganizing the institutional system for child protection was launched.

The next important period in the development of the child protection system in Moldova, from 2007 to 2010, was marked by a large number of changes that significantly reduced the number of children in residential institutions. In 2007, 11,554 children were already living in boarding schools, and another 6562 were in family-type accommodation. During this period, the regulatory framework regulating the procedure for preventing separation from the family is also developing, the so-called "gatekeeping" mechanism. This is a systematic approach and a set of measures and procedures that ensure that alternative child care is used only when necessary. Gatekeeping helps determine whether a child should be separated from their family and, if so, which placement best suits their individual needs and interests. Placement of a residential or family type is preceded by a certain form of assessment of the child's physical, emotional, intellectual and social needs. It is important that the chosen type of accommodation meets the needs of the child. In order to ensure an individual approach to each child and to prevent separation from the family as effectively as possible, a community-based social service was created. In addition to the above, a regulatory framework has been created for the foster care service. An important stage in the process of implementing the reform was the development and approval of the National strategy and action Plan for reforming the residential system for child care for 2007–2012.[3] The main objectives of the strategy were: reducing by 50% the number of children who live outside the family, as well as the reorganization of state institutions of residential type in accordance with the General plan of transformation.

In order to improve the effectiveness of the social service delivery system, a national program for the creation of an integrated social service system for the period 2008–2012 was developed and proposed for implementation. Its main task is to prevent and provide primary assistance to beneficiaries at the community level. In addition, a Strategy for social integration of persons with disabilities for the period 2010–2013 was developed and implemented. In secondary schools, the position of an auxiliary teacher has been created.

It is natural to assume that new services at the community level will require additional financial resources. Therefore, in order to ensure the sustainability of the deinstitutionalization reform and cover the costs of new services, a mechanism for reallocating financial resources from residential institutions to newly created services was developed and implemented.

The system of inclusive education is also being developed. In 2011, the government of the Republic signed a decree approving the program for the development of

[3]Resolution No. 784 of 09.07.2007 on approval of the National strategy and action Plan for reforming the residential child care system for 2007–2012.

inclusive education in the Republic of Moldova for 2011–2020.[4] Inclusive education in the context of this Program provides for continuous change and adaptation of the educational system in order to meet the diversity of children and the needs resulting from this, and to provide quality education to all through integration within the General educational system. Between 2011 and 2012, the national Council for child protection reform and inclusive education was established. In the pilot mode, the model of inclusive education is launched, and specialized schools are included in the reorganization process. In addition, inter-sectoral cooperation is being established to prevent and reduce the level of child mortality, as well as the death rate of children under 5 at home. At the same time, programs are being piloted to promote children's participation in political decision-making processes, as well as in the provision of services.

The implementation of the National strategy for reforming the system of residential care for children in 2007–2012 helped to reduce the number of institutions, reduce the number of children separated from their families by about 62%, as well as the organization and development of social services for children and inclusive education for children with special educational needs.

The period from 2013 to 2016 was also marked by a number of important changes that affected the implementation of the child protection reform. New regulations have been developed and implemented to regulate the work of family support services, the early intervention service, and the psycho-pedagogical assistance service. Already during this period, a model of inclusive education for children with severe disabilities is being tested. In 2014, the education development strategy was approved.

Compared to the previous strategy, the new strategy includes tasks not only to promote the reform, but also to address new pressing issues such as migration, as well as the need for family support through a rethinking of social roles in order to involve both parents in the educational process, as well as support for the work of parents. As a result, an intersectoral strategy for the development of parental skills and competencies for 2016–2022 was approved. The scope of this strategy's intervention is related to the development of an intersectoral system of support for families and future parents in terms of improving parental skills and competencies. In order to develop the concept of the Strategy, consultations were held with experts from ministries competent in the field of parenting skills training and non-governmental organizations operating in this field.

In addition, inter-sectoral cooperation and mechanisms for identifying, assessing, treating, supporting and monitoring children who are victims of violence, neglect, exploitation and trafficking have been strengthened. For example, the educational program of the police Academy included the theme of child protection, and such a discipline as "inclusive education" is included in the program of University training of teachers.

---

[4]Resolution No. 523 of 11.07.2011 on approval Of the program for the development of inclusive education in the Republic of Moldova for 2011–2020.

Since then, various programs of professional development and exchange of experience have been offered to social and medical workers, psychologists and teachers, as well as foster carers, and cross-sectoral cooperation has been strengthened. International development partners and various non-governmental organizations of local, national and international significance are actively involved in the implementation of child protection reform. By the end of 2018, according to official data, out of 10,345 children at risk, only 5337 (51%) are in planned accommodation, of which 4208 (78%) live in family-type accommodation. 56 children live in family-type community homes, and another 592 children are in temporary accommodation centers. Thus, by the end of 2018, only 481 children were living in residential institutions, which is only 9% of the total number of children in the planned placement.

8.7 Grounds for Temporary Placement of Children in Alternative Care Facilities or Substitute Families

According to the Law on special protection of children at risk and children separated from their parents No. 140 of 14.06.2013, the placement of a child can be carried out by the guardianship authorities only if, as a result of assessments, it was found that leaving him with his parents is not possible or contrary to the highest interest of the child.[5] *If the child is separated from the family, the territorial guardianship authority shall place the child in accordance with the priority of placing it under the care of an extended family in comparison with other types of accommodation, and if such placement is not possible, the priority is to place the child in family-type services in comparison with placement in residential services.* Thus, it becomes obvious that the child's residence in a family or family environment is a priority in comparison with other forms of protection. It is important to note that according to the current legislation, the placement of a child in various services should be carried out only if it is impossible to leave him with his parents or threatens his interests.

8.8 Ensuring the Well-Being of Children by Non-profit Organizations, Private or Religious Organizations

The law on public-private partnership No. 179-XVI was adopted in the Republic of Moldova in 2008. On the basis of this law, non-governmental and public organizations have the legal right to deal with issues related to the protection of children's rights, in compliance with legislation on the protection of children's rights. For

[5]Law №. 140 of 14.06.2013 on special protection of children at risk and children separated from their parents.

example, NPOs/NPOs participate in multi-disciplinary multidisciplinary groups. Depending on the organization's goals, NPOs support the creation of social services at the community level. In addition, they are involved in promoting packages of legislation and regulations that affect social policies and strategies, and in protecting the rights of children and families with children. At the same time, representatives of more experienced NGOs are included in the boards of relevant ministries, including the Ministry of labor, social protection and family, health, and education, which provides an additional opportunity to focus on certain issues, influence the policy of ministries, and transmit objective information to colleagues from the non-governmental sector. NPOs also play an important role in developing and conducting research that is used by government agencies to determine strategies in different areas: protection of children's rights, inclusive education, child and young family health, youth policy, and others.[6]

The following are the main non-profit and non-governmental organizations operating in the Republic of Moldova to help socially vulnerable families and children.

8.8.1 UNICEF Moldova

UNICEF Moldova has been working for the realization of the rights of children and women in Moldova since 1995. Thanks to partnerships with the government, members of Parliament, civil society, the media, business and other parties, positive results have been achieved in implementing the rights of the child in a number of areas, and authorized entities are now even more eager to fulfill their responsibilities in accordance with the UN Convention on the rights of the child. UNICEF Moldova supports the government and civil society in ensuring the social integration of those children and their families who are at risk of social exclusion due to geographical differences, poverty, ethnicity, limited opportunities, gender and lack of parental care.[7]

8.8.2 Lumos Moldova

The international charity Foundation "Lumos" ("Lumos Moldova") was founded in 2006 by the world-famous British writer Joan K. Rowling, author of the Harry Potter novels. Also in 2006, the former Executive Director of "Lumos International", Georgette Mulheir, gave a report on deinstitutionalization to specialists from the Republic of Moldova. This laid the Foundation for a long-term and productive

---

[6]Law No. 179-XVI. On public-private partnership of July 10, 2008.

[7]https://www.unicef.org/moldova/ru

relationship in the spirit of cooperation between the international charity organization and Moldova, a small country that had a large number of children in residential institutions, but at the same time had the political will and will to change the lives of socially vulnerable children. The mission of Lumos is to stop the systematic institutionalization of children around the world. Lumos Moldova, along with other organizations, provided assistance To the government of the Republic of Moldova in implementing the National strategy and action Plan for reforming the system of care for children in boarding schools for 2007–2012. Through counselling and training, Lumos Moldova supported the country in reducing the death rate of children and children under 5 years of age at home, ensuring access to education for children with disabilities, and significantly improving the quality of social services.

Lumos Moldova supports the government of the Republic of Moldova, as well as vulnerable children, in several ways. Based on the experience of international experts, measures have been taken to combat high infant and child mortality rates. Lumos Moldova also has significant financial planning experience, which is necessary for the success of the deinstitutionalization process. Work was carried out with the state authorities of the Republic of Moldova to ensure that the funds saved as a result of the closure of residential institutions are redirected to social services that are now provided at the community level. In particular, this has allowed funding for a large number of new support and additional services for children with special educational needs and the inclusion of children with disabilities in secondary schools. Lumos Moldova believes that in practice it is important to demonstrate that deinstitutionalization works. Therefore, the main efforts were concentrated on a few pilot districts - Floresti, Ialoveni, Chisinau and Orhei. Now there are no more residential institutions in the Floresti and Yaloveni districts.[8]

8.8.3 Alliance of NPOs Working in the Field of Social Protection of Children and Families (APSCF)

The "Alliance of NPOs working in the field of social protection of children and families" (Alianța ONG-urilor active în domeniul Protecției Sociale a Copilului și Familiei (APSCF)) is a network of 65 non-governmental organizations operating throughout the Republic of Moldova, including the Transnistrian region. APSCF works to create a consistent and functional framework for decision-making, mechanisms and implementation methods that ensure real respect and protection for the child and family. APSCF members are non-governmental organizations at the international, national and local levels from all over the country that work in the field of child protection. APSCF is guided by statutory principles and promotes the following values: the best interests of the child, democratic decisions, transparency and efficiency in communication, partnership, participation and involvement,

[8]https://www.wearelumos.org/moldova/about-us/

autonomy, flexibility. APSCF is an active member of regional and international communities: ChildPact, Child Rights Connect, national Council for the protection of children's rights, national Council of non-governmental organizations of the Republic of Moldova, national Council for children's participation.[9]

8.8.4 *Amici Dei Bambini*

"Amici dei Bambini" ("Friends of the Child") is an international humanitarian organization for the protection of children's rights, which works in three main areas: international cooperation, international adoption and promotion of the rights of children and youth. Amici dei Bambini also helps families in difficult situations by providing family counseling, organizing support centers for single mothers, providing free food and medical care.[10]

8.8.5 *Ave Copiii*

The AVE Copiii Association for the empowerment of children and families is a public, democratic, politically and religiously independent, non-profit organization. The mission of AVE Copiii is to provide social services. They offer accommodation and rehabilitation for orphans and children left without parental care. In addition, AVE Copiii works with children and their parents to develop their children's independent living and household management skills. Also, work is being done with parents who are in the process of abandoning children, as well as with those who have abandoned children, both in order to prevent such incidents, and in the field of family and social reintegration.[11]

8.8.6 *Caritas Moldova*

On May 10, 1995, the Bishop of Chisinau registered the Religious Catholic Mission "**Caritas Moldova**" as a social Department of the Roman Catholic Church in the Republic of Moldova, which operated through Catholic parishes, consisting of a Director, coordinator, employees and volunteers. In 2015, the Religious Catholic Mission "Caritas Moldova" was reorganized by converting it into the Charitable Foundation "Caritas Moldova". The main activities are: social development, medical

[9]http://roxanatodea.com/apscf/secretariat/

[10]http://www.amicideibambini.it/default_gb.asp

[11]http://avecopiii.md/echipa-noastra/

care, improving social welfare, educational programs for children and young people aimed at preventing school dropouts, emergency response in the event of natural disasters, organizational development and promotion of the Foundation's core values.[12]

8.8.7 CCF Moldova

In 2004, a group of five people, including teachers and doctors, decided to take a more active part in public life with one common goal: to change the lives of children in Moldova for the better. CCF Moldova's mission is to create an atmosphere of hope and respect for children in need, where they can reach their full potential, and offers practical tools for positive changes in the life of the child, family, and society.[13]

8.8.8 CIDDC (Centrul de Informare şi Documentare privind Drepturile Copilului din Moldova)

"Centrul de Informare şi Documentare privind Drepturile Copilului din Moldova CIDDC" ("center for information and documentation on the rights of the child of Moldova") is a non-governmental organization founded in 1999. The mission of the center for information and documentation on children's rights is to help create favorable conditions for the realization of children's rights, develop the abilities of those responsible for the well-being of children, and empower them. The center also undertakes to constantly monitor the state's efforts to fulfill its obligations.[14]

8.8.9 Centrul Naţional de Prevenire a Abuzului faţă de Copii CNPAC

"Centrul Naţional de Preventire a Abuzului faţă de Copii CNPAC" ("national center for the prevention of child abuse") promotes the right of children to be protected from all forms of violence by directing its actions to inform and motivate society in order to stop child abuse. The center's mission is to reduce the frequency of incidents

---

[12]https://caritas.md/ru/istoria/

[13]https://ccfmoldova.org/istorie

[14]http://drepturilecopilului.md/index.php/en/

and minimize the consequences of violence against children through prevention, advocacy, capacity-building and specialized services.[15]

8.8.10 Concordia Proiecte Sociale

Public Association "Concordia Proiecte Sociale" ("Concordia. Social projects") is a non-governmental, non-profit and apolitical organization that started its activities in 2004. The main goal is to promote the harmonious integration of disadvantaged people into society, promote rights and provide necessary social assistance to these people. For 15 years, Concordia has been providing assistance to those who need it most, namely children, orphans, the elderly and low-income people.[16]

8.8.11 Femeia și Copilul: Protecție si Sprijin

The public Association "Femeia şi Copilul-Protecţie şi Sprijin" ("Woman and child—protection and support"), founded in March 2000, arose from the need to promote and provide equal opportunities for access to quality social services for disadvantaged people in partnership with families and the community. From its Foundation to the present, the mission of the Association is to provide access to quality life for disabled people and people with disabilities through the development of services and policy development at the local and Central level in partnership with government agencies and families.[17]

8.8.12 Keystone Moldova

Keystone Human Services International Moldova (Keystone Moldova) was founded in 2004 by Keystone Human Services International from the United States and aims to promote the social integration of vulnerable groups, including people with disabilities. Keystone Moldova supports Central and local authorities in implementing a deinstitutionalization program for people with mental and psycho-social disabilities and their inclusion in the community.[18]

[15] http://cnpac.org.md/rom/about-us

[16] https://www.concordia.md/despre/

[17] http://fcps.md/?page_id=148

[18] http://www.keystonemoldova.md/ro/who-we-are/

8.8.13 Misiunea Sociala "Diaconie"

The "Diaconie" ("Diaconia") is a social structure of the Bessarabian Metropolitan Church that has been active throughout the Republic of Moldova since 2001, starting in October 2003. The organization's vision is as follows: An active society based on Christian values is the result of the constant and consistent activity of the Metropolitan of Bessarabia. The mission of the Diaconie organization is to develop and create a model of social intervention based on the human approach as the face and likeness of God in the relationship of exchange and trust with social partners.[19]

8.8.14 Partnerships for Every Child

"Partnerships for Every Child" (Partnership for every child) is a fairly young organization as a legal entity, but its employees have a wealth of experience, being the most valuable resource of the organization. Partnerships for Every Child is an organization that works with children who are at risk of separation or have already been placed in a foster home or institution. The organization provides various types of assistance, including shelters for mothers and children who, for various reasons, need support in order to prevent separation of the child from the family.[20]

8.8.15 Centrul "Speranța"

The Speranta center (Speranza Center, in Romanian Nadiya) was opened in 1998 as a pilot project of the Association for support of children with disabilities, and in 2000 it was officially registered as an independent organization. The mission of the organization is to create opportunities for growth, development and use of the potential of each child to become a full member of society. The main goal of the organization is to prevent the institutionalization of children with disabilities, especially children with severe disorders of the musculoskeletal system and their integration into society.[21]

---

[19]https://www.diaconia.md/pageview.php?l=ro&idc=305&t=/Despre/Cine-suntem

[20]https://childhood.org/this-is-childhood/projects/partnership-for-every-child-moldova/
https://www.p4ec.md/en/organisation/videnie_i_missiya_organizacii/default.aspx

[21]http://speranta.md/despre-noi/

8.9 De-institutionalization

In many countries, there are other problems in the alternative care system that arise when no attempt is made to reintegrate the child into the family, periodic checks are not carried out to ensure that the conditions in which the child is brought up meet his or her needs, and there is no adequate preparation for independent life after leaving the institution. In this regard, many States have already abandoned "institutional" residential institutions or plan to do so in the near future. There is no significant doubt about the consequences that often result from the specifics of the functioning of a large boarding school. Such consequences can be, among other things, a faceless rigid regime built on a system of organization of life, which initially imposes certain restrictions—for example, strictly shift work of educators. In addition, children do not acquire the skills necessary for independent life. For example, they do not know how to cook food, use many household appliances, keep track of their belongings, plan personal time and money, and so on.

In recent years, increased attention has been paid to the negative impact of residential institutions on young children, especially in the age group up to 3 years. A number of studies have found that if a young child is placed in an environment where they are not given individual attention and, most importantly, are not given the opportunity to form an attachment to the caregiver, there is a high probability of long-term negative consequences for their well-being. According to the UN world report on violence against children,[22] these children may have "poor physical health, severe developmental delays, disabilities, *and potentially irreversible psychological disorders*." These and other observations have prompted many international organizations to act. For example, in 2011, UNICEF, together with the Office of the United Nations high Commissioner for human rights, launched a "Call to action" campaign in Central and Eastern Europe. The main goal of this campaign was to encourage an end to the practice of placing children aged 0–3 years, including children with disabilities, in institutional institutions. According to the prevailing opinion of experts, alternative care for children under the age of 3 years should be provided in family conditions. It is important to emphasize the inadmissibility of placement in any type of residential institutions, and not only in institutions with "institutional" characteristics. In cases involving very young children, choosing a residential institution as a form of arrangement is usually not a constructive solution for them. However, it is also noted that if a child is placed in a residential institution for a short period of time, the likelihood of serious and long-term consequences for their well-being is very low. The results of research show that it is usually possible to talk about a significant, and in some cases irreversible, impact on the development of a child only if the duration of his stay in a residential institution exceeds 3 months. The experience of individual States that have taken steps to implement a policy of partial priority deinstitutionalization indicates that appropriate preventive measures and alternative forms of family arrangement are a prerequisite for this. This will

[22]https://documents-dds-ny.un.org/doc/UNDOC/GEN/N06/491/07/PDF/N0649107.pdf

avoid situations that occur in some countries where the closure of "baby homes" simply leads to the fact that children who were left or abandoned in maternity hospitals are placed in children's departments of hospitals for many months.[23]

8.9.1 Working with Foster Families, Responsible for Preparing, Recruiting, Selecting, and Training Foster Families

The organization and functioning of foster care Services and family homes are regulated by government Regulations, and the minimum standards for these services are the quality of work. The provider of foster care and family-type children's homes is the Department/Department of social security and family protection/Municipal office for the protection of children's rights of Chisinau or a private provider accredited to provide this service in accordance with the law.

8.9.2 Working with a Biological Family: Procedure for Reuniting Children with Their Biological Families

Working with the biological family primarily consists of measures aimed at preventing the separation of the child from the family. For this purpose, there are various forms of family support aimed at preventing separation. In each individual case, the work is carried out on the basis of an individual approach. In order to study the situation and develop a plan of support for each individual family, the social assistant conducts an initial assessment of the situation, and then a comprehensive assessment is carried out together with members of the multidisciplinary group. In the case of a child's reintegration into the family, the social worker evaluates the child's ability to live in the biological family, and provides family support to facilitate the child's reintegration. Based on the highest interest of the child, an assessment of the situation is carried out, on the basis of which it can be concluded whether the family is able to ensure the child's well-being and adequate development. The comprehensive assessment includes multiple home visits, interviews with the child (depending on their age and understanding), individual conversations with each parent/guardian, extended family members, and other people related to the child. This can be neighbors, relatives from other localities, etc. Further, the social

[23]From theory to practice: implementation of the "guidelines for alternative child care".

assistant analyzes the information received during interviews, visits to the family, also based on the recommendations of specialists.[24]

The service provider provides support and primary intervention programs to address risk factors that may affect families with children living in the community, aimed at strengthening the knowledge and skills of child rearing, development, and protection. The purpose of these family support activities is to implement prevention and primary intervention programs, as well as to facilitate access of families and children to services available at the community level. The social assistant regularly conducts activities to inform families with children in order to strengthen the knowledge and skills of upbringing, development and protection of the child. In addition, the social assistant applies prevention and primary intervention programs aimed at strengthening the family environment and protective factors within the family, in cooperation with other specialists, representatives of institutions, and local public organizations. The above-mentioned prevention and early intervention programs are based on knowledge of the needs, risks, problems of individual groups and the General population and cover all families with children living in the community.

In addition to primary support, families with children at risk receive secondary family support based on the results of a comprehensive assessment. As a result of a comprehensive assessment, an individual assistance plan was developed for each child in a risk situation in accordance with the identified needs for assistance. The social assistant ensures that the child and his/her family are informed of the contents of the individual assistance plan and signs an Agreement with the parents/person in charge of the child to provide family support services. The community social assistant monitors the beneficiary's situation and the implementation of the individual assistance plan, ensuring that the individual assistance plan is reviewed. During the implementation of the plan, the community social assistant monitors the situation of the beneficiary and the implementation of the individual assistance plan through home visits and consultations with other relevant persons and specialists. It is important to note that during each control visit, the community social worker must conduct a separate conversation with the child and their family members.

The state provides cash assistance to recipients of secondary family support services based on a needs assessment and based on the positive impact of providing such assistance. The service provider provides a ratio of the size, purpose, and period of cash assistance with data from a comprehensive assessment and an individual assistance plan. The head of the service makes sure that the monetary assistance provided to the recipient is the only possible solution at that time to meet the identified needs. The curator closes the beneficiary's case after completing the tasks set by the individual assistance plan, or if the child's maintenance in the family or its (re)integration is contrary to the child's highest interest. If the risks to the child that led to the provision of family support services are eliminated or significantly

[24]"Serviciul social de sprijin pentru familiile cu copii. Ghid de suport pentru aplicare practică", Partnership for Every Child in cooperation with the government of the Republic of Moldova, approved by order of the Minister of Labor, Social Protection and Family No. 103 of May 30, 2016.

reduced to such an extent that the maintenance or (re)integration of the child into the family is the most appropriate solution for the child's upbringing and upbringing, a decision may be made to close the case. The decision to close the case is made within the framework of the meeting on the revision of the individual assistance plan if it is established that the tasks have been completed. In addition, one of the tasks of the social assistant is to provide access to each child to the information contained in the case, except for information that may affect the child's psycho-emotional state due to the consequences of violence, neglect and exploitation.[25]

8.9.3 Adoption, Procedure, Selection of Adoptive Parents

In the Republic of Moldova, the protection of children's rights through adoption is based on the following basic principles:

- respect for the fundamental rights and freedoms of the child;
- best interests of the child;
- informing the child and taking into account his opinion in accordance with his age and degree of maturity;
- priority of national adoption over international adoption;
- continuity in the upbringing and upbringing of the child, taking into account its ethnic, cultural and linguistic origin;
- quickness in performing all actions in the adoption process;
- guarantee the confidentiality of information received during the adoption process in relation to the identification data of the adoptive parent, as well as the biological parents.

It is important to note that according to the current legislation, throughout the adoption procedure, the authorized body in the field of adoption, in the area where the child lives, must provide him, in accordance with his age and maturity, clear and complete information and explanations about the stages and duration of the adoption process, about the consequences of adoption, about the adopter and his relatives. The purpose of informing the child is to prepare them for adoption and integration into the family environment. The adoption process takes into account the child's opinions, desires, and feelings, depending on their age and ability to understand.

[25]Government resolution No. 780 of 25.09.2014 on approving the Minimum quality standards Of the social family support service for families with children.

8.9.4 *International Adoption*

The adoption of children residing in the Republic of Moldova, persons living abroad shall be in accordance with the legislation of the Republic of Moldova with the legislation of the countries where you reside on the date of filing of application about adoption, and in accordance with international or bilateral treaties, of which the Republic of Moldova. The same procedure is maintained in the case of termination of international adoption due to its cancellation or invalidation.

Adoption of children–citizens of the Republic of Moldova residing outside the country carried out by authorised bodies of a foreign state that is home to the adoptive parent, shall be valid in the Republic of Moldova only if the foreign state is a member of the Hague Convention or a party to an agreement with the Republic of Moldova has bilateral agreements in the field of adoption and with the prior consent of the Central authority of the Republic of Moldova on adoption. Children living in the Republic of Moldova can be adopted by adoptive parents living abroad only if, in accordance with the legislation of the States to which they are to go, they are provided with guarantees and legal norms equivalent to those provided in the case of national adoption.

International adoption of a child residing in the Republic of Moldova can be established if:

- the spouse adopts the child of the other spouse;
- a child is adopted primarily by a relative living abroad up to and including the fourth degree of kinship;
- an adopted child without special needs is adopted by a person living abroad if it is not required by national adoption or guardianship or guardianship within 1 year from the date of its registration as an adopted child. For children with special needs, this period is 6 months.

It should also be emphasized that in the case of international adoption, the Central authority in the process of selecting a suitable adopter takes into account the need to ensure continuity in the upbringing and upbringing of the child, taking into account its ethnic, cultural and linguistic origin, if this does not contradict the best interests of the child.[26]

8.10 Best Practice Models

The Republic of Moldova was one of the first countries where Lumos, an NGO founded by the children's author J.K. Rowling, contributed to the reform and development of the child protection system. Work was carried out in various areas, including lobbying and promoting child care reform, strengthening

[26]Law No. 99 of 28.05.2010 on the legal regime of adoption.

cross-sectoral coordination and cooperation, and developing partnerships with key participants in the deinstitutionalization process. In addition to the above, the government was assisted in developing the legal framework, developing inclusive education and health services, and supporting the promotion of children's participation. In order to ensure the successful implementation of the reform, it was necessary to establish cooperation with Central and local government authorities and work in partnership with international and national non-governmental organizations. Lumos' main partners have also become authorities, communities and services, as well as children and families.

In accordance with the partnership agreements concluded with national and regional authorities, various projects have been initiated, each with a child at the center. Creating a new system that guarantees the well-being of every child involves working at various levels. For example, at the policy level, it is necessary to develop policy documents, legal acts, and methodological resources. It is necessary to develop social services and inclusive education. Professional development of personnel is necessary in the social sphere, as well as in the field of education and health. In order to ensure a holistic approach to the needs of children and their families, it is necessary to work on changing practices. An intersectoral approach is important in the framework of deinstitutionalization reform at all levels.

8.10.1 Problems Encountered in Addressing Issues Related to Child Protection

Based on the experience of implementing the child protection reform, Lumos has identified a number of persistent problems related to the transition from institutional to family and community care and child protection in Moldova. Among them, such difficulties as low family income and, as a result, high level of labor migration of the population were highlighted. At the same time, there is an insufficient level of state funding for the social sphere. It is also necessary to continue intensive work on the development and implementation of specialized and adapted programs for training and strengthening the family institution. A large number of unresolved problems are observed in the field of services and human resources. Among them are such difficulties as the lack of social and educational services for young children 0–3 years, as well as services for children with deviant behavior, children with complex disabilities and sensory disabilities, as well as for former pupils of the alternative care system. Unfortunately, there is an increased turnover of personnel working in social, educational and medical services, as well as a lack of qualified specialized personnel, such as a speech therapist, kinetotherapist, defectologist, psychopedagogue, and others.

8.10.2 Factors Contributing to the Reform of the Social Protection System for Children

Based on the experience of implementing child protection reform, the key factors needed for sustainable change were identified. First of all, it is important to have the political will to carry out reform. It is also advisable to allocate the necessary resources and establish inter-sectoral cooperation. In order to apply methods with proven effectiveness, it is important to cooperate with non-governmental organizations in the development and adaptation of international best practices. Various reform measures should be taken after consultation with all stakeholders, including children and families. It should be borne in mind that local authorities play a leading role in the process of reorganizing the system through coordinated partnerships, and the transformation of the child care system operates in the context of a broader social protection reform. To prepare the General public, it is necessary to conduct information, educational and educational campaigns to change social norms and practices.

8.10.3 Key Aspects of Deinstitutionalization

- A favorable environment for the upbringing and development of each child outside of boarding school;
- The interests of the child are at the heart of the deinstitutionalization process;
- Poverty and special education needs should not be reasons for family separation;
- Eliminating the practice of transferring a child from one institution to another, except for family reintegration or transfer to alternative care, based on a clear assistance plan and for a limited period of placement;
- Mobilizing existing local resources to ensure effective reintegration.

Further Reading

Constitution of the Republic of Moldova. Retrieved from http://lex.justice.md

Convention on the rights of the child. Retrieved from https://www.un.org/ru/documents/decl_conv/conventions/childcon.shtml

Civil Code Of The Republic Of Moldova.

Family Code Of The Republic Of Moldova.

Education development strategy for 2014–2020 "Education-2020".

National Strategy for promoting inclusion of persons with disabilities (2010–2013).

As a result, an intersectoral strategy for the development of parental skills and competencies for 2016–2022 was approved.

Inclusive education development program for the period 2011–2020 (2014).

Action plan for implementing the child protection Strategy for 2014–2020 (2016).

Law No. 123 of 18.06.2010 on social services.

Law №. 547 of 25.12.2003 on social assistance.
Law No. 338 of 15.12.1994 on the rights of the child.
Law №. 140 of 14.06.2013 on special protection of children at risk and children separated from their parents.
Law No. 1585 of 27.02.1998 on compulsory health insurance.
Law No. 547 of 21.07.1995 on education.
Law №. 547 of 25.12.2003 on social assistance.
Law No. 179-XVI. Kishinau, July 10, 2008 About public-private partnership.
Law No. 99 of 28.05.2010 on the legal regime of adoption.
Resolution No. 351 of 29.05.2012 on approval of the Regulation on redirecting financial resources within the framework of reforming boarding institutions.
Resolution №. 410 of 04.04.2003 on approval of The national strategy "Education for all".
Government resolution No. 434 of 10.06.2014 on approving the child protection Strategy for 2014–2020.
Resolution No. 523 of 11.07.2011 on approval Of the program for the development of inclusive education in the Republic of Moldova for 2011–2020.
Government resolution No. 780 of 25.09.2014 on approving the Minimum quality standards Of the social family support service for families with children.
Resolution No. 784 of 09.07.2007 on approval of the National strategy and action Plan for reforming the residential child care system for 2007–2012.
Government resolution No. 591 of 24.07.2017 on approval of the Standard regulation on the organization and functioning of the social service for placement Of children separated from their parents.
Government resolution No. 52 of 17.01.2013 on approval of the Model regulation on the organization and functioning of the social service "Community home for children at risk".
Government resolution No. 760 of 17.09.2014 on approval of the Framework regulation on the organization and functioning of the foster care Service and minimum quality standards.
Government decree №. 51 of 17.01.2018 on approval of the Regulations on a family-type orphanage.
Government resolution No. 1278 of 26.12.2018 on approving the Regulations on the types and specific conditions and care of children placed in guardianship/guardianship services, foster care and family-type children's homes.
Government resolution No. 944 of 14.11.2014 on approval of the education development Strategy for 2014–2020 "Education-2020".
Minimum quality standards for foster care Services (Annex 2 to Government Resolution 760 of September 17, 2014).
Evaluation of the Government of Moldova 2013–2017 UNICEF country programme of cooperation.
MICS questionnaire on children aged 5–17, UNICEF, June 17, 2019.
MICS questionnaire on children under five years of age, UNICEF, June 17, 2019.
Serviciul social de sprijin pentru familiile cu copii. Ghid de suport pentru aplicare practică. Partnership for Every Child in cooperation with the government of the Republic of Moldova, approved by order of the Minister of Labor, Social Protection and Family No. 103 of May 30, 2016.
UNICEF. (2011). *Situation analysis of vulnerable, excluded and discriminated children in Moldova*. Chisinau.
The Declaration on social and legal principles relating to the protection and well-being of children, especially in the case of foster care and adoption at the national and international levels, adopted by UN General Assembly resolution 41/95 of 3 December 1986. Retrieved from https://www.un.org/ru/documents/decl_conv/declarations/childpri.shtml
Report of the independent expert for the United Nations study on violence against children. (2006). Retrieved from https://www.unicef.org/violencestudy/reports/SG_violencestudy_ru.pdf

From theory to practice: implementation of the "guidelines for alternative child care" translated from the English./N. Cantwell, J. Davidson, S. Elsley, And. Milligan, N. Quinn. Great Britain: Center for Excellence for Looked After Children in Scotland, 2012.
http://avecopiii.md/echipa-noastra/
https://issuu.com/unicefmoldova/docs/raport_eng
http://cnpac.org.md/rom/about-us
http://drepturilecopilului.md/index.php/en/
http://fcps.md/?page_id=148
http://old.mmpsf.gov.md/file/studii/indicatori_md.pdf
http://roxanatodea.com/apscf/secretariat/
http://speranta.md/despre-noi/
http://www.amicideibambini.it/default_gb.asp
http://www.euro.who.int/__data/assets/pdf_file/0006/348009/Fact-sheet-SDG-Child-and-adolescent-health-FINAL-en.pdf?ua=1
http://www.keystonemoldova.md/ro/who-we-are/
https://caritas.md/ru/istoria/
https://ccfmoldova.org/istorie
https://childhood.org/this-is-childhood/projects/partnership-for-every-child-moldova/
https://documents-dds-ny.un.org/doc/UNDOC/GEN/N06/491/07/PDF/N0649107.pdf
https://drepturilecopilului.md/files/CDC_2005_final_rus.pdf
https://ru.sputnik.md/economics/20190413/25487813/pervoe-mesto-evropa-dolea-perevodov.html
https://www.concordia.md/despre/
https://www.diaconia.md/pageview.php?l=ro&idc=305&t=/Despre/Cine-suntem
https://www.p4ec.md/en/organisation/videnie_i_missiya_organizacii/default.aspx
https://www.unicef.org/moldova/ru
https://www.wearelumos.org/moldova/about-us/

Chapter 9
Russian Federation

Galina Semya, Alexandra Telitsyna, and Elvira Garifulina

9.1 Introduction: Overview of the Russian Federation

The largest country in the world, the Russian Federation extends from the Baltic Sea in the west to the Pacific Ocean in the east and from the Arctic in the north to the Black Sea in the south. There are 85 federal regions extending across 11 time zones. Founded as the medieval state of the Rus in the ninth century, through conquest and annexation the territory vastly expanded as the Russian Empire into the nineteenth century. In the process the empire acquired a very diverse ethnic and cultural face—European, Slavic, Eurasian, Asian and indigenous groups all comprise what constitutes the citizen of the Russian Federation today. The 1917 Bolshevik Revolution, which gave rise to the Union of Soviet Socialist Republics, fundamentally rocked the modern world. Likewise, the dissolution of the Soviet Union in 1991 set the stage for the creation of 15 new countries.

9.1.1 History of Social Protection of Children

In Russia the earliest models for providing care to children left without parental supervision were largely based on traditional and feudal forms of conventional law

G. Semya
Moscow State University on Psychology and Education, Moscow, Russia

A. Telitsyna (✉)
Higher School of Economics, National Research University, Moscow, Russia
e-mail: atelitsyna@hse.ru

E. Garifulina
E. and G. Timchenko Foundation, Moscow, Russia

I. Earner, A. Telitsyna (eds.), *The Development of Child Protection Systems in the Post-Soviet States*, Child Maltreatment 12,
https://doi.org/10.1007/978-3-030-59588-3_9

embodied in 'Russkaya Pravda'. During Tsar Ivan the Terrible's reign in the fifteenth century special almshouses were built to shelter orphaned children. In the first half of the seventeenth century, under Tsar Mikhail Fyodorovich, whose father was installed as the Patriarch of the Russian Orthodox Church, numerous structural reforms were implemented with the Church notably becoming responsible for almshouses, orphanages and other charitable institutions; the care of widows and orphans was also assigned to the Church and its representatives.

In the eighteenth century, Tsar Peter I laid the foundations of the state system for the care of orphans. He defined categories of people in need, introduced preventive measures to combat social evils, regulated private charity, and codified these relationships and responsibilities into law. The system created by Peter I continued to exist under his successors albeit with less concern for the poor. In 1726, Empress Catherine I issued a decree "on the search for special houses for the reception and care of illegitimate children" and in 1747, Empress Elizabeth issued a decree "on the need to establish houses for the care of illegitimate children". Both Tsarinas were concerned about the illegitimate children of the nobility—their concern did not extend to the children of the poor.

Nevertheless, significant changes in the care of orphans were made under Empress Catherine II. Inspired by the ideas of the Enlightenment, Count Ivan Betskoy, proposed that young Russians of both sexes should be educated in boarding schools to create "a new race of men". The Empress endorsed his ideas and established the 'Society for the Training of Well-Born Girls', later the Smolny Institute, which became the first female educational institution in Russia. Count Betskoy, himself born out of wedlock, went on to establish foundling homes in both Moscow and St. Petersburg. His goal was to create a middle-class through education.

During the reign of Tsar Nicholas I in 1838, the "Committee of the chief guardianship of children's shelters" appeared, which took over control of all existing boarding school shelters (at that time, more than 23,000 children). Initially, these shelters, actually more like boarding schools, gave middle class parents the opportunity to work and at the same time provided their children with basic education. In later manifestations, children's shelters grew to include the poor.

Between 1880 and 1890 models of child protection were expanded to include hospital-based care as well as family foster care. District guardianship authorities identified needy children and placed them in systems of care as they deemed appropriate. An interesting form of arrangement for child protection was represented by the so-called "self-help shelters", which were completely self-sufficient. Children from the age of 12 years old lived in these shelters. A foster mother was employed to help these children learn to manage the house, complete chores and acquire taught vocational skills. These shelters were often of mixed gender.

9.2 Features of the Soviet Period

The 1917 Bolshevik Revolution resulted in many things, not the least which was the increase in the number of orphaned children. The numbers of children left without parents or families increased again during the First World War and then by the millions as a result of collectivization, 'de-kulakization', ethnic cleansing of Cossacks, Tatars and others and the Holocaust. The years of "great terror" under Stalin led to the creation of a new group of orphans-children of "enemies of the people".

Following the 1917 revolution oversight of children's shelters was transferred to the district social welfare departments. The new government began to create a system of state aid, and officially proclaimed the transition to "communist social security, in which everyone with a disability or need... can hope that the state... will come to their aid." The desire of the state to help to children could also be explained by ideological reasons—it was deemed necessary to educate a new kind of person—a person of the Communist society. However, the massive social upheavals that were unfolding created equally massive numbers of children in need. With the destruction of the previous systems of care, the critical shortage of qualified personnel, and the lack of material resources a long period of chaos and confusion ensued.

In the new Code of laws of the USSR, published in 1918, both parents had equal rights and responsibility for the child, and, accordingly, the need for guardianship was recognized only if the child simultaneously lost both parents. Included in the Code is the concept of "parental rights", which are not recognized as something unconditional, and to which parents have the right with the birth of children, and these rights are awarded by the Code to parents solely in the interests of children and for the sake of children. The concept of "abuse of parental rights" appears, and for the first time the state had the explicit opportunity to deprive citizens of parental rights. Among the reasons for depriving parents of their rights to raise children and removing them to a public institution were exploitation and forced labor, harsh treatment, and education that developed anti-social tendencies. The People's Commissariat of Social Security in 1919 included the deprivation of parental rights and the seizure of children if parents were found to be bringing up children "in the spirit that is clearly contrary to the basic principles of communism, inculcating children with hatred to communism and developing in children counter-revolutionary aspirations".

By 1922 it was estimated that there were seven million children who were in need of assistance from the state. A significant group of these children were street children. Regional committees were instructed to immediately create commissions for minors and organize orphanages. In 1927, Anton Makarenko, social worker, writer and education theorist, established self-governing child collectives for homeless street children as well as juvenile offenders. These labor communes were organized for the purposes of re-education, labor training on the principles of self-sufficiency and self-government. Through these efforts, a solid infrastructure was created for the implementation of the state program for the protection of orphans and included children's homes/baby homes, orphanages, boarding schools, labor colonies, and commune schools. The first forms of placing orphans in families began in 1928 in connection with the decree "on the transfer of children from orphanages to peasant families". The term 'patronage family' appeared to describe a guardianship arrangement whereby children were sent to live with a family that provided care and taught children a skill or vocation. In 1942, there were 37,490 'patronized' children with a total of 74,648 during the war years. By 1968 this form of taking care of children had fallen out of favor.

These promising models of child protection that were based on the progressive ideals of Makarenko soon were put to use for far darker and tragic purposes. Between 1937 and 1938 a new group of orphans appeared—children of "enemies of the people" or those whose parents were victims of political repression. The children of "wives of traitors to the Motherland" were either sent to orphanages, if they were under the age of 3 years; and afterwards until the age of 15 years to labor communes which were converted into labor factories.

The Patriotic war of 1941–1945 (World War II) claimed the lives of more than 13 million children. At the beginning of the war a program of evacuating children from cities and areas of conflict was initiated. Much like the evacuation of children from London during the bombing raids; children in Russia were sent to the far Eastern part of the country. Orphanages, boarding schools and kindergartens were among the first to be evacuated. As the war progressed and the conflict created enormous human loss of life and destruction, many evacuated children lost trace of surviving parents or relatives. Tragically, many of these children were never re-united with their families.

At the end of the war new institutional models appeared to address juvenile delinquency. The Union Council of People's Commissars adopted a resolution "on strengthening measures to combat child homelessness, neglect and hooliganism", which declared that in addition to labor colonies for children convicted of crimes, labor and educational colonies would be established for teenagers aged 11 to 16 years. These were secure facilities that housed children with behavioral issues and who had violated the regulations in ordinary boarding schools and orphanages.

One of the most active and popular forms of care for children who did not have parents during the war years was adoption. The number of adopted children in evacuation areas was especially high. This growth was facilitated by official decree that allowed the child to obtain the surname and patronymic of the adoptive parents as well as record them as a 'father' and 'mother' in official records. Some families adopted ten or more children.

Through the second half of the 1950s boarding schools grew in popularity and were considered the most effective institutions for educating the "builders of a new society". In September 1956, by resolution of the Central Committee of the CPSU and the Council of Ministers of the USSR the organization of boarding schools as general education institutions was promoted to solve the problem of training "builders of communism" at a higher level, and by 1960 almost one million students called them home during the week.

Out-of-family upbringing of a child in the Soviet Union was considered more productive for his/her mental development and this attitude remained until the

1970s. This view proceeded from the concept that in a communist society, the upbringing and maintenance of children should not be taken care of by individual parents, but by the entire society as a whole.

By 1991 the system of boarding school institutions in the country consisted mainly of huge facilities with their own large grounds. Many of these institutions became the focal point of the entire community in which they were located. The generally accepted belief was that children were better off in an institutionalized environment. Knowledge about the effects of institutionalization on mental health, attachment, socialization and other theories of human behavior and development that had already existed for decades outside of the Soviet Union were not known to specialists working with children.

9.3 Modern Child Protection System

In modern Russia, there were three main stages in the development of the child protection system as it now exists.

9.3.1 The First Stage from 1991, After the Collapse of the Soviet Union, to 2006

Russia is one of the post-socialist countries that experienced the worst recession in the 1990s. A long period of decline in the Russian economy resulted in a dramatic drop in personal income, increase in prices for housing, food and consumer goods. Families experienced enormous stress; families fractured, alcoholism and drug addiction increased, crime and violence was prevalent. The phenomenon of 'social orphanhood' appeared. These were children who had living parents and relatives but who, for various reasons were unable or unwilling to care for their children. By 1996, the number of children left without parental care exceeded 500 thousand. The problem of 'social orphanhood' was a national disaster. According to statistics, by the beginning of 2000 in Russia there were already 657 thousand orphans; of them without a father and mother—5.6%; "rejected" children (who were refused in the hospital)—2.3%, all other children are orphans with living parents.

By 2006, more than 130,000 children without parental care were identified each year, and at least 40,000 children were sent to orphanages. About 70 thousand parents were deprived of their parental rights every year. In 2005, 375 thousand foster children were registered, 11 thousand were in foster families, and 159 thousand children were in adoptive families.

On average, the number of children decreased by an average of 3% annually, reaching about 27 million in 2006 (31.2 million in 2003), and the percentage of orphans was 2.8%.

According to Goskomstat calculations, in 1996, 60% of the population had incomes below the average level, and the average per capita income of 22.0% of the population was below the subsistence level. Two-thirds of children in Russia are raised in families of the poor or which tend to poverty.

Addressing Social Orphans Through Enhance Social Benefits and De-Institutionalization
Federal law "On state benefits to citizens with children" from 19.05.1995 № 81-FZ established a system of benefits for citizens with children, such as allowances for pregnancy and childbirth, a lump sum payment to pregnant women who registered in medical institutions in early pregnancy, another lump sum payment for child birth and monthly allowances for the period of leave to care for a child until they reach 18 months. These benefits are a system of payments aimed at compensating family expenses related to the birth of a child, and also play a stimulating role in the care and protection of children's health and interests. In order to support families, the monthly child benefit, the largest social transfer program for families with children in the regions, has been paid since 1995. As a rule, in regions with low budget revenues, this type of payment was the main type of social support for families with children. But since 1999, it has been provided on the basis of income control, i.e. only to poor families with children.

In 2008, a new law "on guardianship" was adopted, which officially transferred the patronage to the form of family arrangements for orphans, subject to the adoption of a regional law. Together with it, a new form of family arrangement emerged—the foster family (as a type of paid guardianship), which did not differ from the patronage, but existed on the basis of Federal law. Within 2 years, the patronage practically disappeared in Russia.

9.3.2 *Second Stage from 2006 to the First Half of 2012*

Since 2006, social policy priorities have shifted in favor of families with children. At this stage, the problems of social and demographic development become the focus of state policy and strategic programs. In 2006, the implementation of priority national projects with a pronounced social character was launched: "Health", "Education", "Affordable and comfortable housing". In May 2006, President Putin, in a presidential address to the Federal Assembly of the Russian Federation formulated a large-scale program for overcoming the demographic crisis. A new package of measures to support families with children entered into force, including maternity payments (provided to every woman who gave birth (or adopted) a second (third and subsequent) child, increasing insurance benefits for child care up to 1.5 years, compensating for the payment of preschool services. Since 2007, payments for adoptive parents, guardians, and foster parents have also been significantly increased.

In 2010, again the situation of children became the main topic of the annual address of the President to the Federal Assembly. This message identified the following priorities: increasing the availability and quality of health services for mothers and children; improving the living conditions of large families (families with three or more children); developing measures to improve the availability of pre-school facilities and subsequent social adaptation of children.

In 2007–2008 efforts were made to support the most vulnerable groups of children: orphans and disabled people. The system of benefits created incentives for the development of family forms of placement of orphans, in particular, introduced a benefit for the transfer of a child to a family and increased the amount of other benefits for orphans.

In 2011, the President instructed the government to take additional measures that stimulate the growth of family forms of placement of orphans; the heads of regions to adopt programs necessary for medical, psychological and pedagogical support of families who raise orphans and to complete the development of programs for social adaptation of graduates of orphanages.

To support the development of the family structure, since 2006, funds have been transferred from the Federal level to the regions of the Russian Federation for the payment of a one-time allowance for the admission of an orphan child to a family and remuneration to foster parents. Regions use their own funds to introduce additional payments and establish additional benefits for those families that have adopted orphans for various forms of family arrangement. By 2012, the active placement of orphans in families led to a sharp change in the number of children in institutions. Those who remain in institutional care (difficult to adopt): adolescent children: over 10 years—70%, children with disabilities:—15% (in some regions—up to 30%); children who are brothers and sisters (siblings)—26%. The number of orphans in orphanages decreased from 188,602 in 2006 to 132,790 at the beginning of 2012 (a 30% reduction). In some regions, there are waiting lists for the adoption of small, relatively healthy children left without parental care.

9.3.3 The Third Stage Began on June 1, 2012 with the "National Action Strategy for Children"

The adoption of the National strategy was the beginning of a new stage of modern state policy in the protection of children's rights, which clearly defined its goals, objectives and ways of achieving it. Ensuring a safe and protected childhood and raising a child in a family have become one of Russia's top national priorities.

The National strategy identified six main areas (strategies) for its implementation: (1) Family policy of child-saving, (2) Access to quality education and upbringing, cultural development and information security of children, (3) Health care, child-friendly and healthy lifestyle, (4) Equal opportunities for children who need special care of the state, (5) Creation of a system of protection and ensuring the rights and interests of children and child-friendly justice, (6) Children-participants in the implementation of the National strategy, which is dedicated to the realization of the child's right to be heard.

The adoption of the National strategy marked the beginning of the development and approval of a set of strategic documents to protect and ensure the rights and interests of children, which are not only interrelated and complementary, but also have their own subject of regulation and actions, which define guidelines and measures up to 2025:

Drastic changes are taking place in the sphere of prevention of social orphanhood. Since September 1, 2012, the government of the Russian Federation has introduced mandatory training for people who want to take a child left without parental care into their family. An exception was made for adoptive parents who are stepfathers and stepmothers. At the end of 2012, Federal law No. 272-FZ of December 28, 2012 was adopted, which prohibits US citizens from adopting Russian orphans (the so-called Dima Yakovlev law). In 2012, of the 2604 children placed for international adoption, 746 were adopted by Americans (29%).

At the same time, the Decree of the President of the Russian Federation No. 1688 of December 28, 2012 "on certain measures to implement the state policy in the sphere of protection of orphans and children left without parental care", adopted in order to ensure the right of every child to a family, develop and support various forms of family arrangement of orphans, and reduce the number of children being raised in residential institutions, is being adopted. To implement the Decree, more than 40 normative acts and amendments to legislation are adopted that significantly simplify procedures and reduce the time for family placement of orphans. In material terms, Federal benefits and pensions for disabled children and their caregivers have been increased. Since January 1, 2013, the one-time allowance for the adoption of a disabled child, a child older than 7 years, and siblings has increased 10 times to 100 thousand rubles. Following this, many regions of the Russian Federation adopted regional laws that increase payments from regional budgets. For example, the Kurgan region increased the one-time payment to 800 thousand, and the Sakhalin region introduced a one-time payment of one million for the adoption of a disabled child.

In 2013, an amendment was made to article 123 of the Family code of the Russian Federation, as a result of which the placement of a child in an orphanage becomes a temporary measure until he finds a family, rather than a permanent form of arrangement along with guardianship.

In 2013, Russia joined the International Convention on the Rights of Persons with Disabilities and replaced the medical model of disability with one focused on social integration. In Russia, a large-scale national project "Accessible environment" is being implemented, which affects educational, sports, cultural and other leisure organizations for children. Adapted educational programs are developed and implemented for children with disabilities.

Summarizing the implementation of the National strategy revealed a number of problematic areas: an increase in the proportion of children under the age of 16 living in families with incomes below the subsistence minimum (from 2012 to 2015 it increased from 17.6% to 21.4%); an increase in domestic violence against children in families; an increase in the proportion of sexual violence with a decrease in the number of crimes against minors, a low level of providing housing for graduates from among orphans.

Chapter 10
Tajikistan

Mikhail Petrushkov

10.1 Introduction: Overview of Tajikistan

Tajikistan is the smallest state in Central Asia located in foothills of the Pamir Mountains that create borders with Pakistan, Afghanistan and China. In the thirteenth century Ghenghis Khan conquered the territory and made it a part of the Mongol Empire; in the fourteenth century Tamerlane claimed the area for the Timurid Empire. In 1864 the Russian Empire extended its control of Central Asia, then known as Turkestan; the vassal state of the Emirate of Bukhara controlled a portion of present day Tajikistan. In 1929 Tajikistan became a republic of the Soviet Union; on September 9, 1991 Tajikistan declared independence which was followed by a period of turbulence.

The country is divided into geographical and administrative regions: (1) Autonomous region-Gorno-Badakhshan Autonomous region (GBAO); (2) regions—Khatlon and Sughd regions; 13 Regions of Republican subordination (RRP); and the capital—Dushanbe, which has a special status. Each region is divided into districts, which in turn are divided into 'jamoats' or municipalities. Currently, there are 69 districts and 367 'jamoats' in the Republic of Tajikistan.

10.2 Current Concerns About Children

One of the most alarming statistics in Tajikistan is suicide and attempted suicide by children: In 2018–102 children, in 2017–90 children committed suicide and attempted suicide. Infant mortality rates are also very high; according to the data

M. Petrushkov (✉)
National Association of Public, Policy and Management, Dushanbe, Tajikistan

I. Earner, A. Telitsyna (eds.), *The Development of Child Protection Systems in the Post-Soviet States*, Child Maltreatment 12,
https://doi.org/10.1007/978-3-030-59588-3_10

of the Ministry of Health and Social Protection 3457 children died in the country under the age of 1 year in 2018, 3784 children died in 2017, and 3961 died in 2016.

One of the major threats to the health of children in Tajikistan is their infection with HIV/AIDS. According to the Ministry of Health and Social Protection as of January 1, 2019, 694 children are infected with HIV, 178 children have AIDS.

According to the Ministry of education and science of the Republic of Tajikistan in the 2017–2018 academic year, 42,304 (19,509 girls) orphans and children left without parental care were enrolled in educational institutions, including 1713 (801 girls)—without a father and without a mother, 30,503 (13,905 girls)—without a father, 9646 (4615 girls)—without a mother, 415 (188 girls)—left without parental care.

In Tajikistan, appropriate measures are being taken to ensure that children with disabilities have access to education. In the 2017–2018 academic year, 7571 children with disabilities (2999 girls) were enrolled in the education system of the Republic. Among them, 392 children (144 girls) are trained in 12 pre-school institutions of the Republic, 6584 children (2611 girls) in General education institutions and 595 children (244 girls) were trained at home. Also, there are 13 special institutions for the blind, deaf, hard of hearing, children with diseases of the musculoskeletal system, developmentally disabled, children from disadvantaged families, orphans, 3463 children (847 girls) were trained and received rehabilitation.

10.3 History of Child Protection

The social protection of children evolved under the system of social protection codes that existed in the Russian Empire as well as conventional laws of the regional 'qishlaqs' or settlements. Because of the ethnic and religious diversity of this region, there were differential approaches to social protection of children. Shelters were created for 'native' orphans and the poor, supported by charitable funds from the Tsar. Administrators of these shelters were often the military governors who acted as "honorary trustees". Children received housing, food, medical care, basic education and taught a vocational skill. The Russian Orthodox Church also took an active part in providing charity to the poor and orphans. For example, the nuns of the Holy Trinity St. Nicholas convent willingly accepted underage orphans, provided shelter and food for the poor, the elderly and those "just offended by fate" [Litvinov 1996: 46–47].

A different situation developed in the Emirate of Bukhara, which formally retained, according to the treaties with the Russian Empire from 1868 and 1873, its former form of government, its own administration, but at the same time was dependent on tsarist Russia, being its protectorate. The situation in the Emirate was complicated by the presence of both a nomadic and settled Muslim population. The primary education of children was conducted in 'maktabs' that were run by Muslim clergy and paid for by the parents of students. For the elite, the 'madrassas' education provided an in-depth understanding of Koranic law. Neither of these institutions were accessible to the poor.

The establishment of the Russian Empire in Central Asia made significant changes in the development of the legal system. A new legal culture and legal ideology began to form, connected with the emergence of new legal institutions within the Emirate of Bukhara. All these new legal forms and phenomena in interaction with the medieval means of normative and individual legal influence prevailing in the Emirate of Bukhara, in particular, acted as a means of ordering all spheres of life in the Emirate and both actually and legally significantly modified the legal system of the Emirate of Bukhara.

The institution of marriage and family in the Emirate of Bukhara was regulated by Sharia law. Thus, according to the Sharia, only children born to parents who were legally married were considered legitimate and had property and personal rights in relation to the father. All rights in the upbringing of children born in marriage belonged to the man, including the right to appoint one of his wives to nurse the child of another wife.

The age of marriage depended on the financial situation of girls and boys. Moreover, due to the obligations of the groom's parents to pay for the bride marriage gift (ven, mahr, kalym) as an integral attribute of the recognition of the legality of marriage-there was a so-called intersection: girls from poor families were married earlier than from rich families in order to improve the financial situation of the family, and, sometimes, just to get rid of the "extra mouth". Boys from rich families, whose parents were able to pay kalym, married before their peers from poor families, often did not have this opportunity at all.

On average, boys in the Emirate of Bukhara were married between the age of 15–20 years, girls were married between the age of 10–15 years. Widespread was the practice of 'speaking Bakhsh' ("lullaby marriage agreement"), in which the parents of 2–3 year-old children conspired in advance about the marriage of their children.

To solve the problem of female orphanhood, the law in Bukhara encouraged polygamy: "If you are afraid that you will not do justice to orphans, then marry those female orphans that you like—two, three, four." In addition, the presence of concubines was encouraged. When children inherited the property of deceased parents, the principle laid down by Sharia law was applied: "God commands you with regard to your children: the share of a son is equal to the share of two daughters." In some regions of the Emirate of Bukhara, girls were generally denied inheritance rights if there were male heirs in the family.

10.4 Child Protection in the Soviet Period

The Tajik Soviet Republic (ASSR) was formed from a number of districts of Turkestan and Bukhara. The capital was established in Dushanbe. It was from this moment that the protection of children began to take shape in Tajikistan, based on the unified model of the Soviet Union. State orphanages and other institutions were established in the country under the authority of the People's Commissariat of Education to identify all street children and place them in appropriate institutions and prepare for them for independent life. The Constitution of the Tajik SSR of 1937 granted equality between men and women, equality of rights for all citizens, freedom of conscience, freedom of speech, press, freedom of assembly and meetings, freedom of street processions and demonstrations, the right to association, personal inviolability, inviolability of housing and secret correspondence and the right of foreign citizens to obtain political asylum.

The state also took special care of orphans. By the resolution of the SNK of the USSR "on the arrangement of children left without parents" (January 1942), all state departments, party, trade Union and Komsomol organizations were obliged to take concrete care of orphans. In pursuance of this resolution, the network of children's homes was further expanded. Measures were taken to preserve and improve the material and technical base of children's homes and to supply them with the necessary means, materials, clothing, and food.

Trade unions and Komsomol organizations showed concern for the social protection of children in military conditions. The Central Committee of the Komsomol adopted a resolution "on measures of Komsomol organizations to combat child neglect, to prevent child homelessness" (1942). The newspaper "Komsomolskaya Pravda" published an account of a special Children's Fund, which received funds for the maintenance of children's health resorts, orphanages and for scholarships to students who did not have parents.

In the following years, documents were adopted that develop, specify and detail the CPSU Program on the protection and protection of motherhood and childhood, the financial situation of families with children, and the health of the younger generation. These include "Fundamentals of the legislation of the USSR and the Union republics on marriage and family" (1968); "on further increase in material assistance to low-income families with children" (1974); "on measures to further increase the welfare of the Soviet people" (1976); "on measures to increase the production of goods for children, improve their quality and improve trade in these goods" (1978).

10.5 Modern Child Protection System

The definition of child well-being and the selection of indicators for evaluation are based on the UN Convention on the Rights of the Child. In this regard, despite its universality for all countries that have ratified it, in view of the recognition in the Convention of the need to take into account the specifics of each country in the implementation of the economic, social and cultural rights of children, a single and binding interpretation of the term "child welfare" does not exist today.

Unfortunately, indicators of child well-being, despite the rights of the child clearly enshrined in the Convention, such as, for example, the right of the child to "use the most advanced services of the health system" (Article 24) or to "the necessary standard of living" (Article 27), are highly variable depending on national legal definitions and depend on the political will, public policy, resources of the country in which the child lives, and the interest of society.

Together, this state of Affairs has a negative impact on countries where children's well-being is not the most important, relevant and priority issues on the "agenda". Tajikistan is also no exception. The term "child welfare" has not been introduced into the legislative field of the country. Based on the analysis of normative legal acts of the Republic of Tajikistan, it can be concluded that the main attention of the country's leadership is currently focused on the protection of motherhood and childhood, respect for children's rights and prevention of violence, exploitation and all types of discrimination.

The complex of issues and indicators of "child welfare", of course, including the above-mentioned issues, but not limited to them, due to a number of accumulated problems and the difficult socio-economic situation of Tajikistan, is not a priority at the present stage of development.

Although, based on the provisions of the Law of the Republic of Tajikistan dated March 18, 2015, No. 1196 "on protection of the rights of the child" (as amended by the law of the Republic of Tajikistan dated 02.01.2018, No. 1489), it can be concluded that Tajikistan, though slowly, but consistently advances in the issues of child welfare.

For example, Article 4 introduced the concept of: "state minimum social standards for children", which include the minimum amount of the following social services guaranteed by the Republic of Tajikistan:

- guaranteed provision of free General and primary vocational education;
- provision of free secondary and higher professional education in accordance with the procedure established by the legislation of the Republic of Tajikistan;
- free medical care for the child, in accordance with the minimum social standards;
- guaranteeing the child's right to vocational orientation, field of activity, labor protection, labor in the order established by the legislation of the Republic of Tajikistan;
- social services, including guaranteed material support for children with disabilities, orphans and children left without parental care, through the payment of state benefits, as well as the implementation of measures for their adaptation and social rehabilitation of children in difficult situations;
- ensuring the right of the child to housing in accordance with the legislation of the Republic of Tajikistan;
- organization of measures for health improvement and recreation, including for children living in extreme conditions, as well as in environmentally unfavorable regions;
- taking into account the interests of children with disabilities, orphans and children left without parental care in the development and implementation of state programs of socio-economic development of the country; promoting the physical, mental, psychological, spiritual, moral and moral development of children with disabilities, orphans and children left without parental care;

- providing legal and psychological assistance to a child in accordance with the legislation of the Republic of Tajikistan.

10.6 Promising Practices

It should be noted that several approaches are used in current pilot projects in Tajikistan. One of them provides for the assessment of child well-being based on the methodology of the International Society for Child Indicators (ISCI). The hallmarks of this organization is to improve the measurement, data collection, analysis and dissemination of information on the status of children, and it is in the initial stages of development of indicators of children's well-being; and strengthening linkages between measurement, analysis and policy. Children's well-being is assessed on the basis of 50 indicators grouped into five areas: "Security and physical status", "Personal life", "Social and social life", "Economic resources of children" and "Activity of children".

Another approach, along with assessing the realization of the rights of the child to an appropriate standard of living, to social security and protection from violence and exploitation, to the use of the most advanced health and social services, to equitable access to educational opportunities, pays special attention to the importance of education in a happy and loving family and the subjective perception of the child's level of well-being. In this regard more than 60 indicators are grouped in 6 directions: "Material deprivation"; "Health and safety"; "Education"; "Relationships among children"; "Behavior and lifestyle"; "Subjective well-being".

However, despite all the positive changes and developments, it should be noted that the situation in Tajikistan with child welfare leaves much to be desired. For example, according to the data provided in the UNICEF Bulletin "Early education of children in Tajikistan" (2019), 86% of children aged 3–6 years do not receive pre-school education services.

Recent scientific research in the field of pre-school education, which is supported by UNICEF, provides such statistics for children who have a negative experience and do not receive appropriate pre-school education: 25% are more likely to drop out of school, 40% are more likely to become parents in adolescence, 50% are more likely to go to a special institution, 80% are more likely to not receive a secondary or higher education, 70% are more likely to be prosecuted for various crimes.

One of the most significant recent steps has been the establishment of a special position of the Human Rights Commissioner in 2016 in order to ensure respect, observance, protection and promotion of the rights and freedoms of the child. In order to improve the legislation regulating the system of justice for children, amendments and additions have been made to the family, criminal, criminal procedure codes, the Code of execution of criminal penalties and other normative legal acts of the Republic of Tajikistan.

However, despite these positive developments and presence of separate articles and chapters in documents such as, for example, the criminal procedure code

(Chapter 44, establishing the rules of treatment of juveniles and the order of proceedings in cases of crimes committed by juveniles, as well as, a special procedure of interrogation of minor victim and witness, both at the preliminary investigation stage and the trial stage of the proceedings), the Procedural code of administrative offences of the Republic of Tajikistan (Chapter 16, devoted to the production order on Affairs about administrative offences of minors), the provisions adopted in 2017 the State program of reforming the system of justice for children for the years 2017–2021 and the attached action Plan, we have to admit that a holistic system of juvenile justice in the country today is not formed.

Moreover, there are a number of serious shortcomings.

Thus, the juvenile justice reform Program for 2017–2021 does not take into account the category of minors who have committed administrative offenses, although administrative proceedings provide for the administrative detention of minors.

The criminal procedure code of December 3, 2009 does not contain any time limits for questioning minor victims and witnesses. Mandatory participation of the defender is provided only in cases of minors, suspects, accused or defendants, and minor victims do not belong to this category of persons. In addition, there is no prescription about the separation of children from adults in places of detention, pre-trial detention and other places of deprivation of liberty. Measures to protect participants in the proceedings specified in the Law dated Dec ember 29, 2010 No. 644 "On state protection of participants of criminal proceedings", in "Order to assist the persons subject to state protection, in the change permanent or temporary place of work (service) or study" from the May 2, 2013, No. 213 and in "the Order of protection of information on the implementation of the state protection of participants of criminal proceedings" dated March 1, 2012, No. 101, is not adapted to the protection of underage victims and witnesses of crime.

Tajikistan's legislation does not provide for effective measures to help and protect child victims and witnesses of crime and their family members. In particular, there is no access to permanent support services (material, legal, medical, social, etc.), as well as access to services that promote the rehabilitation and reintegration of the child.

Guardianship in the Republic of Tajikistan is established in accordance with Paragraph 1 of Article 32 of the Civil code of the Republic of Tajikistan of June 30, 1999, "...to protect the rights and interests of incapacitated or not fully capable citizens. In addition," custody and guardianship of minors are also established for the purpose of their education".

Guardianship over minors is established "... in the absence of their parents, adoptive parents, deprivation of parental rights by the court of parents, as well as in cases where such citizens for other reasons were left without parental care, in particular, when parents evade their education or protection of their rights and interests".

According to article 36, Paragraph 4, of the Civil code of the Republic of Tajikistan of June 30, 1999, "...these institutions are the Trustees of citizens who are or are placed"... in appropriate educational, medical institutions, social protection institutions or other similar institutions...".

The age limit for guardianship of minors in the Republic of Tajikistan is set out in Article 34. Civil code of the Republic of Tatarstan of June 30, 1999: "...guardianship is established over minors aged from fourteen to eighteen years...". **There is no age limit for the appointment of guardianship over adult citizens**, and guardianship can be established at any age over adult citizens "... limited by the court in capacity due to abuse of alcoholic beverages, narcotic drugs, potent or other intoxicating substances" (in the wording of the law of the Republic of Tatarstan from 18.03.2015, No. 1178).

10.7 De-institutionalization

In Tajikistan, placing a child in a residential institution is a priority form of placement of children, including a priority form of placement of vulnerable children, including children with disabilities, and support for large and low-income families by the state. Insufficient support for vulnerable families by the state, which forces children of single mothers, low-income families, families of migrant workers, families with children with disabilities to be placed in boarding schools, leads to violations of children's rights to life and upbringing in a family environment.

In Tajikistan, mostly children in boarding schools are "social orphans" i.e. they have one or both parents. However, due to the fact that their status is not regulated, and the parents are not deprived of parental rights, such children can not be arranged in other families.

An equally important reason for the institutionalization of children is the low awareness of the community about the negative impact of the institutional environment on the social and mental development of the child and the lack of alternative social services. Deinstitutionalization is not currently considered a priority by the Government, despite the recommendations of the UN Committee on the rights of the child. In addition, the gatekeeping system is not fully functional. The problems are that the child rights Departments lack staff (there is no one responsible for the family structure), and the existing staff has a low capacity to conduct a full assessment of the situation of the child and the family, and children are simply sent to orphanages and boarding schools.

The Ministry of Health and Social Protection supported the initiative of international non-governmental organizations Caritas Germany and "Handicap/Interneyshl" on the implementation of a project aimed at the development of social services at the community level for people with disabilities, including for children with disabilities to provide services at the local level. In order to teach parents with children with disabilities how to care for such children a children's early intervention center "Kishti Center for Disabled Children" was opened in 2013 located at the entrance to one of the largest orphanage institutions in Dushanbe. The center provides support to parents to prevent abandonment of disabled children and provides different types of therapy, counseling and crisis intervention. One of the most profound benefits of the Kishti Center is a sense of fellowship, acceptance and support that is provided to the parents of disabled children.

10.8 Challenges for the Future

In Tajikistan, to date, there is no systematic approach or clear legislative regulation in the field of child protection, rehabilitation of children/adolescents who have come into conflict with the law, or previously were in conflict with the law or protection from child labor. Institutionalization of children, especially disabled children, is still a primary form of services.

Data on child abuse, neglect, abandonment of children is not readily available and therefore it is difficult to use data to influence policy.

There are a very small number of state centers in the country, where children who have come into conflict with the law, or previously were in conflict with the law, can receive rehabilitation services (psychologist, social worker, lawyer, medical worker), as well as domestic and material assistance and support.

Establishing effective coordination between responsible state bodies, cooperation and coordination between state bodies and non-governmental organizations to create a full and effective system of rehabilitation of children in conflict with the law, the treatment of disabled children and addressing labor exploitation of children is a major problem at the present stage and one of the main tasks in the future.

Chapter 11
Turkmenistan

Shohrat Orazov

11.1 Introduction

The country of Turkmenistan is one of the largest but most sparsely populated countries in Central Asia. Bordered on one side by the Caspian Sea, it is largely situated within the Karakum Desert. Mysterious Indo-European tribes roamed the territory in ancient times; Alexander the Great, Ghengis Khan and Tamerlane laid claim to the land at various points in history. Like much of Central Asia, the Russian Empire incorporated portions of present-day Turkmenistan in the nineteenth century by building the Transcaspian Railway that followed the Silk Road. In 1924 Turkmen became a republic of the Soviet Union; on October 27, 1991 Turkmenistan declared independence. For centuries the inhabitants of the territory were nomadic tribes; the current population is evenly divided between rural and urban environments. 50% of the population is under the age of 30 years; the capital city is Ashgabat.

11.1.1 Social Protection of Children

Social protection and child protection are closely intertwined. Income or in-kind support helps to address poverty and economic shocks and programs that increase access to services (such as health, education and nutrition) also help to realize the important human rights of children and families. Social protection is also an effective policy tool in addressing adverse economic conditions and strengthening the resilience of children, families and communities to deal with future uncertainty. While reducing income poverty and smoothening economic shocks, social protection also

S. Orazov (✉)
Ashgabat, Turkmenistan

I. Earner, A. Telitsyna (eds.), *The Development of Child Protection Systems in the Post-Soviet States*, Child Maltreatment 12,
https://doi.org/10.1007/978-3-030-59588-3_11

addresses social vulnerability, taking into account the inter-relationship between exclusion and poverty.

UNICEF perceives social protection as a powerful tool to achieve greater progress in child outcomes, especially for vulnerable and disadvantaged children and their families. Investing in children means an investment in the future. Child sensitive social protection does not only benefit the children, allowing them to develop to their full potential. Improving child outcomes also means an investment in the future of a country, as better educated, nourished and healthier children become better educated, healthier and also more productive adults, who are less exposed to social and economic risks and are more resilient to face future uncertainties. In this respect, social protection is a powerful tool in reducing social and economic inequalities.

In order to respond to the global economic change and smooth the effects of the transition from planned to market economy, the Government of Turkmenistan has embarked on a comprehensive economic, social and political reform process since 2007. This reform process encompasses social protection, reflecting the commitment of the Turkmen government to reach vulnerable groups and accelerate social development. Recent favorable economic growth has allowed the government to substantially increase public spending on social policy, including measures targeting families and children.

11.2 Regulatory Framework

According to the constitution of Turkmenistan all citizens are entitled to social security payments in connection with old age, illness, disability, loss of ability to work, loss of a breadwinner and unemployment.

These entitlements are specified in a set of different legal frameworks, notably

Social Security Code (2007): It provides the main regulatory framework for the provision of social protection, including insurance, social allowances, as well as state benefits. It regulates all aspects of social protection, including eligibility, the calculation of benefits, as well as modes of delivery for different target groups and contingencies (old age, childcare, disability, loss of breadwinner, loss of employment, pregnancy, etc.).

The code defines social protection as follows "*Social protection represents the state system of material provision and social service of non-able-bodied people, disabled and families with children* and others through payments in the form of pensions, state benefits and social allowances[1]" (New code on social protection, 2012).

The development of the code in 2007 provided a major milestone regarding the social protection for children and families, including children with disabilities. A

[1]Own translation.

child birth grant and a child care allowances have been introduced, the size of disability allowances significantly increased. The Code also guarantees access to education and vocational training programmes, as well as to individual rehabilitation programmes and employment opportunities for people with disabilities.

The code has gone through a series of amendments, the most recent one (2012) being the result of a major pension reform.[2] The recent changes have also seen the introduction of a voluntary cumulative pension scheme with the objective to increase the number of insured workers who are working outside the formal labour market.

The provision of social benefits and social allowances in Turkmenistan seems to be quite extensive compared to its neighbouring countries in the region, which given the broad resource base of the country does not come as a surprise. However, the principle of subsidiarity, in particular in the form of family support is also emphasized on in the Social Security Code which confirms the role of the extended family as a key stakeholder in the provision of social support in the country.

Labor Code (2009): The labor code contains a whole set of regulations concerning overall employment conditions including important social protection measures. In 2009, the code has been substantially amended. As a result of the UN-conventions on prevention of child labour and the convention on the rights of the people with disabilities that Turkmenistan has ratified in 2005 and 2008 respectively, the code has been expanded to provide regulations on workers younger than 18 and workers with disabilities. Furthermore the labour rights of women have been substantially improved, including regulations that allow women to work shifts and go on duty travel which before severely limited the employability of women. The code also contains a regulation stipulating equal salaries for both men and women in the same labour branch. It also sets a basic minimum income for public enterprises (currently at 440 TTM). For the first time, the law guarantees also equal labour rights to citizens working for private employers, home-workers and employees of religious associations.

Family Code (2012): The recently amended family code stipulates the right of families to receive support from the state, including family allowances, housing and maternity, paternity and child protection policies. In compliance with international standards, the definition of childhood has been extended from hitherto 0–16 to 0–18. This has major impacts on other regulatory frameworks, including education and social protection. While in education the extension of mandatory education until 18 is already under way, the social security code has not yet been adapted. This concerns in particular the payment periods for allowances and social benefits targeting children. So is the disability allowance for children currently paid out until the age of 16 only.

Turkmenistan has also signed a range of international conventions. In terms of children's rights, Turkmenistan has ratified the United Nations Convention on

[2]Due to the recent reform of the Turkmen pension system, which has changed from a classical *pay-as-you-go* scheme to a notional defined contribution scheme and

the Rights of the Child and its two Optional Protocols, as well as the Convention on the Rights of Persons with Disabilities and its optional protocol. It also committed to the principles and goals of the Millennium Development Summit and UN Special Session on Children.

The changes that have been made to the national legislative framework, in the Law on Guarantees of the Rights of the Child (2002), the Child Labour Law (2005), as well as the new family code, the labour code and the law of education are direct consequences of this.

In addition, there are several national development strategy papers which identify focus areas for social and economic development over the next 15–20 years: The national development strategy, 'National Programme of the President of Turkmenistan on the Development of Social and Living conditions of people residents in villages, communities, towns and regional centres for the period up to 2020' which aims at increasing the living standards of the population, in particular in rural areas, and the 'National Programme for Social and Economic Development of Turkmenistan for the period 2011–2030' with the overall goal of strengthening the human capacity development of the country.

An important policy document for social protection for children is the early childhood development programme which has been developed as part of the 2020 strategy and its priority on human capacity development. Aiming at improving the learning and development capacity of children from an early age onwards, the early childhood development programme focuses on increasing the number of children in pre-school facilities. In addition, the programme aims at the establishment of integrated services for young children and their families in order to prevent developmental delays in children through parental counselling. It also foresees the introduction of inclusive education models in pre-school facilities.

This very comprehensive and advanced legislative framework in terms of child protection standards is however, stands in stark contrast with its very low implementation level. The existence of a legislative framework is an important pre-condition for implementing concrete policy measures. More importantly it guarantees a rights-based approach to social protection and social security guaranteeing citizens a certain independence of the windfalls of politics and donor support. However, it appears that in Turkmenistan there is a strong discontinuity between the development of the legislative framework and its transformation into concrete policy measures.

A report by UNICEF Turkmenistan on institutions dealing with child rights mentions three major obstacles to the realisation of child-based policies: (a) the weak implementation of laws and policies due to a limited capacity of institutions of executive power and poor cross-sectoral coordination, (b) lack of a human-rights culture in which children are viewed as personality with inherent dignity and, (c) weak ordinary citizens' and civil society organizations' engagement in exacting accountability.

11.3 Institutional Framework of Social Protection of Turkmenistan

The various ministries responsible for social protection elements play critical roles in the development and implementation of social policies. *TheMinistry of Labour and Social Protection* (MLSP) is responsible for core elements of social protection, particularly in terms of vulnerability and social exclusion as well as in terms of labour market protection. MLSP has recently gone through a reform process. By Presidential decree dated of 8 April 2011, former Ministry of Social Welfare has been renamed into Ministry of Labour and Social Protection of Turkmenistan (MLSP), which expanded the functions of Ministry to cover the issues of employment, labour, and occupational health and safety. This is a clear indication of the importance the government now gives to employment issues.

As part of the Ministry's structure, Pension Fund was established to ensure implementation of rights of citizens for social protection, state social insurance and pension insurance through provision of pensions, state allowances and other cash benefits.[3] At the regional and local levels the respective departments of the Pension Fund are responsible for the management and implementation of social protection programs at their level of jurisdiction.

Under the structure of the Ministry, a network of Labour Exchange offices established at local level to provide job search assistance for unemployed and to maintain a register of individuals in need of social benefits. In 2010, there were 110,670 officially registered job seekers (25% women). In the same year, 74,255 people found employment (23.8% women and 76.2% men). Of the total number of people registered in 2010, 67% found employment (62.7% of women).[4] However, there is no data on whether the data is disaggregated based on family status and number of children in families in need of job search assistance.

The institutional reform in the social protection sector implies streamlining the linkages and better coordination of employment issues, social assistance and social services. This will also have certain implications on human resource and administrative capacity of the newly established Ministry, a challenge yet to be addressed in the near future.

In addition to the key social protection institutions mentioned above, there is a number of other ministries and public agencies, which have responsibilities in their respective domains for protection of family and child rights and service delivery (Ministry of Health and Medical Industry, Ministry of Education, Ministry of Finance, Ministry of Interior, Youth Organization, Women's Union, local state

[3]Regulation N 11991 on Turkmenistan Pension Fund, January 6, 2011.

[4]Turkmenistan: Overview of vocational education and training and the labour market, European Training Foundation, 2012.

administrations and commissions on minors, guardianship and trusteeship bodies and commissions of state support), and local self-governance bodies.[5]

Ministry of Health and Medical Industry (MOHMI) is responsible for implementation of state healthcare programmes and provision of healthcare services to population as well as undertakes the functions related to approval of state norms and standards in healthcare system, infrastructure development, monitoring of provision of population with drugs and quality health services. MOHMI is also assigned with provision of medical services for disabled and older people in special facilities such as infant homes for children under the age of three and a neuropsychiatric child's home.

The Ministry of Education (MoE) is the lead advisor to the Government on the education system, covering early childhood, primary, secondary, upper-secondary education and higher education. The Ministry also has a role in administering the institutions for children without parental care.

The *Ministry of Finance* plays several important roles in the areas of policy formulation, resource allocation and coordination. These various ministries have certain implementation responsibilities for which harmonized delivery systems may improve effectiveness and efficiency.

In addition, there are several **specialized bodies**, such as the commission on minors, guardianship and trusteeship bodies, as well as the commissions of state support at sub-regional (etrap) level. They are attached to the local state administration. The commission of state support at the sub-regional level has an important oversight function regarding the application process for social allowances. In an effort to improve the efficiency of administrative processes in delivering social allowances, this institution might be removed.

According to a UNICEF report on the role and effectiveness of child rights institutions there are around 100 **NGOs** in Turkmenistan that provide social support and social services. However, this estimate appears to be fairly high. They are quasi NGOS that are government sponsored or otherwise supported by the government, such as the National Association of the Blind and the Deaf who have extensive specialized programmes for their target group, including a special boarding school and special workshops. The Youth Organization of Turkmenistan and the Women's Union play an important advocacy role in the provision of support.

The local councils or ***Gengeshes*** provide support to the local community in a range of matters. They are not part of the government systems, but act as a quasi -local self -government structure to central government. They consist of a communal council which is elected for a period of 5 years. Council members usually are the most important stakeholders in a community, including doctors, teachers and representatives of the famers' association. Depending on the size of the community, a

[5]See more detailed information on insitutions dealing with child and family protection issues in the report "Roles and Effectiveness of Child-Rights Accountability Institutions in Turkmenistan", UNICEF Turkmenistan, 2012.

council may have 9 and 11 members. In addition, the state employs 3 to 4 civil servants who are in charge of the administrative tasks. These include amongst others the issuing of birth certificates, solving issues in regard water or gas supply, soliciting of funds for infrastructure measures with the sub-regional level (etrap). To a certain extent they can be compared to a one-stop-shop for citizens for accessing services for which they would otherwise need to travel to the next larger municipality. Local Councils also play a role in identifying extra resources at local level for ad-hoc support needed, such as improvement of local infrastructure or support for the poorer families in the community. In regard social protection they have a very important role in as much as people use to apply with them for social transfers and social services.

11.4 Social Protection: Cash Transfers

Turkmenistan inherited quite developed system of administration of social transfers, which were primarily geared towards the provision of pensions for the elderly. However, the state policy of family support has been broadly reflected in a number of state benefits to ensure economic support and wellbeing of families.

There are few universal benefit schemes delivering in-cash, exclusively targeting children and families, which is extensively described in Table 11.1.

Social protection of the most vulnerable groups of population has also envisaged cash benefits to support vulnerable groups such as orphans and disabled.

Table 11.1 Cash benefits for children and families

Type of benefit	Description
Maternity leave	100% of earnings (56 days before and after the expected date of childbirth). State benefit for maternity leave shall be calculated based on the average monthly and the average daily wage for the last 12 calendar months, which preceding the month of maternity leave. State maternity benefit is paid to women at a time of prenatal and postnatal periods at the place of their primary work (service). (Social Security Code, article 83)
Childbirth grant	Birth grant is paid as a lump sum to one of the parents, foster parent or guardian regardless of whether parents are employed or not. In case of the birth of two or more children at one time allowance is paid for each child. The size of the birth grant is: For each of the first two children—1.3 times the size of base value For the third child—2.5 times the size of base value For the fourth child—5 times the size of base value
Child care allowance	State benefit for child care is established for each child up to 3 years in the amount of 65% of the base value established for the calculation of public benefits State benefit for child care is paid on a monthly basis to one of the parents, foster parent or guardians
Survivor pension for half orphans	Survivor's pension is calculated based on the number of dependents and the base value established for the calculation of the minimum pension, and is: For one dependent—65% For two dependents—125% For three dependents—145% For four dependents—170%
Sickness benefit	Persons who temporarily lost labour ability during the period of employment due to a general medical condition, employment injury (trauma), occupational disease and who submitted medical certificate issues by the health care institution are entitled to state benefits for temporary disability State benefit for temporary disability shall be calculated based on the value obtained by multiplying the average daily wage and the number of calendar days of temporary disability. Regardless of the length of work experience the benefit is paid at 100% of the value, among other groups specified in law, to a person under 18 years of age; and the mother who is raising a disabled child under 16 years, or with dependent three or more children under the age of 16 years
Tax breaks Other	Income tax exemption of 50 TMM per child for the families with children An annual provision to young people of under 23 years of age attending school or a higher learning institution to purchase school related items

Base value is a standard, which is applied for calculation of state benefits. It is approved by Ministry of Finance and Cabinet of Minister of Turkmenistan. The recent base value is equal to 150 TMM

Survivor allowance for full orphans	1 child—1.5 times the size of base amount 2 children—2.3 times the size of base amount 3 children and more—2.9 times the size of base amount
Disability (with onset of partial or total disability)	Size of the disability benefit is a percentage of the base value established for the calculation of state benefits, and is: (1) children with disabilities under the age of 16 years—160% (2) disabled from childhood first, second and third groups—200% (3) persons with disabilities who do not have work record (length of service): (a) 1st group—160% (b) 2nd group—140% (c) 3rd group—120% Disabled of 1st and 2nd groups, with dependent minor children are entitled to supplement payment for each child in the amount of 20% of the base value Disabled people of 1st group and lonely visually impaired disabled of 2nd group, who are in need of outside help, are entitled to supplement allowance for caretaking at 20% of base value Disabled workers are entitled to 30 days of unpaid leave Parents with a disabled child are given a priority in scheduling vacation period and also entitled to a day-off once a month at any convenient time

11.4.1 Challenges

Turkmenistan faces numerous challenges in addressing the social protection of children. The situation of children is often reflective of overall socio-economic conditions. While education is free there is unequal access across the country which leaves children of minorities and those living in remote rural areas at disadvantage. The Ministry of Education has implemented educational reforms at the primary and secondary level which has been restructured to reflect Western influences in order to make graduates competitive on the global market.

Child labor remains a problem, especially in the agricultural areas where children are routinely expected to work alongside adults.

Children under the age of six represent 16%; 7–15 years 75% and over 16.9%. Disabled children are routinely institutionalized in specialized boarding school.

Chapter 12
Ukraine

Galina Bevz, Tatyana Melnychuk, Yulia Melnychuk, Nadezhda Kondratyuk, and Yulia Udovenko

12.1 Introduction: Ukraine

The country of Ukraine is the second largest in Europe. Since the Middle Ages the territory of present-day Ukraine was the seat of Slavic culture and power. Fragmented by the thirteenth century, a Cossack republic emerged in the seventeenth century but, was again split between Poland and the Russian Empire. After World War II the entire country became a part of the Soviet Union. On August 24, 1991 Ukraine declared independence.

G. Bevz
Laboratory of Communication Psychology, Institute of Social and Political Psychology of the National Academy of Sciences of Ukraine, Kiev, Ukraine

T. Melnychuk
Laboratory of Social Psychology, Institute of Psychology named after G. S. Kostyuk APN of Ukraine, Kiev, Ukraine

Y. Melnychuk
Decision Coordination Department, European Court of Human Rights, Coordinating the Implementation of Decisions of the European Court of Human Rights and Informing the Committee of Ministers of the Council of Europe, European Court of Human Rights of the Ministry of Justice of Ukraine, Kyiv, Ukraine

N. Kondratyuk (✉)
Association of Mentoring for Children and Youth, Mentoring Programs in Ukraine, Kyiv, Ukraine

Y. Udovenko
Department of Social Rehabilitation and Social Pedagogy, Taras Shevchenko National University of Kyiv, Kyiv, Ukraine

I. Earner, A. Telitsyna (eds.), *The Development of Child Protection Systems in the Post-Soviet States*, Child Maltreatment 12,
https://doi.org/10.1007/978-3-030-59588-3_12

12.2 The Context of Child Protection

The historical path of society's attitude to children began quite pragmatically: children were interpreted in terms of objectivity: they were an exchange fund, they were sold, and in a situation of undesirability, they were killed (Firsov 2007). The period of childhood began to be singled out as special only from the sixteenth century, and in the twentieth century began the discussion about children receiving the status of subjectivity as bearers of law. The recognition of the child's subjectivity has led to a revision of a number of norms related to culture, everyday life, family relations, social and legal relations. In the arena of social life, the child was periodically viewed as a value, the weight of which began to grow steadily over the years, up to the point of "shifting" towards "super-value" with subordination and competition with the position of self-sufficiency of the adult. Historically, the dynamics of changes in the attitude to the child and its place in society can significantly swing the pendulum of social development, initiating one or another trends. The environmental integration of *child safety issues* into the system itself will help to balance these processes.

Scientific views on the historical development of the protection of children's rights from the end of the nineteenth century to the 1920s are divided into two groups. The first group includes legal studies based on trends aimed at combating child crime and limiting parental authority. To the second—the views of teachers who pointed to the need for free development of the child's personality, the recognition of the child's right to individuality, the right to creative development, the need to replace punishments with educational measures.

The modern stage began with the adoption of the UN Convention On the Rights of the Child (1991), which is associated with the growing attention of scientists to the problems of protecting the rights and freedoms of the child. Modern research is characterized by the recognition of the child as an object of special protection and guardianship, which in the process of development becomes an active subject of the rights and freedoms that belong to it.

12.3 Child Protection in Ukraine

The Constitution of Ukraine (article 51) declares that "the family, childhood, motherhood and fatherhood are protected by the state". In Ukraine, a system of state and local government bodies has been formed to address issues of ensuring the rights of the child, as well as to help prevent negative phenomena in the child's environment. This is in line with the requirements of article 3 of the UN Convention on the rights of the child, according to which States parties must ensure that institutions, services and bodies responsible for the care or protection of children meet the standards established by the competent authorities, in particular in the field of safety and health and in terms of the suitability of their personnel, as well as competent supervision.

In recent years, the state system of child protection in Ukraine has undergone a number of reorganizations. So, during the years of independence of our state, issues of child protection were in the departments of various ministries—the Ministry of education and science, the Ministry of family Affairs, youth and sports, and the Ministry of social policy.

Ensuring the implementation of the requirements of the Convention, as well as responding to new challenges to children's rights, Ukraine is constantly improving the state system of child protection. Today, the issues of ensuring the rights of the child are assigned to the competence of several ministries and departments, among which the main one is the Ministry of Social Policy of Ukraine.

In Ukrainian legislation, the term "*childhood*" is provided for only in one legal document-the Law of Ukraine "on child protection" (Law of Ukraine "on child protection" 2001). Thus, the concept of "childhood" is understood as "the period of human development before reaching adulthood". The term "*child*" provided in several legal acts including the Law of Ukraine "On state assistance to families with children", the Law of Ukraine "On citizenship of Ukraine", Law of Ukraine "On protection of childhood", the Law of Ukraine "On combating human trafficking" and the decree of the Ministry of internal Affairs of Ukraine "on approval of the Instruction about the procedure for interaction between the Ministry of internal Affairs of Ukraine and Administration of State border service of Ukraine concerning the acceptance and return of the children to the country of permanent residence," the Family code of Ukraine and the Civil code of Ukraine. According to this law, a "child" is a person under the age of 18 (of majority) who, according to the law, does not acquire the rights of an adult earlier. In Ukrainian legislation, there are some grounds on which a child acquires the rights of an adult earlier, and is actually deprived of the status of "child" (Law of Ukraine "on child protection" 2001).

One of the main directions of every modern state in the world, both in national legislation and taking into account international treaties, is the protection of the rights of the child and childhood in general. The Convention on the rights of the child (hereinafter referred to as the Convention) is the first and main binding international legal instrument dealing with a wide range of children's rights.

By resolution of the Supreme Council of Ukraine No. 789-XII of February 27, 1991, Ukraine ratified the Convention, which entered into force for our state on September 27, 1991 (Convention on the rights of the child 1989). Also, in 2003 and 2005, respectively, the Ukrainian Parliament ratified the two optional protocols to the Council of Europe Convention on measures to combat trafficking in persons, child prostitution and child pornography and on participation in armed conflict, which have since become part of national legislation (Council of Europe Convention 2005). In addition, the main legal acts regulating children's rights in Ukrainian legislation are the Constitution of Ukraine, the Family code of Ukraine, the Civil code of Ukraine and the Laws of Ukraine "on child protection", "on ensuring organizational and legal conditions for social protection of orphaned children and children deprived of parental care" (Civil code of Ukraine 2003; Law of Ukraine

2005; Law of Ukraine "on child protection" 2001; Constitution of Ukraine 1996; Family code of Ukraine 2002). Our state also has a number of other ratified instruments, including the United Nations Convention on the elimination of all forms of discrimination against women (12 March 1981), the Convention on the prohibition and immediate action for the elimination of the worst forms of child labour (5 October 2000), the optional Protocol to the Convention on the rights of the child on the sale of children, child prostitution and child pornography (3 April 2003), The United Nations Convention against transnational organized crime (4 February 2004), the optional Protocol to the Convention on the rights of the child on the involvement of children in armed conflict (23 June 2004), the Convention on cybercrime (from September 7, 2005).

At the same time, five priority areas for ensuring the rights of the child, defined by the Council of Europe Strategy on the rights of the child (2016–2021), are crucial for Ukraine: (1) equal opportunities for all children; (2) participation of all children; (3) a life free of violence for all children; (4) justice is friendly to all children; (5) child rights in the digital environment (Council of Europe strategy in support of children's rights 2016). The action plan for the implementation of the Council of Europe Strategy on children's rights for 2018–2021, approved by the Committee of Ministers of the Council of Europe in cooperation with Ukraine, provides for one of the main goals of protecting and promoting children's rights (The action plan of the Council of Europe for Ukraine 2018). Children are a special category whose status and well-being depend not only on the volume of available resources and investment in their development, but also directly on the actions and decisions of families, society, and the choice of priorities of the state's policy on the distribution of resources. Therefore, the elimination of various types of child deprivation, ensuring full-fledged conditions for the development of each child is possible through the introduction of effective and transparent policy instruments and the creation of a full-fledged institutional environment (Cherenko et al. 2009).

The rights and freedoms of the child are legal ways of realizing their interests, that is, the interests of the child are a broader concept than rights and freedoms, because they are claims to social benefits that are not always covered by the content of rights and freedoms. The age characteristics of the child can be divided into two types:

1. The interests of the child that he is not aware of are subjectively determined needs of the child in favorable conditions of its existence and development. Such interests of the child are realized through the fulfillment or observance by the parents or persons replacing them of the rights of the child and their obligations under the law;
2. The interests of the child, which he is aware of, are subjectively determined needs of the child in favorable conditions of its existence and development, which can be provided by parents, or persons replacing them, as well as by the child himself through the implementation of his rights and freedoms.

Thus, in the Law of Ukraine "On protection of childhood" defined the concept of "best interests of the child", which is understood as the actions and decisions aimed at meeting the individual needs of the child according to his age, sex, health status, special needs, life experiences, family, culture and ethnicity and consider the views of the child, if he reached an age and level of development that can Express the (Law of Ukraine "on child protection" 2001).

According to this Law, the concept of "*child protection*" is defined as a system of state and public measures aimed at ensuring a full life, comprehensive upbringing and development of the child and protecting his rights. The purpose of legislation on child protection is to expand social and legal guarantees for children, ensure the physical, intellectual and cultural development of the younger generation, and create social, economic and legal institutions to protect the rights and legitimate interests of children in Ukraine. All children on the territory of Ukraine, regardless of race, skin color, gender, language, religion, political or other beliefs, national, ethnic or social origin, property status, health status and birth of children and their parents (or persons replacing them) or any other circumstances, have equal rights and freedoms as defined by this Law and other legal acts. The state guarantees all children equal access to free legal aid necessary to ensure the protection of their rights, on the grounds and in accordance with the procedure established by the law regulating the provision of free legal aid.

In accordance with the Law of Ukraine "on bodies and services for children and special institutions for children" of 24 January 1995, coordination of the work of all Executive authorities in addressing issues of social protection of children and organizing work to prevent child neglect is carried out by the services for children (Law of Ukraine "on bodies and services for children and special institutions for children" 1995). Therefore, if a violation of children's rights is detected, it is first necessary to report it to the children's service. The main tasks of children's services are:

- work on social and legal protection of children, prevention of neglect and delinquency among them, and social and psychological rehabilitation of the most vulnerable categories of children;
- monitoring the conditions of children's maintenance and upbringing in institutions for orphans and children deprived of parental care, special institutions and social protection institutions for children, regardless of their form of ownership;
- keeping records of children in difficult circumstances, orphaned children and children deprived of parental care;

  – ensuring the placement of orphans and children deprived of parental care, and others.

Shelters and centers for the social and psychological rehabilitation of children are subordinate to the children's services.

In accordance with the Laws of Ukraine "on social work with families, children and youth" of 21 June 2001 and "on social services" of 17.01.2019, social work with families, children and youth, the provision of social services to them is carried out by the Centers of social services for families, children and youth (Law of Ukraine "on social work with families, children and youth" 2001; Law of Ukraine "on social services" 2019). The main tasks of the centers are (Resolution of the Cabinet of Ministers of Ukraine 2013):

- carrying out social and preventive work aimed at preventing difficult life circumstances of families, children and youth;
  - conducting an assessment of the needs of individuals in order to determine the types and volumes of services;
- implementation of social inspection, support, rehabilitation, maintenance and other measures to restore social functions, psychological and physical condition of families, children and youth in difficult life circumstances and in need of assistance;
  - training of candidates for foster parents, parents-educators, guardians, Trustees, improving their skills, and others.

The centers of social services for families, children and youth control and coordinate the work of social dormitories for orphaned children and children deprived of parental care, and social centers for mothers and children.

In addition to the above-mentioned main state bodies, there is an extensive network of other state bodies in Ukraine that also have the responsibility to take care of children, in particular:

- *the educational and scientific bodies* that provide educational services have a whole system of state educational institutions under their control;
  - *health authorities* that provide medical examination, treatment and prevention of children's diseases. At the disposal of these structures are medical, medical, sanatorium and other institutions.
- *social protection agencies* that provide all types of state assistance to children and families with children and have institutions for children with disabilities under their control;
  - *authorized divisions of internal Affairs bodies* that work to prevent offenses among children, conduct activities to solve criminal crimes committed by children, search for children, work with parents who evade their duties, and so on. These structures are subordinate to the receivers-distributors for children;
- *state Executive services* that ensure the recovery of alimony from parents who evade the upbringing and maintenance of their children;
  - Prosecutor's offices that monitor compliance with the law and the implementation of legislation in the field of children's rights protection;
  - Judicial bodies that consider cases and make decisions to protect the rights and interests of children.

However, as practice shows, despite the existence of an extensive system of bodies and services designed to ensure the rights of the child, their rather large number, the rights of the child in many cases remain unprotected, in particular, due to the lack of certainty of areas of competence, duplication of functions, unavailability and lack of transparency of services, low level of competence and responsibility of employees.

The main directions of state policy in the field of protection of children's rights are:

- health care and promotion of a healthy lifestyle for children;
- providing quality education and upbringing;
- improving the economic conditions of children's life;
- increasing the effectiveness of the state support system for children in difficult situations.

The law of Ukraine "on ensuring organizational and legal conditions for the social protection of orphans and children deprived of parental care" of 13 January 2005 No. 2342 defines the legal, organizational, social bases and guarantees of state support for orphans and children deprived of parental care, and is an integral part of legislation on child protection.

Article 1 of this Law defines the following terms (Law of Ukraine 2005):

- *the status of an orphan child and a child deprived of parental care* is a child's status determined in accordance with the law, which grants him the right to full state support and benefits provided for by law, and which is confirmed by a set of documents certifying the circumstances under which the child does not have parental care;
- the status of children—an orphan child and a child deprived of parental care:
  - *an orphan child* is a child whose parents have died or died;
  - *children deprived of parental care*—children left without parental support in connection with deprivation of their parent rights taken away from the parents without deprivation of parental rights, recognition of parents is unknown absent or incapacitated, their announcement died, serving the sentence in places of imprisonment and their stay under guards during the investigation, tracing their internal Affairs agencies connected with evasion from payment of the alimony and lack of information about their location, prolonged sickness of parents that prevent them from fulfilling their parental responsibilities, and children separated from their families, abandoned children whose parents are unknown, children abandoned by their parents, and street children;
- *forms of placement of orphans and children deprived of parental care*—adoption; establishment of guardianship, guardianship; transfer to a foster family, a family-type orphanage, institutions for orphans and children deprived of parental care:

- *adoption*—adoption by the adoptive parent of a child in his family as a daughter or son, carried out on the basis of a court decision. Adoption of a child is carried out in its interests to ensure stable and harmonious living conditions;
- *establishment of guardianship and care*—placement of orphaned children, children deprived of parental care, in families of citizens of Ukraine who are mainly in family, kinship relations with these orphaned children or children deprived of parental care, in order to ensure their upbringing, education, development and protection of their rights and interests. Guardianship is assigned to children under 14 LEM, guardianship is assigned to children from 14 to 18 years;
- *transfer to a foster family*—voluntary acceptance for a fee by a family or an individual who is not married, from institutions for orphans and children deprived of parental care, from one to four children for upbringing and cohabitation;
- *transfer to a family-type children's home*—acceptance into a separate family, which is created at the request of the spouses or an individual who is not married, for the upbringing and cohabitation of at least five orphaned children and/or children deprived of parental care. The total number of children, including relatives, in such a family can not exceed ten people;
- *mentor*—an adult capable person who is engaged in providing a child living in an institution for orphans and children deprived of parental care, another institution for children, individual support and assistance, primarily in preparing for independent life;
- *mentoring* is a voluntary free activity of a mentor to provide a child living in an institution for orphans and children deprived of parental care, another institution for children, with individual support and assistance, primarily in preparing for independent life.
- *institutions for orphans and children deprived of parental care*—medical, educational, educational institutions, other institutions and institutions where orphans and children deprived of parental care live.

Practical activities point to the insufficient resources of existing family forms of education to ensure the realization of the right of every child to be raised in a family, including children with disabilities. The analysis confirms that the number of orphaned children and children deprived of parental care, who are arranged in family forms, significantly exceeds the number of such children in institutional institutions in percentage terms. And state statistics only count "status" children, while parents' children fill boarding schools almost at full capacity.

Despite a certain legal norm on the priority of family forms of education, the number of families of foster caregivers, foster families and family—type orphanages in the field does not allow for the implementation of the rights of children to be raised in a family by 100%. When placing orphaned children and children deprived of parental care in family forms of education, significant difficulties arise with the placement of adolescent children (11–18 years old), children from large families, children with special needs and disabilities. Citizens who want to adopt children prefer healthy children aged from birth to 10 years and intend to raise one or sometimes two children. That is, the current forms of family education for orphaned children are not ready to meet the needs of all children for development and upbringing in the family.

The Institute of the presidential Commissioner for children's rights is functioning in Ukraine. It was established by presidential decree No. 812/2011 of August 11, 2011. The emergence of such an institution has had a positive impact on the overall state of child rights protection in Ukraine. Also, it is worth noting that this Institute now plays a significant role in improving the policy on child protection and protection of children's rights in our country, although its main function is to monitor the situation of child rights in Ukraine, and not to implement the policy. Recommendations based on the monitoring results were used as the basis for Presidential acts that form the state policy on child protection.

Of course, the child, his rights, freedoms and legitimate interests should be the subject of constant attention of the state, society, scientists, teachers and, above all, parents. At the same time, modern philosophical approaches to defining the role of childhood in society are based on the idea of " avoiding design", on understanding the other essence of the relationship " adult–child", based on dialogue and mutual understanding (State policy in the field of health care: Col. monograph 2013).

12.4 Challenges

Studying the issue of unequal opportunities for children in Ukraine, experts identify three interrelated elements: (1) the economic viability of families raising children; (2) the availability of services in the main sectors of the social sphere (health and education) for all categories of children; (3) the possibility of inclusion in the social protection system and obtaining high-quality and effective support from the state for socially vulnerable categories (Unequal opportunities for children in Ukraine: Analysis and recommendations for policy (based on monitoring economic inequality in households and children's access to social services)).

The complexity of the problem requires systematic actions to solve it. Therefore, the government developed and approved the legal strategy for implementing the state policy towards families with children (Decree of the Cabinet of Ministers of Ukraine "On approval of the Concept of State social program" national action plan for the implementation of the UN Convention on the rights of the child for the period up to 2021, from 5 April 2017 No. 230-p) based on the Concept of state family policy of Ukraine since 1999 and the National plan of action for the implementation of the UN Convention on the rights of children.

Resolution of the Cabinet of Ministers of Ukraine of May 30, 2018 No. 453 was approved the program "On endorsement of State target social program" national action plan for the implementation of the UN Convention on the rights of the child "for the period until 2021", which aims to ensure the consistent implementation of the provisions of the UN Convention on the rights of the child, development of an effective system of protection of rights and interests of the child at the level of territorial communities in the conditions of decentralization, creation of child friendly environment in accordance with international standards and priorities of the Strategy of the Council of Europe on the rights of the child (2016–2021), and achieving the Sustainable development Goals approved by UN Resolution 70/1 "Transforming our world: an Agenda for sustainable development to 2030", in terms of children's rights (Resolution of the Cabinet of Ministers of Ukraine dated May 30, 2018).

During the execution of the Program, the following is provided:

- determination of priorities, main tasks and principles of implementation of the state policy in the field of child rights protection;
- development and approval of child welfare and safety standards;
- development of indicators (indicators) at the national and regional levels to ensure the protection of the rights and interests of the child;
- modernization of the system for protecting the rights and interests of the child;
- improvement and harmonization of national legislation in the field of child rights in accordance with international obligations;
- defining the role of the territorial community in the conditions of decentralization of power to ensure the rights and interests of the child;
- ensuring the protection of the rights and interests of the child in situations of war or armed conflict;
- development of a strategy for creating a safe information space for children.

However, for the time being, the implementation of legislative acts, adopted strategies and programs remains almost the main problem for Ukraine. Strategic and policy documents today are mostly declarative. They cover a wide range of activities in various fields of activity, often duplicating each other. Although monitoring of their implementation is carried out, it is often formal, since it does not include specific indicators of the implementation of all tasks. In addition, most strategies and programs do not have targeted funding. Scientists studying the issue of human development in Ukraine have come to the conclusion that one of the most problematic aspects of the social environment, which should be paid attention to, is the spread of social orphanhood. This is the most dangerous is the situation with social orphanhood in Eastern Ukraine, where fighting continues and in Western Ukraine, where a high level of adult employment abroad.

A fairly high priority of the state policy of Ukraine in relation to children who are at risk of social orphanhood is the reorganization of boarding schools, the allocation of resources to prevent children from entering boarding schools and the organization of assistance to families to create appropriate conditions for raising children in blood families. For this purpose, Ukraine has undertaken the development of a number of programs on "Basics of parenting skills", "formation of parental competence", etc.

For orphans and children deprived of parental care, active measures are being taken to adopt children, place them in foster families, family-type orphanages, and provide mentoring for children of adolescent and youth age. Since foster families and family—type orphanages must be a professional sphere of activity with the appropriate requirements, standards, and criteria, it is mandatory for such parents to have professional training at the state level.

In Ukraine, unfortunately, there are no separate specialized courts for conducting family cases or considering cases against minors. However, according to the law of Ukraine "on the judicial system and status of judges", article 18 provides that local General courts and courts of appeal specialize in the implementation of criminal proceedings against minors (paragraph 3). Judges (judges) authorized to conduct criminal proceedings against minors are elected from among the judges of the relevant court by the Assembly of judges of this court on the proposal of the President of the court or on the proposal of any judge of this court, if the proposal of the President of the court was not supported, for a term not exceeding 3 years and may be re-elected A judge who is authorized to conduct criminal proceedings against minors may be elected with at least 10 years' experience as a judge, experience in conducting criminal proceedings in court, and high moral, business and professional qualities. If there are no judges with the necessary work experience in the court, the judge authorized to conduct criminal proceedings against minors is elected from among the judges who have the longest work experience as a judge (paragraph 6).

Today in the Ukrainian state there are more than 700 services for children, but the total number of social workers involved in child protection issues is only about 4000 people.

During the 28 years of independence of the country since 1991, the child population has almost halved and today it is 7,600,000 children. Every third child today lives below the poverty line. At least one in seven children suffer from domestic violence. 150 thousand children have disabilities and cannot go to school or kindergarten. Every second child lives with one of the parents, usually the mother. With the birth of every second child in the family, 80% of families fall below the poverty line. We are in the top rankings for child mortality. Ukraine now ranks 186th in the world in terms of birth rate and 13th in the world in terms of national extinction. Every 50 children live in a special institution like a boarding school. Almost 106,000 children, or 1.5% of the country's total child population, are raised in boarding schools, but only 8% of them are orphans—the remaining 92% have parents. Every 3 days, 250 children are sent to boarding schools mainly because of poverty and the inability to provide the necessary services for the child. Approximately 600,000 children are in the occupied territories. Almost 250,000 children are displaced. About 100 thousand children live in the conflict zone and this is a matter of national security (Commissioner of the President of Ukraine for children's rights N. Kuleba).

On January 19, 2017, the people's deputies adopted the draft law "on amendments to article 4 of the Law of Ukraine" On bodies and services for children and special institutions for children concerning the improvement of the legal status of services for children, one of the necessary normative acts to strengthen the protection of children in Ukraine. And on February 8, 2017, law No. 1824-VIII on strengthening state guarantees for the protection of children's rights was signed.

In Ukraine, on the one hand, there are no specialized courts to ensure the rights of children: family courts, courts for minors, but now there are 10 educational colonies for minors. More than half of the convicted teenagers are between the ages of 14 and 17. A third are serving time for theft, a third for robbery and robbery, and 13% of young prisoners are convicted of premeditated murder. In addition to the specified number of convicts, 70% of the convicts led an asocial lifestyle, 24% of them did not work or study, and 22% were orphans. However, 30% of the convicts were from fairly well-off families. These figures are given by the first Deputy Chairman of the State Department of Ukraine for the execution of sentences Mykola Iltiai (2018).

The specifics of guarantees of the rights and freedoms of the child in Ukraine is that they function through a system of various factors, United by the category of the mechanism for ensuring the rights of the child. Depending on the spheres of activity of society, they are divided into socio-economic, political, spiritual and legal guarantees.

Socio-economic security are the basic measures of a social nature, as well as conditions, ways and means economic system of the state to create the appropriate environment in which a child grows, social stability in society, an adequate standard of living, family education, a broad set of healthcare institutions, the education system, and recognition and equal protection of ownership.

Political guarantees to ensure the rights of the child are the state's policy aimed at ensuring an adequate standard of living for the child, at protecting, implementing and protecting the rights and freedoms of the child.

Spiritual guarantees of the rights and freedoms of the child are a system of spiritual values of society, which are based on the promotion of cultural and intellectual development of the child, the formation of a system of spiritual values and ideological orientations based on respect for their country, human rights and freedoms.

Legal guarantees of the rights and freedoms of the child are ensuring the competence of state bodies and officials in the field of child rights protection, establishing responsibility for violations of the rights and freedoms of the child, as well as the legally established procedure for protecting violated or disputed rights and freedoms of the child, the right to receive qualified legal assistance (divided into guarantees of protection and guarantees of protection).

Examining the process of formation and implementation of state policy in the field of protection of children's rights and welfare in a retrospective analysis, we can talk about significant progress over the years of independence of Ukraine in addressing issues of social protection of children: a number of international legal acts have been ratified, system-defining Ukrainian laws and other legal documents have been adopted, the best foreign experience of developed countries in building a modern national system of child protection is being studied and applied.

However, the existence of a legal framework for the protection of children's rights does not mean that the provisions of Ukrainian legislation are effectively implemented. On the contrary, the practice of the children's Ombudsman shows numerous violations of children's rights. In particular, the analysis of appeals to the presidential Commissioner for children's rights found a growing need for legal protection and protection of children, among which the most typical were: protection of housing and property rights of children; protection of the rights of orphans and children from large families, minors in conflict with the law; protection from violence against children; from threats to the life and health of children in the zone of military conflict; resolution of conflicts between parents about the child's place of residence; complaints about the actions or omissions of local authorities, etc.

Permanent changes in the functions, powers and subordination of state authorities responsible for protecting the rights and welfare of children do not contribute to improving the effectiveness of state policy in this area. The state of implementation of the rights of children from the category of internally displaced persons, children of ATO participants who died or became disabled requires increased attention.

In Ukrainian legislation, sanctions for violations of children's rights are collected in the Family, Criminal and Civil codes, but some violations are not statistically taken into account, which indicates that there are no mechanisms for responding to violations, so a detailed analysis is required by state mechanisms for protecting children's rights.

Thus, respect for children's rights in Ukraine is ensured by increasing public awareness of these rights; the creation of state institutions and institutions to help minors exercise their rights. However, there is still many problems, which are aggravated; the system of child rights protection in Ukraine remains uncoordinated; the responsibility is divided between different ministries and agencies, cooperation between them inefficient. It is possible to solve these problems only by optimizing the functioning of Central and local Executive authorities, coordinating the activities of state and public structures, and close cooperation between officials, scientists, practitioners and the public. The formation and implementation of state policy on the protection of children's rights in Ukraine should be held on legal, regulatory, target-oriented and organizational-administrative levels and rely on legal mechanisms aimed at the early detection, prevention, and, if necessary, and prosecute persons who violate children's rights; on effective government structure that possesses the necessary authority for interagency coordination and implementation of state policy in the sphere of protection of children; the coordination structure of civil society organizations focused on protecting the interests and rights of children; for training, training and accreditation of personnel social workers in the sphere of protection of rights and interests of children and minors; the system of channels and media of communication that allows discussion of socially important problems in the field of the health and safety of children and adolescents, but also influence the formation of public opinion, the functioning of public organizations, in particular those composed of parents and social workers.

Further Prospect In the context of decentralization of power, an approach should be developed to determine the optimal number of services for children, social services to provide social services to families with children at the local level, the number and qualifications of those working in these institutions. The current trend of reducing them in order to save financial resources may lead to a significant, and possibly irreversible, deterioration of child protection indicators in General.

Bibliography

Cherenko, L. M., Polyakova, S. V., Reut, A. G., et al. (2009). Poverty and unequal opportunities for children in Ukraine. In M. Libanova (Ed.), Institute of demography and social science. Research. NAS of Ukraine, Children's. United Nations Foundation (UNICEF), Ukr. Social Center. Reform, 288 p.

Civil code of Ukraine from 16.01.2003 № 435-IV. Retrieved from https://zakon.rada.gov.ua/laws/show/435-15

Constitution of Ukraine from 28.06.1996 № 254k/96-BP. Retrieved from https://zakon.rada.gov.ua/laws/show/254к/96-вр

Convention on the rights of the child of 20.11.1989. Retrieved from https://zakon.rada.gov.ua/laws/show/995_021

Council of Europe Convention on measures to combat human trafficking of 16.05.2005. Retrieved from https://zakon.rada.gov.ua/laws/show/994_858

Council of Europe strategy in support of children's rights (2016–2021). Retrieved from https://rm.coe.int/-2016-2021-/1680931c99

Family code of Ukraine from 10.01.2002 № 2947-II. Retrieved from https://zakon.rada.gov.ua/laws/show/2947-14

Firsov, M. (2007). *History of social work: Studies*. Manual for children. School, Moscow, Publishing House of Acad. Project, 2007.

Hart, P. (1991). *Children's participation*. York: Joseph Rowntree Foundation.

Law of Ukraine "on providing organizational and legal conditions for social protection of orphaned children and children deprived of parental care" dated 13.01.2005 No. 2342. Retrieved from https://zakon.rada.gov.ua/laws/show/2342-15

Law of Ukraine "on bodies and services for children and special institutions for children" of 24.01.1995 N 20/95-BP. Retrieved from https://zakon.rada.gov.ua/laws/main/20/95-%D0%B2%D1%80

Law of Ukraine "on child protection" from 26.04.2001 № 2402-III. Retrieved from https://zakon.rada.gov.ua/laws/show/2402-14

Law of Ukraine "on citizenship of Ukraine" from 18.01.2001 № 2235-III. Retrieved from https://zakon.rada.gov.ua/laws/show/2235-14

Law of Ukraine "on combating human trafficking" dated 20.09.2011 No. 3739-VI. Retrieved from https://zakon.rada.gov.ua/laws/show/3739-17

Law of Ukraine "on social services" from 17.01.2019 № 2671-VIII. Retrieved from https://zakon.rada.gov.ua/laws/show/2671-19

Law of Ukraine "on social work with families, children and youth" dated 21.06.2001 No. 2558-III. Retrieved from https://zakon.rada.gov.ua/laws/main/2558-14

Law of Ukraine "on state assistance to families with children" dated 21.11.1992 No. 2811-XII. Retrieved from https://zakon.rada.gov.ua/laws/show/2811-12

Nichols, M. (2004). *Family therapy: Concepts and methods*. Moscow: EKSMO Publishing House.

Order of the Cabinet of Ministers of Ukraine "on approval of the Concept of the State social program" national action plan for the implementation of the UN Convention on the rights of the child for the period up to 2021, dated April 5, 2017 No. 230-p. Retrieved from https://zakon.rada.gov.ua/laws/show/230-2017-%D1%80

Order of the Ministry of internal Affairs of Ukraine, administration of State border service of Ukraine "On approval of the Instruction about the procedure for interaction between the Ministry of internal Affairs of Ukraine and Administration of State border service of Ukraine concerning the acceptance and return of the children to the country of residence" from 25.11.2003 № 1426/267. Retrieved from https://zakon.rada.gov.ua/laws/show/z1171-03

Resolution of the Cabinet of Ministers of Ukraine dated August 1, 2013 No. 573 "on approval of the General regulations on the center of social services for families, children and youth". Retrieved from https://zakon.rada.gov.ua/laws/main/573-2013-%D0%BF

Resolution of the Cabinet of Ministers of Ukraine dated May 30, 2018 No. 453 "on approval of the State social program" national action plan for the implementation of the UN Convention on the rights of the child "for the period up to 2021". Retrieved from https://www.kmu.gov.ua/npas/pro-zatverdzhennya-derzhavnoyi-socialnoyi-programi-nacionalnij-plan-dij-shodo-realizaciyi-konvenciyi-oon-pro-prava-ditini-na-period-do-2021-roku

Resolution of the Supreme Council of the Ukrainian SSR "on ratification of the Convention on the rights of the child" No. 789-XII, 27.02.1991. Retrieved from https://zakon.rada.gov.ua/laws/show/789-12

State policy in the field of health care: Col. monograph: At 2 o'clock [Col. auth.; comp. Prof. I. F. Radish; pered. and the General editorship of Prof. M. M. Bilinskaya, prof. I. F. Radish]. Moscow: NAGU, 2013. Part 1. – 396 p.

The action plan of the Council of Europe for Ukraine for the years 2018-2021. Retrieved from https://rm.coe.int/coe-action-plan-for-ukraine-2018-2021-ukr/1680925bec

Unequal opportunities for children in Ukraine: Analysis and recommendations for policy (based on monitoring economic inequality in households and children's access to social services) [Electronic resource]. Retrieved from http://www.idss.org.ua/monografii/nerivni%20mojlivosti.pdf

Chapter 13
Uzbekistan

Marifat Ganieva, Nadira Latipova, and Victoria Alekseeva

13.1 Introduction: Overview of Uzbekistan

In ancient times the first known settlers of this high plateau territory in Central Asia were the Scythians, nomads from eastern Iran. In the fourteenth century Tamerlane, who established the Timurid Empire, made Samarkand his capital. During the nineteenth century parts of the area were incorporated into the Russian Empire; in 1924 the territory became the Uzbek Soviet Socialist Republic. Uzbekistan declared independence on August 31, 1991.

The social protection of children is one of the most crucial directions in the social policy of the state. This is motivated both by the need to ensure the wellbeing and protection of all members of society as a whole, and by the necessity of improving the quality of life of vulnerable groups of children, mitigating the consequences of the lack of security, poor health, and economic and social vulnerability, and helping preserve a basic quality of life for everyone.

The implementation of a strong social policy is the chief principle of the national model of market reform in Uzbekistan. A key component of the reforms is the bolstering of the efficiency of the system of social protection for various groups, including families, women, children, and youth.

Marifat Ganieva was deceased.

N. Latipova · V. Alekseeva (✉)
Department of Social Work, National University of Uzbekistan named after Mirzo Ulugbek, Tashkent, Uzbekistan
e-mail: n.latipova@nuu.uz; v.alekseeva@nuu.uz

I. Earner, A. Telitsyna (eds.), *The Development of Child Protection Systems in the Post-Soviet States*, Child Maltreatment 12,
https://doi.org/10.1007/978-3-030-59588-3_13

A system of social protection which is focused on the interests of the child is one grounded in the principle of children's wellbeing, directly linked to the economic, social, and spiritual resources of the family, and the availability of basic services. A functional system of social protection is conducive to the prevention and elimination of social and economic problems for children and their families.

In the past 3 years, the President of Uzbekistan has implemented a number of new laws and decrees aimed at resolving specific social problems, and has tasked the Cabinet and pertinent agencies with taking stronger action to raise the efficiency of social services. In the National Strategy for 2017–2021 the development of the social sector, the provision of security were noted among the country's key political priorities.

Children are a significant socio-demographic group in any society. In a broad sense, children serve the functions of demographic, social, and cultural reproduction, and the renewal of society; in the narrower sense—the functions of development and personal development of the identity of an adult, the satisfaction of a multitude of the most varied needs. From the standpoint of the economy, children are the human capital of society, defining the future of social reproduction, its scale, growth rate, and quality.

Uzbekistan belongs to the list of countries with high rates of natural reproduction. Its high natural population growth is mainly the result of high birth rates among the native population of the republic, which traditionally orients its reproductive behavior towards large numbers of children. Children under the age of 18 comprise 40% of the population of Uzbekistan.

In Uzbekistan the birth of children has been considered, since ancient times, to be a divine gift, the treasure of the family, and the more children there were—especially boys—the more wealth and power the family was seen to possess. These traits of the people are reflected in the proverbs and sayings which express that relationship to a newborn child, love for it and concern for its future: *Bolali uy—bozor, bolasiz uy—mozor* (A house with children—a market, a house without children—a cemetery); *Bol shirin, boldan ham bola shirin* (Honey is sweet, and a child is sweeter than honey); *Davlatning boshi farzand* (Wealth begins with a child).

Despite this reverent attitude towards children, however, in traditional families it was the rearing of children that constituted the family's chief attribute: *Bola aziz, adabi undan aziz* (The child is precious, but the upbringing is more precious). Here, too, we find an element of cultural heritage—the recognition of one's great responsibility for a child's proper upbringing.

A significant indicator of the structure of the contemporary family is the average number of children in the family. The state policy of Uzbekistan is aimed at strengthening the family as a social institution, improving the health of the mother and child, and at the promotion of a healthy lifestyle among the youth, which influences the formation of positive reproductive conditions. It appears that there are more urban families with one or two children, while rural families are more likely to have five or more (Fig. 13.1).

Multigenerational bonds are equally preserved, and the guiding principles of an Uzbek family are the sanctity of marriage, the parents' responsibility for the children's upbringing and the children's debt to their parents, mutual respect and accord, the protection of family honor and dignity. Traditions form an integral part of the Uzbek national culture and way of life, and rank highly in the system of values and beliefs.

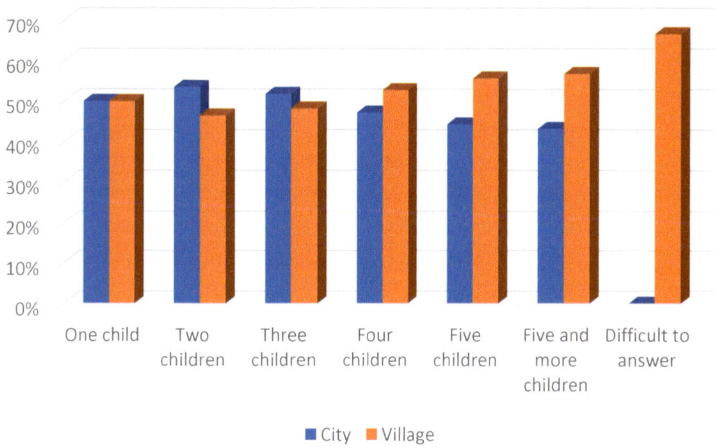

Fig. 13.1 The number of children in the family, depending on the place of residence, in %

13.2 Cultural and Historical Traditions

Care for those in need has taken various forms over the course of its historical development on the territory of contemporary Uzbekistan, ranging from charity to the organization of a state system of social protection. The first instances of social aid were natural impulses, manifesting in care for those who could not support themselves. Such care was largely practiced within clan structures, as household assistance, mutual aid, and the protection of the clan, family, community. The clan structure ideally served to generate solidarity and mutual ties between clan members formed on the basis of tradition.

The tradition of charity, directed at the provision of material aid to the poor, consisted of the willing and uncalculating donation of money, goods, and services to the needy. The ruling motivations behind charitable deeds in the community were both religious and spiritual, guided by the desire to assist the well-being of others on simple humanitarian grounds. It is also important to note that those actions were voluntary and deliberate, and not in the least the result of external pressure.

The first written source that allows us to evaluate the system of social activities is the Avesta—the holy book of Zoroastrianism. It contains information on the structures and social policies of states which practiced the religion. Charity as a means of providing targeted assistance was a traditional mode of conduct for regular citizens, while the clergy and cult organizations took on the functions of social services: the provision of aid and support and the running of charitable events. Rulers, wealthy citizens, and temples set up charitable lunches and alms giving to the poor and to relatives in difficulty. Communities provided material support to families in need from a collective fund.

The distinctive characteristic of the mechanism of social aid in the community was the fact that each person was under the protection of the social structures to which they belonged. Those structured included the family and the community which provided support to their members. In this manner, the most ancient community on the territory of Uzbekistan could in large part resolve such problems as childrearing, employment and leisure, and became a sort of collective center for the provision of social support on the level of the individual, the family, the group.

The Muslim period in the history of the peoples of Central Asia both carried on and diversified the participation of the clergy in social life. Despite the secular form of government, Islamic religious leaders played a significant role in the functioning of the state, and Islamic values would, accordingly, influence the modes of social support provision at the level of the state.

The forms of social support were extended as the community required new types of cultural values. The functions of social support and aid were placed with the mosques, as well as other socio-religious groups. The most common form of individual aid is the Zakat: as one of the five pillars of Islam, it requires each Muslim to give alms to the poor.

Other ethical categories in the socio-cultural system of the country are the *savob* (good deed) and *himmat* solidarity, which served as an 'instrument' for social support. At their core, they indicated that support was provided unselfishly, often in secret. Among the collective forms of social aid, the most frequent were alms, medical support, the organization of special free hospitals.

Ethnocultural traditions have done and continue to bear on childrearing practices. As a result, the latter have come to reflect the dichotomy between East and West. Although both the western and the eastern approaches to childrearing have evolved beyond their dialectically opposed roots, the East continues to take pride in its traditions—in the respect for its elders, the reverence towards ancestors, the polite, if not downright subservient attitude towards adult relatives. In many ways, those represent a correct, sensible mode of conduct, wherein children listen to their parents, respect them, and value the opinions of their elders. In contrast, the childrearing model characteristic of the West is based on tolerance and the development of the child's individuality. The psychologist N. Kozlov argues that what is prioritized there is not the bringing up of the child, but rather the idea that children owe nothing to their parents.

The civil rights and liberties attained in the past decades go hand in hand with spiritual, moral, and ethical values that have evolved over the course of historical development. In this mode, the focus on universal agreement and calm, which manifests, in particular, in the desire to smooth over conflicts and be content with one's lot, is a distinct, inherited trait of the eastern mentality.

One of the traditional forms of local self-government in Uzbekistan is the *makhalla*—the neighborhood commune. The history of the Uzbek makhalla goes back one thousand years, to its root in the provision of social help to those in need. In the community, familial and household customs and rituals are carefully preserved and related, there is moral and material support for widows and their children, and particular attention is given to rearing orphans and teaching them specific crafts.

Contemporary Uzbekistan has not only retained the charitable functions of the makhalla, but also continually works to perfect them. The legal basis to serve that specific purpose, since one of the state priorities that arise from the national model of development of Uzbekistan is the gradual and incremental transference of certain function to local government bodies—and their heart is the makhalla self-governing structure.

Consequently, the makhlalla is becoming a key player in the development of social work. It has become the keeper of the traditions of culture and morality of the Uzbek people, the legally acknowledged mechanism of civic self-governance. The network of over 10,000 makhallas spans the entire country and serves as an important link in the chain of a stronger civil society. The whole population of Uzbekistan considers it to be an effective form of social organization.

The charitable functions of the makhalla are perpetually being refined. Members of the community attempt to bolster young families at times of conflict and divorce. The makhalla committees make every effort to reconcile the spouses before granting the courts the right to rule on the a divorce.

The special role played by the makhalla in the provision of moral and material assistance clearly manifests on days of mourning. The makhalla organizes the funeral, informs the inhabitants of the neighborhood and those close to the deceased, and the chairman of the makhalla personally takes part in and oversees the process. If the grieving family is of low means, then in addition to the aforementioned moral support it also receives a measure of material aid from the makhalla social support fund. As has been made clear, the makhalla is a prime example of targeted social work and assistance.

13.3 Development of System of Social Protection of Children under Soviet Conditions

The systems of state social protection of the population in each country have been shaped in relation to its historical conditions and, in spite of the similarities of social problems, show marked differences in approach, method, and organization.

In Soviet conditions the social protection and support of the population was administered through a system of social security and insurance. That period in the republic saw the formation of a normative and legal basis which mimicked the one that functioned across the USSR, as well as the creation of institutions whose activity was directed towards aiding and supporting children.

The model of social protection that existed in Uzbekistan was financed, in large part, by the state budget (95%) through a system of distribution of social security funds, as in the rest of the country. Alongside institutional children's organizations where children left without parents were brought up, there existed a network of boarding schools with free room and board for children with different profiles, as well as free meals and school clothing for children from poor families.

Alongside pensions and subsidies there existed various other types of provisions, including professional technical training and reeducation for people with disabilities, employment, free prosthetic/orthopedic aid, specialized transportation, etc. Studies show that by the mid-80s, the country had developed a multi-stranded system of social security with clear benefits, which allowed one to feel socially protected and certain of the stability of one's individual situation.

After gaining independence in 1991, Uzbekistan oriented its policies towards economic reform in order for the country to enter the united global space and to build a market economy. During the implementation of market reforms the strategic aims of the government's social policy were, first and foremost, improved quality of life and family and individual welfare. These targets are at the core of both the transitional social policy, and the subsequent reform strategy.

13.4 Development of System of Social Protection of Children in Independent Uzbekistan

From the first years of its independent existence, Uzbekistan has paid particular attention to ensuring the comprehensive protection of the interests of socially vulnerable sectors of the population: low income families and families with many children, elderly people without caregivers, orphans, people with disabilities. A new mechanism for social protection was created to account for the real economic situation, the available resources and capacities.

Among the key directions of the mechanism in Uzbekistan are the formation of a normative and institutional base which can ensure the protection of the rights of all citizens, as assured by the Constitution of the Republic of Uzbekistan and the laws, as well as the creation of a working mechanism and conditions for the activation of the potential of 'social self-defense' and the provision of a normative and institutional base for the targeted protection of specific social sectors. The realization of this policy involves multiple social systems: social insurance, unemployment support, assistance for low-income families, subsidies for particular groups of citizens, etc.

As Uzbekistan was transitioning into a new economic system, the majority of the population found themselves in a very difficult social situation. This led to the development of a system of social security which took into account every step in the shift to a market economy. One of the main principles of the reforms during this transitional stage became the "strong social protection" concept, which was practically implemented through monetary or in-kind payments via the system of social insurance and assistance.

Taken together, the measures taken by the government forestalled a sharp decline in the population's quality of life. The transition to a market economy was likewise not marred by a steep drop in social indicators—in fact, some parameters actually demonstrated growth: there was, for instance, no 'shock' stratification on the basis of income, though the economic reforms did destroy the equalizing distribution of goods and services.

As the economic reforms intensified, a mechanism of targeted social protection which supposed the identification of the most vulnerable groups was implemented with the mentality and lifestyle of the people in mind. The central part in the mechanism is played by the traditional institution of local self-governance, the makhalla, which allocates aid to those most in need. Such an approach has centuries-old roots in the population and ensures the most targeted distribution of resources meant for the support of vulnerable segments of the population. It does not, however, diminish the role of the state, especially in the sphere of resource provision for social protection activities. The 1991 Law for the Social Protection of People With Disabilities (passed in a new version in 2008) laid the foundation for the formation of a national model of state social support for handicapped people. Uzbekistan has joined the main international agreements, pacts, declarations, and conventions dealing with the rights and liberties of children and people with special needs, and conducts its policies accordingly.

Practically every newly adopted code and law in the Republic of Uzbekistan takes into account the principle of optimal provision for the interests of the child. Uzbekistan's Guarantee of the Rights of the Child law sets out the guarantees of children's rights in the spheres of healthcare, education, social provision, and well-rounded development. The law places particular emphasis on the guarantee of the rights of socially vulnerable children and children with disabilities.

In difficult social and economic conditions Uzbekistan has succeeded in creating an entire network of new social institutions where citizens in need can receive the necessary aid and support. Care for the elderly, children, and people with disabilities is largely accomplished through the system of the Ministry of Labor and Social Protection, as well as all other ministries and departments, the makhallas, and the institutions of the Ministry of Internal Affairs. Among them are centers for social services for different categories of citizens, centers for psychological and educational assistance, social rehabilitation centers for underage youth and women, territorial centers for social assistance to families and children, etc.

The country puts extensive efforts into increasing the efficiency of the system of social protection, giving greater attention and care to children without caregivers, taking measures to improve the material/technical base of orphanages and specialized boarding schools, bolstering support for low income and in-need segments of the population.

Equal access to education is particularly important for children with special needs. The child's social rehabilitation, adaptation, and their integration into society directly relies on their education level. In recent years special attention has been given to the inclusive education of children with different psycho-physical development, promoting joint efforts both on the part of the child, and of their milieu. The first steps in that direction have already been taken, and a gradual policy of incremental incorporation of inclusive education into the general education system is being implemented.

Naturally, further development of inclusive education depends on the resolution of a number of problems, including the creation of a legislative base, scientific and organisational support for the process of integration, psychological preparation of all concerned, the creation of a national model of integrated education and its pedagogical and methodological implementation.

The non-governmental sector is taking on an ever greater role in the provision of social support for the population and the social protection of citizens. It addresses the social needs of individuals with the utmost flexibility and speed. In the past few years the number of local NGOs has exhibited a consistent increase.

As a result of the recent reforms in the sphere of child protection the country has been giving a lot of attention to the training of social workers. The cornerstone document in the sphere of child protection is the Guarantee of the Rights of the Child law of the Republic of Uzbekistan, passed in 2008. The law affirms all the rights listed in the UN Declaration of the Rights of the Child. Regarding the need to prepare workers, Statute 4 states that training, raising of qualifications and re-training of workings in the sphere of the protection of children's rights is one of the key directions of the state's social policy.

Uzbekistan puts a great deal of effort into promoting social work, and each year passes under one or another social banner and is pronounced the year of social protection for a specific part of the population. The government purposefully enacts the policy of social protection through activating an "issue" every year: thus, the Year of the Interests of the Person, the Year of the Family, the Year of the Woman, the Year of a Healthy Generation, the Year of the Mother and Child, the Year of the Older Generation, the Year of Social Protection, the Year of Youth, the Year of the Harmoniously Developed Generation, the Year of the Healthy Mother and Child, the Year of Dialogue with the People, the Year of Active Investments and Social Development and so on.

13.5 Promising Practices

In 2018 UNICEF, in partnership with the research team of the Social Intervention Group of the Columbia University School of Social Work (SIG), the Oila Center of Academic and Applied Research, and the National University of Uzbekistan (NUUz) looked into the current functions and capacities for the provision of social services to children and families on the part of Uzbekistan's social protection sector. In February 2019 the research team presented its "Social Service Workforce in Uzbekistan: Strengths, Challenges and Ways Forward. Final Report" (UNICEF 2019). The main targets of the study were as follows:

- Determining the content, functions, capacities, and readiness of the system of social protection of the Republic of Uzbekistan for the administration, regulation, monitoring, and support of professional staff for the realization of social programs and the provision of social services to the population.
- Identifying the complications and gaps in the existing system of social protection and defining the priorities of its development in Uzbekistan, including that of the growth of social work as a profession.
- Suggesting solutions for the elimination of problems and gaps inhibiting further bolstering of the system of cadres of social protection.

The analytical survey of 35 reports presented to UNICEF and over 65 laws, edicts, and decrees of regional governments conducted by the research group has shown that the system of social support of families and children in Uzbekistan includes numerous ministries and departments. Thus, no fewer than 13 state and non-governmental structures take part in the development and realization of social programs for vulnerable individuals, families, and children: the Ministry of Health, the Ministry of Public Education, the Ministry of Preschool Education, the Ministry of Higher and Secondary Special Education, the Ministry of Employment and Labour Relations, the Ministry of Internal Affairs, the prosecutor's office, hokimiyats, local self-governing bodies (the makhallas), the Women's Committee, the Oila Center and the Youth Union, as well as local and international NGOs, such as the National Center for Social Adaptation of Children and SOS-children's villages of Uzbekistan.

The report notes that the realization of the laws, edicts, and decrees of the President and the Cabinet of Ministers dealing with social services has been particularly intensified in the past 2 years. Almost half all reviewed legislative acts are dated between October 2016 and December 2018. Due to recent legislative measures, contemporary social problems such as migration, domestic abuse, mental disorders (including suicides), crimes and offences among women and youth, as well as human trafficking, have become open to public discussion and the generation of suitable measures. There is a range of new services, such as social housing and the provision of employment to socially vulnerable families, women, and youth, and services aimed at preventing domestic violence and suicides among youth and women, including crisis centers and hotlines. Many decrees and edicts are aimed at bolstering the role of national agencies, such as the Women's Committee, the Makhalla, the Youth Union, and the Oila Center, in regulating the needs of vulnerable families, children, and women.

The study uncovered the strong points in the current system of social security in Uzbekistan, which consist of the following:

- Solving the problems of social vulnerability and providing social support to families and children are priorities of the State policy, and, accordingly, have been reflected in legislation and in the structures, functions, and goals of institutions.
- In the past 2 years the structure, quantity, posts, and professional requirements for social services employees have increased. This particularly pertains to specialists working with women and families, specialists in the social protection of children, prevention inspectors, and specialists working with youth.
- More attention has been paid to the unique body of self-government—the makhalla—on the part of the government. Further investments in the raising of qualifications of the personnel of the communes can ensure the makhalla's becoming the key provider of preventive services for families and children on the level of the commune. Of particular note has been the overall potentiality of cadres in the sphere of the provision of children's and family welfare in Uzbekistan.

13.6 Challenges

Special attention in the evaluation of the system of cadres of the social sector has been given to the existing gaps. Thus while Uzbekistan invests significant resources in the social protection of vulnerable groups of the population, the effectiveness of these measures remains insufficient due to the absence of a single government body responsible for the support of families and children. Many duplicate departments are involved in the sector of the provision of social services to families, children, and youth. The system of cadres of social protection is extensive, but fragmented and composed of numerous functions, specialists, workers without specialized education, and representatives from related professions (Table 13.1).

It is clear that the cadre composition of the system of social protection is disproportionate in its degrees of qualification and range of services. The majority is composed of rehabilitation and medical/social institutional organization workers (highly specialized services), while the minority is made up of specialists who provide direct services to families and children in district agencies and on the level of local communes. Employees working on preventative measures on the level of the makhalla are largely without specialized education, lacking in professional skills and the oversight (supervision) required to provide social support services to vulnerable groups at the necessary level.

An institutional medical model of care is likewise prevalent in the system of children's protection. The healthcare sector carries out an extensive and diverse collection of functions, including medical, pedagogical, and social/psychological services in various formats, all under the umbrella of regional and district healthcare departments. Para-professional employees of the system of the Ministry of Public Health, who provide services in the home (and are mistakenly termed social workers) provide specific services to the elderly and people with disabilities, but purely household services are inadequate for this category. Homecare nurses from family clinics are not trained in screening, detecting social problems, and providing preventative social support. On the whole, the healthcare sector lacks professional standards for the provision of social/psychosocial services, although the Ministry is the main government body for the oversight of social services. PCC, first and foremost, follows legal codes.

In the sphere of education social services are primarily provided for children of preschool age (The Ministry of Preschool Education) and school age (The Ministry of Public Education), including children deprived of parental support or children from low income families placed in institutional organizations. In spite of certain attempts to deinstitutionalize and reform the organizations into small homes or family establishments, the institutional mode of care remains the main type of services. Alternative care and preventative programs continue to be limited.

The main purpose of the Ministry of Public Education is the 'determination and realization of a unified state policy in the sphere of secondary and extracurricular education for the spiritual, moral, intellectual, and physical education of students. Its target groups are children (ages 0–18) deprived of parental care, children with

Table. 13.1 Social sector stakeholders responsible for social support services and social services (Human resources of the social protection system in Uzbekistan: strengths, problems and further development, UNICEF 2019)

Responsible Ministries and Departments	Main Social Services								
	Healthcare	Education	Labor and Employment	Juvenile Jurisprudence and Prevention	Social Protection	Children's Protection	Youth Support	Family Support	Women's Support
Ministry of Health	v			v	v	v		v	v
Ministry of public education	V	v		v	v	v	v	v	
Ministry of preschool education	V	v				v		v	
Ministry of higher and secondary special education	V	v		v	v	v	v		
Ministry of labour			v	v	v			v	
Ministry of internal affairs		V	v	v	v	v			v
Makhalla	v	V	v	v		v	v	v	v
hokimiyats	v		v	v		v	v	v	v
Women's Committee	v		v	v				v	v
Oila Center	v	v	v	v			v	v	
Youth Union	v	v	v	v			v		
Republican Center of social adaptation of children	v			v		v		v	
SOS Children's Villages Uzbekistan—SOS	v					v	v	v	

disabilities/special needs/health problems, children from socially vulnerable families/low income families, children in trouble with the law, or those belonging to the at risk group.

The workload of a specialist in children's social protection (the SPON bodies for custody and guardianship which form part of the system of the Ministry of Public Education) has represented a significant problem for many years. A single employee of SPON can service a district or city with a population of 50–400 thousand. In addition, the number of functions and tasks they must perform demands various levels of competencies: for instance, conducting psychological evaluations, social accompaniment, consulting, investigations into questions of child protection, aid with adoption and alternative rearing, help in crisis situations, participation in a multidisciplinary team, court cases, drawing up of documents, and carrying out of administrative functions. It is obviously impossible for one employee to be responsible for all of the above functions.

The Ministry of Preschool Education (MPE) is the central government body coordinating the provision of education services to children of preschool age (3–7), as well as those with special needs. Established by the President in September 2017, this is the newest government organ. Until 2018 preschool services were included in the Ministry for Public Education. The aims off the Ministry are the development and realization of a unified government policy in the sphere of preschool education. The website can be found at http://mdo.uz. The main social services of the MPE are the services of preschool social education and kindergartens. The services are coordinated by the department for the coordination of the activity of specialized preschool educational institutions, rehabilitation and children's health of the MPE.

There exist 188 kindergartens for children with special needs, including 14 facilities of the isolator type for children ill with tuberculosis or having previous contact with those ill with tuberculosis. The other kindergartens are intended for children with various type of mental and physical disorders, analogous to specialized schools included in the system of the Ministry for Public Education (e.g. children with severe speech impediments, auditory or visual impairment, mental disorders, disorders of the musculoskeletal system). There are both kindergartens for children with multiple disorders and kindergartens specializing in a single condition. In total 20,012 children between the ages of 3 and 7 are being serviced.

Services include specialized education/correction; rehabilitation; health support; support of mental development; in some cases, round-the-clock care. Nevertheless, there are no social workers on staff—even in kindergartens where children remain overnight.

Short staffing in the system of social protection and lack of social services for the prevention of social orphanhood generate a situation wherein children from low-income or troubled families who have suffered severe or negligent treatment, children with limited capabilities, with at-risk behavior—the most vulnerable and in-need of support—find themselves in boarding schools and correctional facilities which are not conducive to rehabilitation, but, rather, lead to further trauma.

The personnel of the system of prevention of delinquency on the part of minors in the Ministry of Internal Affairs consists of prevention inspectors, as opposed to specialists in social work. The functions of the inspectors are, in many ways, analogous to those of social workers in the system of minors, but inspectors have no training in work with families and children who find themselves in conflict with the law, or children from an at-risk group. Furthermore, territorial and family rehabilitation services to which inspectors and schools could be directing youth from at-risk groups do not exist. In order to increase the effectiveness and quality of social services for vulnerable families, women, children, and youth, there is a need to consider creating of a unified government department for the social protection of the population, inclusive of children and families. In particular, such a department could provide services for the protection of children (including reacting to severe or negligent treatment, alternate forms of care), for the support of the family, preventive services for children and youth, social programs based in local communities for children and youth from at-risk groups.

Further Reading

UNICEF (2019) Human resources of the social protection system in Uzbekistan: strengths, problems and further development. (This assessment was carried out at the request of UNICEF in Uzbekistan by the Social Research Group of the School of Social Work of Columbia University (New York) with the support of the Oila Research Center and the National University of Uzbekistan).

Index

I. Earner, A. Telitsyna (eds.), *The Development of Child Protection Systems in the Post-Soviet States*, Child Maltreatment 12,
https://doi.org/10.1007/978-3-030-59588-3

Printed by Printforce, the Netherlands